Hitler's Armed
Forces Auxiliaries

ALSO BY JEAN-DENIS G.G. LEPAGE
AND FROM McFARLAND

*Medieval Armies and Weapons in Western Europe:
An Illustrated History* (2014 [2005])

An Illustrated Dictionary of the Third Reich (2014)

*British Fortifications Through the Reign of Richard III:
An Illustrated History* (2012)

*Castles and Fortified Cities of Medieval Europe:
An Illustrated History* (2011 [2002])

The Fortifications of Paris: An Illustrated History (2010 [2006])

*Vauban and the French Military Under Louis XIV:
An Illustrated History of Fortifications and Strategies* (2010)

French Fortifications, 1715–1815: An Illustrated History (2010)

Hitler Youth, 1922–1945: An Illustrated History (2009)

Aircraft of the Luftwaffe, 1935–1945: An Illustrated Guide (2009)

The French Foreign Legion: An Illustrated History (2008)

*German Military Vehicles of World War II:
An Illustrated Guide to Cars, Trucks, Half-Tracks,
Motorcycles, Amphibious Vehicles and Others* (2007)

Hitler's Armed Forces Auxiliaries

An Illustrated History of the Wehrmachtsgefolge, 1933–1945

Jean-Denis G. G. Lepage

McFarland & Company, Inc., Publishers
Jefferson, North Carolina

LIBRARY OF CONGRESS CATALOGUING-IN-PUBLICATION DATA [new form]

Names: Lepage, Jean-Denis G.G., 1952–
Title: Hitler's Armed Forces auxiliaries : an illustrated history of the Wehrmachtsgefolge, 1933–1945 / Jean-Denis G.G. Lepage.
Other titles: Illustrated history of the Wehrmachtsgefolge, 1933–1945
Description: Jefferson, North Carolina : McFarland & Company, Inc., Publishers, [2015] | Includes bibliographical references and index.
Identifiers: LCCN 2015037851| ISBN 9780786497454 (softcover : acid free paper) | ISBN 9781476620886 (ebook)
Subjects: LCSH: Germany. Wehrmachtsgefolge—History. | Organisation Todt (Germany) | Deutsche Arbeitsfront—History. | Germany. Reichsarbeitsdienst—History. | Nationalsozialistisches Kraftfahrkorps (Germany) | Nationalsozialistische Deutsche Arbeiter-Partei. Deutscher Volkssturm. | Forced labor—Germany. | World War, 1939–1945—Economic aspects—Germany.
Classification: LCC D757 .L48 2015 | DDC 331.6'2094309043—dc23
LC record available at http://lccn.loc.gov/2015037851

BRITISH LIBRARY CATALOGUING DATA ARE AVAILABLE

© 2015 Jean-Denis G.G. Lapage. All rights reserved

No part of this book may be reproduced or transmitted in any form or by any means, electronic or mechanical, including photocopying or recording, or by any information storage and retrieval system, without permission in writing from the publisher.

Front cover illustrations by the author

Printed in the United States of America

McFarland & Company, Inc., Publishers
Box 611, Jefferson, North Carolina 28640
www.mcfarlandpub.com

ACKNOWLEDGMENTS

The author wishes to thank Jeannette à Stuling, Simone and Bernard Lepage, Eltjo de Lang, Ben Marcato, Hervé François, Siepje Kroonenberg, Jan à Stuling, Nicole Lapaux, and Antoinette Gennesey, as well as Alex Dekker, Peter de Laet, Rudi Rolf, and Monique Brinks of the OVMG (War and Resistance Documentation Center at Groningen).

TABLE OF CONTENTS

Acknowledgments v
Introduction 1

Chapter 1: Organisation Todt 5

Fritz Todt 5
Autobahns (Motorways) 6
The West Wall 9
Fritz Todt's Mysterious Death 13
Albert Speer and Xaver Dorsch 16
The OT During the War 20
Structure of the OT 21
OT-Militia (OT-SK) 25
Ranks of the OT 26
Uniforms and Insignia 27
Cadres and Slave Labor 33
Fortifications 38
U–Boat Pens 43
Protection of Industry 48
Revenge Weapons 49
Hitler's HQ Bunkers 52
Public Shelters and Anti-aircraft Towers 54
Aftermath 57

Chapter 2: Deutsche Arbeitsfront (DAF) and Reicharbeitsdienst (RAD)— German Labor Front and National Work Service 59

Creation and Purposes of the DAF 59
Robert Ley 60
Organization of the DAF 62
DAF Werkscharen 67
Schönheit der Arbeit 68
Kraft durch Freude (KdF) 68
Reichsarbeitsdienst (RAD) 73
Women's Labor Service 77
Structure of the RAD 78
Prewar Tasks of the RAD 81
The RAD at War 84
Pro-Nazi Foreign Labor Services 86
Militarization of the RAD 87
Ranks of the RAD 89
Uniforms of the RAD 91
Insignia, Flags and Dagger of the RAD 100

Chapter 3: Nationalsozialistisches Kraftfahrer Korps (NSKK) 104

Origins of the Motorized Corps 104
Structure of the NSKK 107
Prewar Tasks of the NSKK 108
Marine-NSKK 114
NSKK and Organisation Todt 114
The NSKK at War 115
Foreign Volunteers 117

Transportkorps Speer   120
Militarization of the NSKK   122
Ranks   123
Insignia   124
Uniforms   129
Aftermath   136

Chapter 4: Deutscher Volkssturm (German Popular Home Guard)   138

Situation in the Winter of 1944–45   138
Creation of the Volkssturm   138
Command   141
Organization   142
Uniforms   144
Ranks   149
Weapons   149
The Volkssturm at War   154
Aftermath   156

Chapter 5: Other Military Affiliated Units   158

Sturm Abteilung (SA)   159
Waffen SS   162
Hitler Youth (HJ)   168
Nazi Flyers Corps (NSFK)   170
National German Railway Company (DRG)   178
Ordnungspolizei (Orpo)   182
German Postal Service   185

Conclusion   189
Appendix: World War II Chronology   193
Bibliography   201
Index   203

INTRODUCTION

The Wehrmacht was the official name of the German armed forces of the Third Reich (1933–1945). Created in May 1935, it replaced the Reichswehr, a term used to describe the 100,000-man army of the Weimar Republic in the post–World War I period. The term Wehrmacht is often used as if synonymous with the German ground forces, but actually it referred to all three armed services: the Heer (ground force), the Kriegsmarine (navy) and a newly created arm, the Luftwaffe (air force).

The Oberkommando der Wehrmacht (OKW, High Command of the Armed Forces) was set up by Hitler in February 1938 to replace the Reichskriegsministerium (War Ministry). With the consent of high army leaders, Hitler made himself supreme commander of the OKW and required all members of the military to take an oath of personal loyalty to him. The organization of the OKW underwent several changes in the period 1938–1945, all modifications strengthening Hitler's grip on the German armies.

The OKW had three major branches: the Oberkommando des Heeres (OKH) was the high command of the ground forces replacing the Allgemeine Heeresamt (General Army Office); the Oberkommando der Marine (OKM) was the high command of the navy; and the Oberkommando der Luftwaffe (OKL) was the high command of the air force. As chief of the OKW staff, Hitler had appointed General Wilhelm Keitel (1882–1946). Keitel—a loyal and subservient worker to the Führer—attended all significant conferences on the conduct of the war and signed operational orders, including those for the execution of hostages and prisoners of war as well as the *Nacht und Nebel* decree of December 1941 by which those said to endanger the regime were to vanish into "night and fog," that is to be detained without trial in concentration camps. Keitel was sentenced to death and hanged at Nuremberg in 1946.

Originally, the OKW directed all military operations, but at the end of 1941, Hitler altered the chain of command again and increased his power. The domain of the OKW was then limited to Western Europe, the Mediterranean Sea and the Balkans, and the front in Russia was then directed by the OKH and Hitler himself.

The Wehrmacht had been rapidly expanded by Hitler after 1933, and a large-scale rearmament was done after 1935, when all limitations of the Versailles treaty of 1919 had been repudiated. Although ill prepared for a long war, the German forces achieved tremendous and quick victories in the period 1939–1941. Hitler's increasingly unrealistic strategic plans—notably the invasion of the Soviet Union—led to heavy losses and dramatic failures culminating in the defeats of El Alamein (November 1942) and Stalingrad (February 1943). The losses suffered by the Germans after 1943 could not be made up for, and divisional establishments within the army were greatly reduced. Second-class formations were often deployed as front-line troops.

To support the German armed forces, Hitler had created several organizations and agencies. The topic of World War II German auxiliary forces is a complex one. These organizations were by their very nature not regular armed forces, but auxiliaries to them. In fact, the only true auxiliary forces were four Wehrmachtsgefolge, or armed forces auxiliaries, serving important, even essential, support roles. These included the Organisation Todt (OT, construction company), the Reichsarbeitsdienst (RAD, Work Service) and the Nationalsozialistisches Kraftfahrer Korps (NSKK Drivers' Corps). When the Allies intensified their air bombardments on Germany, several units were also engaged in repair and rescue duties. In September 1944, with defeat looming, a fourth Wehrmachtsgefolge, the Deutscher Volkssturm (Popular Home Guard), was hastily created in order to draft all German manpower into a final fight. Construction workers, drivers, policemen, rescue teams and civilians became part of paramilitary formations, and many of them took arms in one way or another.

These organizations were given the status of Wehrmachtsgefolge (Armed Forces Auxiliaries) to put their members under the protection of the Geneva Conventions. Should members of these troops be taken prisoner, they could officially benefit from having the status of Prisoner of War. The Geneva Conventions—negotiated in 1864, 1906 and 1929—were international agreements, protocols, and treaties that extensively defined the basic wartime rights of prisoners (civil and military), and established protections for the wounded and for civilians in and around a war zone.

The total strength of the German armed forces auxiliary paramilitary organizations was about 1,200,000 in 1939, peaking in 1944 at about 3,800,000. By that time, they represented 40 percent of the size of the armed forces, and their contribution to Hitler's Third Reich war effort was far from negligible.

Yet the story of the Wehrmachtsgefolge units is much less familiar than the stories of the other branches of the Wehrmacht such as the Panzer divisions, the planes of the Luftwaffe or the U-Boats of the Kriegsmarine. Many books dealing with World War II mention these auxiliary formations, but very few focus exclusively on them. This book is an attempt to bring some light to their history, organization, regalia, and technical data and to the role they played in World War II.

Finally, due to the sensitive nature of the topic of this book, the author would like to close this introduction with the following. The German Army Auxiliaries, as is true for

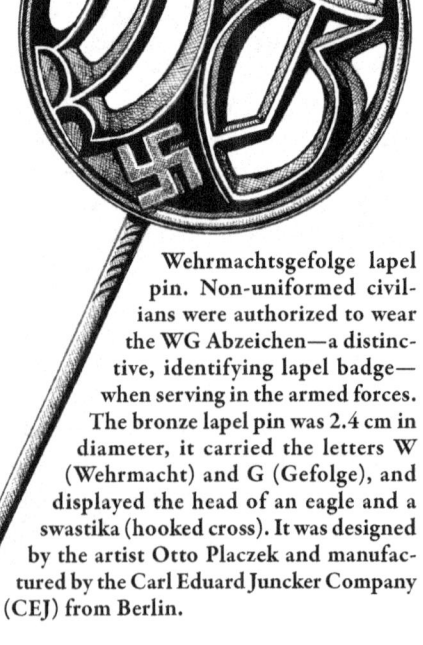

Wehrmachtsgefolge lapel pin. Non-uniformed civilians were authorized to wear the WG Abzeichen—a distinctive, identifying lapel badge—when serving in the armed forces. The bronze lapel pin was 2.4 cm in diameter, it carried the letters W (Wehrmacht) and G (Gefolge), and displayed the head of an eagle and a swastika (hooked cross). It was designed by the artist Otto Placzek and manufactured by the Carl Eduard Juncker Company (CEJ) from Berlin.

all other aspects of Hitler's regime, is a historical subject in which claims to absolute objectivity and technical detachment sound somewhat artificial and forced, not to say dishonest. Let there be no misinterpretation: the author has no truck with attempts at apologism for Nazism; justifying Nazi crimes; encouraging any form of neo–Nazism, racism, or anti–Semitism; or championing any ideology based on violence, racism, hatred or totalitarianism.

Most measurements in this book are given in the metric system.
1 centimeter = 0.393 inches
1 meter = 0.328 feet
1 kilometer = 0.612 miles
1 hectare = 2,471 acres
1 cubic centimeter = 0.061 cubic inches
1 cubic meter = 1.308 cubic yards
1 kilogram = 2.205 pounds
1 tonne = 1.102 short tons

Chapter 1

Organisation Todt

The Organisation Todt (OT) was a German conglomerate of public construction companies developed by the Nazi regime. From the start, the OT was a connecting body, a kind of government agency between the Nazi authorities, who decided what public and military works were to be done, and civilian building companies and firms, whose task it was to realize them.

Fritz Todt

The driving force behind the Organisation Todt was Hitler's architect and engineer Fritz Todt. Fritz Todt was born in Pforzheim (Baden) on September 4, 1891, to a prosperous upper-middle-class family, the son of the owner of a jewelry factory. After having attended the humanist Gymnasium (high school), the young Fritz studied at the college of technology in Munich in the period 1911–1914. During the First World War (1914–1918), he served in the artillery until 1916, then in the air force as a flying observer officer. He was wounded in an air battle. After the war, he completed his education at the Technical University in Karlsruhe. After graduation in 1920, Fritz Todt worked as a construction engineer in the firm Sager and Wörner in Munich and specialized in tar and asphalt roads. Like his successor at the head of the OT, Albert Speer, Todt was a technologist who loved nature, ski tours, hikes and holidays in Alpine mountains. Politically Todt was not an extremist but—like many ex–World War I servicemen—a moderate nationalist embittered by the defeat of 1918. He was impressed by Friedrich Naumann's vision of a European economic community under the leadership of Germany and was attracted by the Nazi ideology. He joined the Nazi Party in January 1923 and founded a NSDAP local branch at Eitting, where he was working. After Hitler's failed coup of November 1923, the NSDAP was banned and the prudent Todt devoted himself to his career and his family. His political zeal went into abeyance until the end of 1931, when he resumed activities by joining the SA reserve regiment R16. He took part in the customary propaganda activities and became an active proselytizer within middle class circles for the candidate Adolf Hitler during the elections of 1932. During the next decade the modest, unassuming technologist gathered into his hands significant responsibility in the German construction business. First he took over the leadership of the engineers' section of the Kampfbund Deutscher Architekten und Ingenieure (KDAI, the Fighting League of German Architects and Engineers)—tightly related to the Nazi Party—and worked as consultant and accessor for the NSDAP's Office for Economic Technology, run by the Nazi theorist Gottfried Feder. In August 1934, at

Organisation Todt

Todt's suggestion, the Nationalsozialistischer Bund Deutscher Technik (NSBDT, the Nazi League of German Technology) was created—a para-governmental propaganda unit that exercised a decisive influence on the development of technology and the orientation of engineers in the Third Reich, the furtherance of technical and scientific projects, and the responsibilities and status of technical personnel. From March 1936, Todt directed the academy of Plassenburg near Kulmbach, which was to become a stronghold of the National Socialist concept of technology and science. Todt's techno-political approach embraced the holistic "spiritual revolution" of the regime—man, machine and nature in aesthetic harmony—and developed administrative tools to propagate it among fellow German engineers and the broader public.

Fritz Todt (1891–1942).

Autobahnen (Motorways)

Hitler was keen on cars and planes. He was one of the first politicians in Germany to campaign extensively by automobile and airplane. As early as 1925, he owned a Dürkopp car, then an Opel and finally a Mercedes-Benz. He liked speed but never learned to drive, being afraid that an accident would bring his political career to an end. In the early times, his chauffeur was Julius Schreck, who formed the first group of bodyguards, later to become the Schutz-Staffeln (SS protection detachments). The Nazi Party rapidly realized the potentialities of motoring and gave a great deal of attention to modern means of transport. As a promotion, an important auto show was created in Berlin in 1933 and, in June of the same year, a large-scale construction scheme, the Autobahnprogram, was launched.

The idea of constructing modern, broad, multilane and limited access highways had been initiated by the Weimar Republic. Begun as early as 1924, the construction was intended to reduce unemployment and create a modern national transportation infrastructure. A year before Hitler became chancellor, a highway linking Cologne to Bonn was opened for traffic. Cologne's mayor, Konrad Adenauer, solemnly opened the new motorway on August 6, 1932, with these prophetic words: "So werden die Straßen der Zukunft aussehen [This is how the roads of the future will look]." Today this segment is part of the A555 autobahn. Konrad Adenauer (1876–1967) became West Germany's first chancellor, serving as Bundeskanzler (federal chancellor) from 1949 to 1963. So the truth is that Hitler did not create the concept of modern highways; he simply continued the practice. However, the Nazis found it easy to take credit for the earlier work of others and make it seem that it was all Hitler's idea.

The autobahn freeway system quickly became a symbol of Nazi Germany, and it was considered a major element of Germany's economic resurgence under Hitler. The National Motorway Enterprise was founded, and Hitler appointed the highly regarded engineer Fritz Todt as Generalinspekteur für das Deutsche Straßenwesen (inspector-general of the German Roads) in July 1933. Todt then became the supreme commander in all matters related to highway planning and construction in the Third Reich, second only to Hitler himself.

Todt committed himself enthusiastically to the project and set to work with unprecedented energy. He commissioned a large number of building companies, later to be known as the Organisation Todt, named after him—an unfortunate name indeed, as it closely resembled the German words for death (Tod) and dead (tot). Work began on the Frankfurt-Darmstadt-Heidelberg stretch in September 1933 in the presence of Hitler himself, who inaugurated the site. The Frankfurt-Heidelberg motorway was completed in 1935.

The purpose of the motorways was to establish an efficient and unified network of transport routes under the control of the Reich. The autobahns were intended not only to revolutionize transportation, but also to connect the metropolises to the countryside, and reconcile nature and technology. They were meant to encourage motorization and encourage the use of the private automobile. Indeed, according to Nazi propaganda, each German family would soon possess its own personal car, the famous Volkswagen (see chapter 2, "Kraft durch Freude"). The highways became the obvious symbol of Germany's renewed strength and economic recovery.

The autobahn program served several goals. Socially, the motorways created jobs to fight unemployment after the 1929 economical crisis; in 1936 there were 125,000 workers employed on the building sites, 120,000 working in quarries and many others employed in the road-building equipment industry. They were only a small fraction of the millions of German unemployed, but they were symbolic and gave a sense of equal opportunity among a work force with reinvigorated morale. The official propaganda pictures of thousands of eager workers building the "Führer's Roads"—as the minister of propaganda named them—had the added impact of suggesting a united community in which class and privilege had been abolished for the common good. The perception of the German people in the period 1934–1938 was that life was safe again. After the chaos of the 1930 crisis, more and more people thought Hitler might not be perfect, but said that at least he gave jobs and something to eat, and had restored hope, tranquility, social order and national pride.

Politically, the motorways were prestige objects for the Nazi regime, and Hitler was quick to see the propaganda value of the program. The new roads were intended not only to convey travelers as quickly as possible from one place to the other, but also to show them the beauties of Germany—a dynamic Nazi Germany presented as working for peace, modernity and international friendship. It was Todt's ambition to make the motorways not only technically perfect, with long acceleration and deceleration lanes, gentle curves, and durable surfaces, but also artistically pleasing. The whole program was formally delivered as an "artistic commission" intended to merge with nature and to embellish the landscape. The roads were designed as four-lane, limited-access highways, with central medians, hard shoulders, and concrete road surfaces in each direction normally 24 meters (79 ft.) wide (widened on some major segments immediately before the war). In addition to having no intersections, the roads were to have limited grades as much as possible, no more than 8 percent, and curves were to fall within a range of 600 meters (660 yd.) and 1,800 meters (2,000 yd.) in radius. They were not to have perfectly straight courses but rather always be slightly curved after a maximum of two kilometers of straight line. However, a section of an autobahn near Dessau (with a length of about 10 km) was designed as a straight stretch and used for prestigious speed-record attempts. For example, Ernst Henne used that section to set a new land-speed record on a motorbike of over 134 mph in 1929. Another record stretch between Frankfurt and Darmstadt saw the death of driver Bernd Rosemeyer in January 1938 when he attempted to drive a streamlined Auto Union car at 432 km/h (268 mph).

The autobahns were to blend into nature and be suited to the form of the landscape through the alignment of the curves, harmonic and rhythmic lines of construction, unity of style, elegant bridges, the correct management of topsoil, suitable plantings, and the restoration of the berms and edges of forest that had been torn up. Todt's masterpieces were the symbol of the rise of the Third Reich, and the token of the rebirth of Germany. The autobahns were largely exploited by propaganda, and the "Führer's Roads" were commented on by hundreds of journalists and correspondents. In the 1930s a drive on the prestigious motorways was often part of the tourist agenda of many foreign visitors, journalists and reporters, ambassadors, and political representatives and VIPs. More than economic products, the autobahns were a heroic Nazi achievements and considered national artistic monuments, which the propaganda machinery did not fear to compare to the great monuments of Ancient Greece and Rome and to the medieval cathedrals.

Besides the economic recovery, love of nature, respect of landscape, national prestige and Nazi glamor presented by the Ministry of Propaganda, the autobahn program served other purposes. Like virtually every other aspect of life under Hitler's regime, the construction of superhighways proved to be a double-edged sword. The autobahns served the internal political security of the Reich, enabling the rapid intervention of the SS security forces to crush any attempt to overthrow the regime. External security was also served, as Germany is a rather large continental land without real natural barriers. The new roads enabled the army to mobilize fast and with efficiency. Their east-west axis would make a two-front war a manageable proposition. The highways were suitable for armored vehicles and made the transport of military troops quicker and easier from one part of the Reich to another, for instance in Pomerania, where the bad roads could turn to mud after heavy rains. To overcome this problem, the Nazi government ordered the construction of an autobahn running from Berlin to Breslau, Stettin, Königsberg and Elbing. Another autobahn ran from Berlin to Frankfurt-on-the-Oder, making possible rapid reinforcement of the defensive positions of the eastern border. Furthermore, some straight sections could possibly be used not only as tracks for breaking speed records, but also as temporary airstrips for the air force.

On the subject of road construction Fritz

Autobahn. The idea for the construction of the autobahns was first conceived during the days of the Weimar Republic, but construction was slow, and most sections did not progress much beyond the planning stage due to economic problems and a lack of political support. Upon assuming power in January 1933, Adolf Hitler enthusiastically embraced an ambitious autobahn construction project under the supervision of Fritz Todt.

Todt wrote a long essay, "*Der Strassenbau im nationalsozialistischen Staat* [Roads Construction in the Nazi State]" in volume three of the publication *Grundlagen, Aufbau und Wirtschaftsordnung des nationalsozialistischen Staates [Foundation, Construction and Economic Order in the Nazi State]*, which was published by Hans H. Lammers and Hans Pfundner in 1937 in Berlin.

In the end, Hitler's marvelous project came to naught. Historians continue to debate the military value of the autobahns in the Second World War. The Nazis clearly considered the network of German expressways of some military value, and even included the military in autobahn planning. But tanks and trucks were very hard on highway surfaces and the bulk of German military traffic, men and materiel, went by rail. The much vaunted German autobahn network was still incomplete, and much of what existed was made useless by neglect and by Allied bombing during World War II. The Third Reich was not able to finance both the war and its planned autobahn system. The regime also failed to mass produce cars for the population. In 1938, although the autobahn linking Karlsruhe-Stuttgart-Munich-Salzburg was completed, Hitler's goal of a network of about 12,000 km (7,300 miles) of four-lane highways was not reached. At the beginning of World War II, only 3,065 kilometers of motorway were ready and 1,689 under construction. By 1941, only another 800 km (500 miles) had been added to the autobahn total since 1938. Ironically, the war prevented the completion of the motorways that were supposed to help support it. Even with the use of slave labor provided by Russian prisoners of war, Germany's resources were strained to the limit. With 3,860 km completed, all

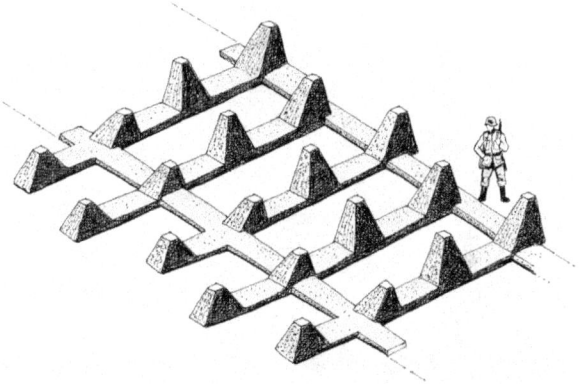

Dragon's teeth, Model 1938. The Höckerhindernis (dragon's teeth) were anti-tank obstacles made of several tiers of concrete blocks whose distance and height were calculated to make crossing impossible for any tanks. About 280 km of this efficient but very expensive obstacle were installed in the West Wall, mainly in the sector south of Aachen.

autobahn construction was halted in December 1941. By the end of the war, the embryonic great motorways, which stretched across Germany from the Rhine to the Oder, were strategically useless, since there was no petrol for large-scale movement of troops by road. As it turned out, however, it was not the German armies but those of the Allies that found their movement facilitated by Hitler's uncompleted Autobahn network. In postwar Germany, it was recognized that the Reichsautobahn network had been a white elephant.

THE WEST WALL

Nazi Germany's wartime strategy, at least up to 1942, is generally associated with a policy of all-out, mobile offense. It is curious to find, therefore, that bombproof concrete protection on a huge and sometimes indiscriminate scale was, even before the start of World War II, one of the main features of the country's military program. In 1938, Fritz Todt received a new mission, this time directly connected with the military. In collaboration with the Festungspionierstäbe (army engineering corps), his conglomerate of companies was commissioned to build bunkers in the West Wall

Organisation Todt

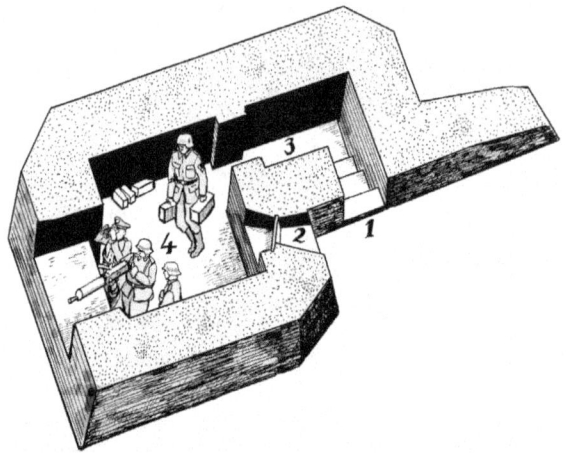

MG pillbox, type B1-1. The small West Wall standard machine-gun post, B1-1 MG Schartenstand (pillbox), was built with roof and walls 1 m (3.28 ft.) thick. It was 5.90 m wide and 8.00 m long. It took 167 cubic meters (218 cubic yd.) of concrete to build it. It included one entrance (1) at the back, defended by a small, close-range crenel (2), and a small corridor (3) leading to the firing chamber (4). This faced the direction the enemy were expected to come from, and was armed with one machine gun. The combat chamber also served as an observation and resting room for the crew of four.

(Siegfried Line) at the western border of the Reich.

After the reoccupation of the demilitarized Rhineland in 1936, in defiance of the Treaty of Versailles, German military engineers focused their attention on fortifying the border of the Reich with France. The Czechoslovak crisis of May 1938 made Hitler speed up the building of the fortified belt as a defense against Czechoslovakia's ally, France. The West Wall served two main purposes. First, in 1938, it was supposed to mark Germany's western border, and that was part of a deceitful plan showing France that Germany had no intention of aggressive conquest. Second, when the war was declared in September 1939, the line was intended to repulse any French or British attack, freeing the Wehrmacht to invade Poland without the need to worry about the western borders. The defensive line was called the West Wall by German propaganda. The French and the British nicknamed it the Siegfried Line during the "Phoney War" from September 1939 until May 1940. By that time, as a mockery and a morale-booster, there was a popular song composed by Jimmy Kennedy and Michael Carr with the line, "We're agonna hang our washing on the Siegfried Line!"

The West Wall was a gigantic task monopolizing some 400,000 workers including military personnel of the Engineering Corps, Organisation Todt workers and Deutsche Arbeitsfront (DAF German Labor Front) conscripts. From May 1938 until August 1939, eight million tons of concrete were poured, and one million tons of metal and as much wood were used to build about 22,000 bunkers. The cost of those defenses was estimated to 3.5 billions Reichmarks, and they had a considerable deleterious effect on the construction sector of the German economy, resulting in shortages of raw materials, transportation disruption, labor shortages, rising wages, price increases and fierce competition.

In the north, the West Wall began at

View of infantry shelter type B1-10.

The West Wall

Emmerich near the Dutch border, extended along the Rhineland (protecting the vital industrial Ruhrgebiet region), passed west of Aachen, stretched through the Eifel mountains, faced the French Maginot Line in Palatinate and continued south along the Rhine Valley down to Lörrach on the border with Switzerland. The vast length of the West Wall—about 600 km—together with the relatively limited amount of time available for its preparation and construction, resulted in rigorous constraints being imposed on the design and the building of the bunkers, so giving it a unique character and a remarkable unity of style. The bunkers were designed by the German army engineer corps directed by General Otto-Wilhelm Förster, but overall strategy and tactics were in the hands of Major Erich von Manstein-Lewinsky (head of the General Staff), Fieldmarshal Werner von Blomberg (minister of defense) and General Werner von Fritsch (commander of the army). Between them, there were many disagreements about the nature and the structure of the line, but the real arbiter of debates was Hitler himself. Planned as early as 1934, the construction of the West Wall was completed in two main phases. The Pioneerprogramm was launched in early 1938 by the Army Engineer Corps. The first part of the program was modest and rather small-scale. It consisted of about 1,400 small and monofunctional bunkers. The second phase of construction, the so-called Limesprogramm, was

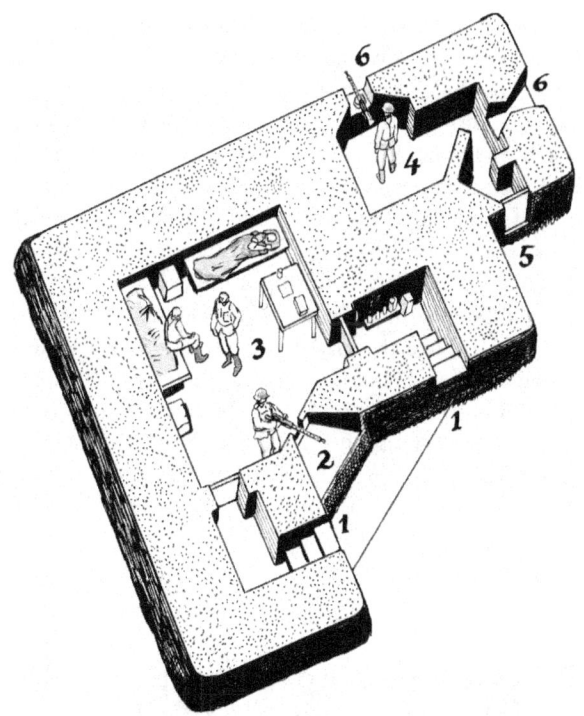

Ground plan, infantry shelter type B1–10. This standard infantry shelter, built with roof and walls 1 meter thick (3.28 ft.), was 11.10 m long and 9.80 m wide and demanded some 287 cubic meters (375 cubic yd.) of reinforced concrete for its construction. It included two entrances (1) placed at the rear of the building, and defended by a close-range defense crenel (2). The troop chamber (3) could accommodate a Gruppe (a squad of nine soldiers). There was also a small combat chamber (4) with its own entrance (5) fitted with two loopholes (6) for machine guns. Some 3,471 type B1–10 bunkers were built in the West Wall.

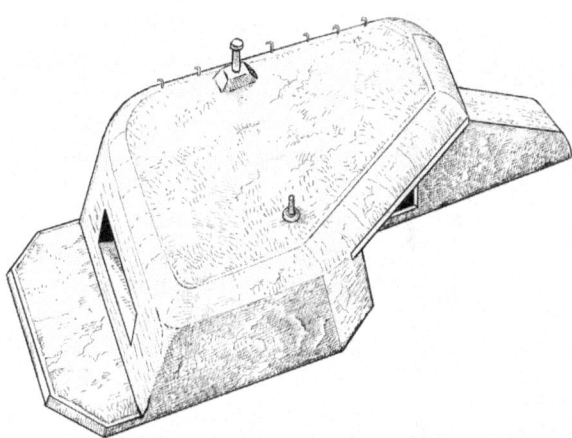

View of MG pillbox type B1–1.

more ambitious because it was directly connected to the political and military tensions caused by the Czech crisis, the Polish campaign, and the Anglo-French threat during the Phoney War. The Limesprogramm was launched at the end of 1938, and work continued until May 1940. Since the fortification pioneers of the army did not think they were capable of building bunkers in the numbers required by the Führer in the prescribed schedule, Hitler was impatient and dissatisfied. He transferred the commission to implement the project to the inspector for German roads, Fritz Todt. Hitler was enthusiastic about Fritz Todt's achievement in the autobahn program. The Führer's commission to Todt to build the West Wall was seen by the military as an unprecedented assault on its authority. Hitler took every opportunity to make clear to the army generals that Todt was to take the credit for the West Wall, arguing that if he had given this task to the army alone, the fortifications would still not have been ready in ten years. As the Organisation Todt had no experience yet with constructing bunkers, and to help speed up construction on the West Wall, the German Inspectorate for Fortifications established the so-called Regelbau system (Standard Design). The Regelbau system provided easy-to-handle designs without too many technical complications. It allowed a simplified documentation process that could be displayed on maps and gave all the information necessary to understand the fortifications displayed. It facilitated design, organization, construction and utilization. Standardization was raised to an obsession by Fritz Todt and later by his successor, Albert Speer. Standardized methods allowed the creation of types and sub-types of bunkers with variants and options as well as the prefabrication of many elements, for example doors, furniture, ventilation systems, cupolas, armored turrets, communication systems and observation devices. Standardization allowed precise planning of required materials, manpower, and timing of construction. The West Wall bunkers were all standard designs that could be duplicated over and over with sometimes only a few individual, non-standard designs being selected to match specific local conditions.

Fritz Todt directed the 22 senior building executive committees, which were commissioned to undertake the construction work from the Central Office for Western Fortifications in the Hotel

Advertisement in *Signal*. A book about "Fritz Todt as man, engineer and National-Socialist," written by a certain Ed. Schönleben and edited by the People Publishers Westland from Amsterdam, was published in the German propaganda magazine *Signal* (Dutch edition).

Kaiserhof in Wiesbaden. Along with the army Pioneers and the Deutsche Arbeitsfront (DAF, German Labor Service), about 1,000 firms with their depots and staff worked under his overall direction on the West Wall. An overhead coordinating company was then created called the Organisation Todt (OT). Todt's associated building companies existed already, but the name Organisation Todt was used by Hitler for the first time at the National Nazi Party Convention at Nuremberg in 1938. Fritz Todt's conglomerate of civilian building companies was unique in Germany, as it had no ministerial or military standing. It did not even have an official name, other than the designation that Hitler casually gave it. There was also no official foundation day. Yet the conglomerate grew into a huge force and administration, a massive, quasi-autonomous, semi-governmental organization tasked with creating the necessary conditions for massive construction. This included recruiting, transporting, accommodating, paying, feeding and clothing workers.

From then on Fritz Todt assumed many of the prerogatives of the transport minister, exercised substantial legislative authority, and dominated the construction industry. The Organisation Todt soon became a formidable fiefdom within the German state. The conglomerate of building companies organized and led by Fritz Todt had grown from 700 employees in 1933 to 300,000 in 1938, and about 1.4 million during the war.

Fritz Todt was to contrive the chain of West Wall fortifications according to the military and tactical plans of the Pioneer Staff, employing the Motorway Directorates in such a way that 5,000 concrete structures were completed by October 1, 1938. In November 1938 plans were drawn up for 14,600 additional bunkers. In early 1939 the numbers were increased and more workers were involved. In September 1939 when World War II started, the West Wall formed a long, almost continuous barrier. It was, of course, not a proper wall but rather a succession of loose hedgehogs, strongholds with concealed minefields, camouflaged concrete shelters, bunkers armed with machine guns, mortars and artillery pieces, numerous obstacles and field fortifications in the intervals. Although quite substantial, the West Wall was nowhere near as massive and strong as its opposite, the French Maginot Line, which included deep, underground fortresses. Working and upgrading the quality of the positions continued during the Sitzkrieg (Phoney War) until the offensive in the West in the spring of 1940.

FRITZ TODT'S MYSTERIOUS DEATH

With the West Wall, Todt proved that he was able to fulfill commands that were regarded as impossible by the standards of normal technical expertise. After this achievement, Hitler's trust in Todt was as great as for few others within the National Socialist leadership circle. Fritz Todt was already chairman of the Verein Deutscher Ingenieure (VDI, Association of German Engineers) and, in December 1938, he was appointed to the function of plenipotentiary for the regulation of the construction sector, which was a part of the Four-Year Plan commissioned by Hermann Göring. Fritz Todt was appointed national minister for weapons and munitions in March 1940 to centralize all war productions. In July 1941 he became inspector general for water and energy.

Although at the peak of his career, the famous road and bunker builder had remained a modest man dwelling in a small, unpretentious house off the beaten track at Hintersee near Berchtesgarden in the Bavarian Alps, where he lived a quiet and withdrawn life totally dedicated to his work and functions and to his family. Fritz Todt had no personal contacts with Nazi Party circles and kept clear of all political intrigues. He rarely appeared at Hitler's dinners, suppers or parties. His modesty enhanced his pres-

Organisation Todt

Dr. Fritz Todt ring. The ring, housed in an impressive casket, had an oval face featuring the letter T surrounded by oak leaves and interlinked swastikas on the outside body.

armament with the rank of honorary general. As head of construction and industrial production within the framework of the Four-Year Plan, Todt had, however, frequent clashes with the incompetent, conceited and boastful Hermann Göring. Indeed, things were not that rosy at the top of the Nazi hierarchy. The German organizational method was based on having as many independent units as possible; every branch of construction, tige, and even Hitler showed him and his accomplishments a profound respect. In reward for his achievements, he was the first person to receive the prestigious medal of the German Order, created by Hitler for individuals who had rendered "special services to the German People." Fritz Todt was a loyal NSDAP party member but always maintained his personal independence in his relations with the Nazis. In the autumn of 1937, Lord Wolton (who had been invited as guest of honor to visit the work on the motorways) expressed the wish that Todt be appointed as ambassador to London in the place of Ribbentrop, who was not considered to be the right man for the job of improving relations between Britain and Germany. Hitler heard of the remark but did not react, as Fritz Todt was too badly needed in Germany.

In 1940, the Organisation Todt became a Werhmachtsgefolge (paramilitary structure), and its men, materials, machinery and transport fleets were put at the disposal of the army. Fritz Todt was promoted to minister of

Dr. Fritz Todt Prize. The badge had a length of 68 mm and included an eagle with down-folded wings placed upon a ribbon scroll with the inscription "Dr. Fritz Todt" and a swastika inside a cogwheel.

production, industry and the military was eager to achieve the greatest possible self-sufficiency in every area. Thus there were, in the OT, autonomous subdivisions. Clothing, food, communication, supplies and transportation were all organized separately. The result was unnecessary delays and waste of manpower and material.

At the end of 1941 Fritz Todt was at the top of his career, being the supreme head of all road-building operations; he was also in charge of all navigable waterways and improvements on them, as well as of all power plants. As Hitler's direct envoy, he was minister of armaments and ammunitions. Within the framework of Hermann Göring's Four-Year Plan, he headed the construction industry and the Todt Organisation, which was already busy building the Atlantic Wall and the U-Boat shelters in occupied France. He was also responsible for road building and communication in conquered Russian territories.

But Fritz Todt was also a realistic man who disapproved of Hitler's aggressive policy. After two years of war, he was aware that Germany could never win the war—especially when Russia was not defeated and when the United States entered the war in December 1941. By that time Hitler was convinced that the Russians were on the edge of defeat. This self-confidence was not shared by the pessimist Todt, who knew a lot about the weaknesses of the long-term German economic and industrial potential, and also of the deteriorating military situation. Responsible for increasing the equipment of the army, Todt was close to despair. He had done several tours of inspection on the Eastern Front, where he had seen stalled hospitals filled with wounded, had witnessed the misery of the front troops, had endured the harshness of the climate and had been struck by the discouragement and despair among the German soldiers. He became opposed to Hitler's policy of conquest and tried to convince the dictator of the hopeless situation of the Reich. In spite of Hitler's refusal to hear his complaints, Todt remained a loyal servant of the regime and continued performing his task.

Fritz Todt met Hitler for the last time on February 7, 1942, at his headquarters at Rastenburg (East Prussia). What happened during the conversation remains unclear. It seems at times to have been a noisy and brisk discussion. The following morning, Todt flew back to Munich. Right after take-off his two-engined Heinkel He 111 crashed, killing crew and passenger. In 1988 the historian Franz W. Seidler, in his biography of Fritz Todt, made it clear that Todt was the victim of an accident caused by a navigational error by the pilot of the plane, but way back in 1942 there circulated uncertain stories. Had Todt been deliberately assassinated for pessimism and defeatism? There were rumors of sabotage of his plane by the SS on Hitler's order. Had the Führer ever forgiven the fact that Fritz Todt was a faithful Catholic, not a convinced and fanatic Nazi? Was Todt the victim of quarrels at the top of the Nazi hierarchy? Some spoke of an army plot to stop Todt's interfering in military concerns. Others suspected that Martin Bormann—remembering the flight of Hitler's deputy Rudolf Hess to Britain on May 10, 1941—feared that Fritz Todt would take off for Sweden to negotiate peace, and for this reason had ordered an explosive charge placed into his plane. Given the criminal nature of the Nazi regime, nobody was certain whether Todt's death was caused by an accident or was a deliberate assassination. Anyway, his death came at the right moment. An overworked man who could no longer cope with his immense responsibility, a defeatist lacking radical Nazi conviction, had been swept out of the way. Officially the tragic and deadly accident was attributed to a technical fault, the icing up of the plane's wings. Todt's mortal remains were taken back to Berlin, where he was honored with a grandiose national funeral and became a posthumous hero of the Nazi cause.

In November 1943 Hitler instituted the Dr. Fritz Todt Preis (Doctor Fritz Todt Prize) to honor the memory of his great civil engineer. The award was to be conferred on people who furthered the war effort. The Badge of Honor for Doctor Fritz Todt carried with it a payment and was awarded in three classes, denoted by gold (with a sum of 50,000 RM), silver (30,000 RM), and black steel (10,000 RM). The gold badge was awarded on the combined recommendation of Robert Ley (head of the DAF, the German Labor Front), and Albert Speer (minister of armament), the silver and the steel badges on the recommendation of the *Gauleiter* (senior Nazi Party district administrative leader) and senior DAF leaders. The badge was worn on the lower left breast.

To honor the memory of Fritz Todt, there was also a ring sponsored by the National Socialist Union of German Technology, NSBDT. The Fritz Todt ring was awarded to Albert Speer by Hitler in person in June 1943. Thereafter, conferments were made by Speer himself, and only to two persons: the Minister of Transport and Director-General of the German State Railways Julius Dorpmüller, and to Minister of Posts Wilhelm Ohnesorge.

In Fritz Todt's honor the important Channel gun, Batterie Siegfried, with its four huge casemates located at Audighen near Cap Gris Nez in Northern France, was renamed Batterie Todt and was often used in Atlantic Wall propaganda.

Albert Speer and Xaver Dorsch

Fritz Todt, who had gathered in the course of the past several years the major technical tasks of the Reich into his own hands, seemed irreplaceable. He was, however, replaced by Hitler's architect, Albert Speer (1905–1981).

Speer, born of a wealthy, middle-class Mannheim family, had studied architecture in Karlsruhe and Berlin. In the summer of 1927 he passed the architect's license examination and became assistant to the highly regarded architect and urban-planning professor Heinrich Tessenow (1876–1950). In January 1931, he joined the Nazi Party more because of Hitler's determined personality than through adherence to the ideology. With his conventional, moderate-right-wing political opinions, Speer might have joined any other conservative political party that offered him a career. Speer was a respectable young man, very middle-class, cultivated, well-educated, polite, good-mannered, handsome and always elegantly dressed. A healthy friend of art and nature, fond of camping, sailing and rafting, mountain climbing and skiing, he was intelligent, balanced, sober, noncorrupt, and faithful to his loving wife—Margarete Weber, whom he had married in 1927 and with whom he would have six children. He symbolized a type that became increasingly important: the pure technician, the successful winner, the respectable and bright man with a decent background, with no original aim than to make his way in the world and no other means than his talent, technical skills and managerial ability.

In the period 1931–1932, the skilled and industrious Albert Speer performed several minor architectural commissions for the Berlin Nazi authorities. Notably, he converted and furnished in only three months a building for Gauleiter Joseph Göbbels. As a relatively wealthy car owner, he was involved in the newly created National Socialist Party Motorist Association. Speer's great opportunity came when he attracted Hitler's attention by making—with inventiveness and skill—the technical arrangements for the Berlin NSDAP party rally in May 1933. Speer used oversized swastika flags and employed army searchlights, creating a kind of gigantic and impressive "cathedral of light" above the audience.

In the period 1933–1942, he became Hitler's favorite architect. He was appointed general architectural inspector and charged with designing grandiose schemes for the rebuilding and improvement of German cities. Hitler, who had started out in a career as a painter, was particularly concerned with imposing his tastes on the fine arts. A frustrated artist and architect at heart, Hitler saw in Speer a means of fulfilling his own aborted, youthful dreams. Speer was attracted by Hitler's personality, rather than by the Nazi Party itself, to which he was always an outsider. Something of a friendly collaboration was established between the two men. Speer soon belonged to the Führer's artistic entourage, took part in his bohemian lifestyle, traveled with him and moved to be close to Hitler's alpine home on the Obersalzberg. Given a free hand and huge means, Albert Speer worked tirelessly to convert Hitler's megalomaniacal dreams into stone. Using a pompous, monumental, neoclassical style, Speer designed state offices, stadiums, superpalaces, huge monuments and parade grounds and esplanades for the grandiose future of Nazi Germany, including the new Reich Chancellery in Berlin and the Nazi Party palace in Nuremberg.

Albert Speer (1905–1981).

After Fritz Todt's death, it was indeed reckless and frivolous of Hitler to appoint an architect and city planner to one of the most important ministries upon which the existence of the Nazi regime depended. Albert Speer—aged only 37 in 1942—was an artist, but also a complete outsider to the army and to industry. But Hitler distrusted professionals and preferred to choose non-specialist amateurs as his associates. After all, he had already appointed a wine salesman (Joachim von Ribbentrop) as his foreign minister, a hazy party philosopher (Alfred Rosenberg) as his minister for eastern affairs, an engineer (Fritz Todt) as minister for armament and munitions, and an erstwhile air force pilot (Hermann Göring) as overseer of the national economy.

With this appointment Speer changed from a master architect to a complete technocrat and became a very important man in Hitler's Reich. Overnight, he was the virtual leader of the German war economy, the man who actually directed the giant power machine. Speer became the man charged with drawing from it the maximum effort under maximum strain, the very epitome of "managerial revolution." Speer jettisoned the regime's commitment to a specific Nazi technical ideology in favor of the war effort. The "reactionary modernist" element in Nazi ideology, personified by Todt, disappeared as a result of the war.

With Speer, Hitler made a judicious choice, as the young and ambitious architect proved a skilled and talented technocrat, a remarkable manager of industrial enterprise on a gigantic scale, and an exceptionally capable administrator, raising production levels of armaments to previously unattained heights. In spite of massive Allied bombing attacks and the bureaucratic opposition of other Nazi leaders, Speer kept the German war machine in the field—thereby prolonging World War II by at least two years.

As minister of production and armament, Albert Speer entrusted the direction of the OT to Xaver Dorsch. The civil engineer Franz Xaver Dorsch (1899–1986) had been a soldier in World War I, had joined a paramilitary *Freikorps* in May 1919, and became a member of the Nazi Party in 1922. He also took part to Hitler's failed Beer Hall Putsch in November 1923. Dorsch qualified as an architect in 1928, and from 1929 to 1933 he was a close colleague of Todt and his deputy. The relationship between Speer and Dorsch, however, was strained. A major bone of contention was the fact that the OT only had responsibility for building projects outside the Reich. It was now increasingly being employed for construction work at home and needed to have control of the domestic construction industry. Dorsch and Speer fought a bitter battle over the issue, with Dorsch demanding that he be put in charge of all building activity inside the Reich so that new projects could be managed by the OT. Dorsch was secretly an ally of Speer's archenemy, Martin Bormann, who recruited him as an agent of the Parteikanzlei (the Nazi Party head office) to spy on Speer. On several occasions, Dorsch instigated moves and plots to oust Speer, and although Dorsch was unsuccessful, Speer's position was seriously weakened. In April 1944, Hitler took command of the OT away from Speer and gave it to Dorsch. Dorsch was invited to submit proposals for a scheme, which Speer vigorously opposed, to move German industrial facilities into concrete factories or underground facilities to protect them from Allied bombing. Hermann Göring, the Reich minister of aviation, also ordered Dorsch to undertake the construction of underground aircraft hangars and plants for the Luftwaffe. Dorsch was put in charge of the armaments ministry's building office and served, in his role as the minister's deputy, as general commissioner for construction industry matters, as well as retaining his existing post as the head of the Organisation Todt. He was thus in charge of virtually all the Third Reich's building projects in the final year of the war, while Speer concentrated on armaments production. Hitler's directive to build bombproof factories gave Dorsch the authority he needed to take control of the whole German construction industry. By September 1944 he headed a workforce of 780,000 people, mostly foreign, forced laborers who were engaged in construction projects within the Reich.

After the war, although he had been a major Nazi, and responsible for the employment of forced laborers, Xaver Dorsch avoided prosecution and started another very successful career. He was commissioned by the United States Army to write a 1,000-page study of the Organisation Todt, which was published in 1947. In 1950, he set up the firm of Baumeister Xaver Dorsch, Ingenieurbüro (engineering office), which became the consulting engineering company Dorsch Consult in 1951, located at Offenbach am Rhein (province of Hessen). Franz Xaver Dorsch died in November 1986, but his company became the Dorsch Gruppe GmbH in 2006. Today it is one of Germany's largest independent planning and consulting companies, employing some 1,600 persons.

Back in 1942, Speer and Dorsch, in spite of their strained relationship, made the OT directly responsible to Hitler, therefore avoiding a takeover by the Deutsche Arbeitsfront (DAF, the German Labor Front) and insisted—in August 1943—that field armies and staffs include an OT Generalingenieur (engineer-general), usually the local OT corps commander, to coordinate all building projects.

Although the OT was militarized, orders were issued not by the OKW (German Armed Forces High Command) but by Speer's Minister of Armament, a situation that gave rise to numerous frictions and rivalries between the two leaders, and also between the military and civilians.

In the end, Speer's skilled efforts as minister of war production and armament were desperate short-term measures and expedients that undermined the structure of the German economy and accelerated its eventual collapse. Through the better management of this board, together with drastic rationalization, the massive closure of small firms and the redistribution of skilled labor, factories producing war materials worked under high pressure. War industries were dispersed to enable large-scale prefabrication, and components for war machines were produced in many different parts of the country and brought together only when ready for assembly.

In the short term, Speer was able to maintain, and in some cases increase, the output of essential weapons and ammunition. In 1944 Germany produced more armaments than in 1940. Yet the so-called "Speer miracle"—which was able to answer the Allied bombing offensive with a considerable increase of war production in 1943–44—was not realizable without the ruthless exploitation of human and material resources from occupied Europe. While Dorsch was a convinced Nazi, Speer was a realistic technocrat, not a political fanatic; but he showed no scruples in exploiting slave labor, and his role indirectly caused the expansion of the system of SS concentration camps. German workers, including women, and foreign workers—including prisoners of war, forced laborers, and Jews and concentration camps inmates—were driven to the point of exhaustion by Speer's expedients. His position was such that he was not directly involved with the cruelty in the administration of the Nazi slave labor program, but he was plainly responsible for and aware of its existence. For example, at meetings of the Central Planning Board he was informed that his demands for labor were so large as to necessitate violent methods in recruiting; however, he insisted that the slave laborers be given adequate food and working conditions so that they could work efficiently. Albert Speer's level of involvement in the persecution of the Jews and his level of knowledge of the Holocaust have always been matters of dispute. The German historian Matthias Schmidt (in his book *Albert Speer: The End of a Myth*, 1983) has unraveled facts that seem to provide evidence of Speer's knowledge of the Nazi extermination of the Jews. Several historians and biographers (notably Adam Tooze and Gitta Sereny) have argued that Speer's ideological commitment to the Nazi cause was greater than he claimed. In mitigation it must be recognized that by the end of the war, Speer became increasingly opposed to and disillusioned with Hitler's policy of victory or annihilation, and did his best to protect German industry from Hitler's Nerobefehl—the Nero Decree of March 1945—which ordered drastic, scorched-earth tactics, in fact the total destruction of all infrastructures and facilities in areas threatened by the advancing Allies that could be used by them in the continuation of the war against Germany. This included all military and civilian traffic, communications, industrial and supply installations. As it was Speer's ministry that would have to implement all measures geared toward mass destruction, thus Speer could also go far in blocking Hitler's crazy plans. Feeling a mixture of abhorrence, pity and fascination, Speer also claimed to have (vainly) attempted to kill Hitler in early 1945 by envisioning the insertion of poisonous gas in the ventilation shaft of the Führer's bunker at Berlin.

After the war at the Nuremberg Trials, Speer was one of the few accused to admit his guilt and declare regret for his crimes. He cunningly confessed that he had made a pact with the devil and realized much too late the implications of his agreements. He admitted that without his commitment, Germany might have lost the war by 1943. Cleverly, Speer partially distanced himself from Hitler's inhumane regime and genocidal system. He presented himself as an apolitical technocrat who had not planned or initiated the war. He developed a modest, remorseful and "respectable" image of himself as a man who was essentially only ambitious in an artistic sense. That he later became a technician who had acted in an immoral way was (according to him) precisely because of his limited insight. For his commitment to the Nazi regime and his involvement in the slave labor program, Speer was found guilty of war crimes and crimes against humanity. His repentant attitude, however, allowed him to save his head, and he was sentenced to 20 years' imprisonment in 1946. Speer served his full sentence at Spandau Citadel near Berlin, together with other high-ranking Nazis, notably the enigmatic and deranged Rudolf Hess. Speer was released in 1966 and wrote a very interesting autobiographical book, *Erinnerungen (Memories)*, published in Berlin in 1969 by Verlag Ullstein GmbH. Translated in English as *Inside the Third Reich*, Speer's book gives a unique portrait of Hitler and a vivid description of the Nazi regime, and also made him a rich man. Albert Speer, the deceitful and controversial "good repentant Nazi," died at age 76 on September 1, 1981, of natural causes.

The OT During the War

During World War II the OT became a huge paramilitary body. Its tasks became various, and all were connected to the war effort: building, repair and establishment of roads, and support of army engineers. After the end of the war on the Western Front in 1940, OT personnel repaired railways, roads, bridges, ports, canals and airfields, but soon the tasks became even broader. In summer 1941, the OT was engaged in Russia and, following the conquering Wehrmacht, carried out repair work in occupied territories, and built railways, roads, bridges, and facilities. Because Germany and Poland used standard-gauge rail lines (1.435 m) and the Soviets continued to use the Czarist era's wide-gauge lines (1.528 m), Germany was obliged to construct two special gauge-conversion yards on the German-Soviet border. German rail conversion efforts were completed relatively quickly. In many cases, the Germans only had to remove one of the rails and move it closer in. Alongside maintaining the transport system in all occupied territories, the OT took over the exploitation of sources of raw materials, the extraction of oil, the installation of factories and the transportation of (looted) strategic products back to the Reich. The OT also managed farms in Ukraine; supervised the harvest; and constructed harbor facilities, dams and dikes in marshy districts. It ran ammunition, vehicles and tank factories, and established electric power grids.

Because of the experience gained from the West Wall, the OT was commissioned to build large-scale fortifications such as the Atlantic Wall and many other defensive lines, notably in northern Italy and Russia. The OT was also the key builder of the gigantic Kriegmarine's U-Boat bases on the Atlantic coast, as discussed later.

The huge achievements of the OT, based on private enterprise, improvisation, slave labor, technical rationality and standardization, were largely due to technocrats Albert Speer and Xaver Dorsch. The OT had to supply all working sites with material and manpower, and had to build according to contradictory policies and within demanding deadlines imposed by impossible schedules. The Organisation Todt's achievements were colossal and astonishing, but it must be remarked that slave labor was widely used and that the German economic system was completely devoted to war. Besides, the Germans utilized all the resources of the lands they occupied to support their war effort. In fact, occupied lands were treated and ruthlessly exploited just like colonial possessions. Unlimited looting and methodical plundering became common practice. On a large scale, the OT requisitioned all material, tools, plants, equipment and transportation means.

Under Todt's leadership the OT had greatly increased but basically remained a German undertaking. With the accession of Dorsch and Speer at its head, the organization gained a European dimension. In all occupied lands, the OT subcontracted local firms and employed individuals to help construct military installations and bunkers. Working with the German OT often meant good wages and attractive premiums, and many (e.g., French, Dutch and Belgian) building companies made significant profits. Collaborating with the Organisation Todt offered the guarantee for the personnel to keep their jobs, and also to avoid being rounded up and send to work in Germany. However, this guarantee was not always respected. In June 1943, many OT volunteers working on the Atlantic Wall were arbitrarily drafted and transferred to the Ruhr region in Germany in order to repair the damages done to the Eder and Möhne dams by Allied air raids on May 16. This measure put a dark shadow on the OT and discouraged voluntary workers.

From mid-1943 onwards, the Germans were forced to wage a defensive war, and the OT had to build fortifications intended to hold the enemies at bay. As the war progressed in 1944, the German forces had to withdraw everywhere. Then, the OT formations were often obliged to carry out the destruction of the installations and facilities, many of which they had themselves built during the period of victory and occupation.

Structure of the OT

After Fritz Todt's death in 1942, his successor Albert Speer and his deputy Xaver Dorsch brought some changes to the structure to the OT. Speer created the OT-Zentrale, a coordinating body directly answering to the Ministry of Armament. The OT became a part of the ministry but kept a large measure of independence, notably the power to requisition what it needed, the right to subcontract other firms and the right to have its armed militia. OT men were "front line workers," and wherever they were deployed, the company links of the OT were generally maintained. The contractor, workforce, cadres, and machinery stayed together. Transport and mobility were guaranteed by the Organisation itself through an affiliated organization, the National Socialist Drivers' Corps (see Chapter 3). Until 1942 the administrative unit of the OT was the Einsatz (working place), but after Dr. Todt's death Speer redesigned the OT into formations that were organized on a paramilitary basis with units and ranks typical of the Nazi hierarchy as used by NSDAP, SA and SS.

The largest unit, corresponding to an army corps, was called an Einsatzgruppe (EG) and was placed under the command of a major general. The corps was divided into Oberbauleitungen (OBL, Main Construction Command, roughly of brigade strength), each about 5,000–15,000 strong, headed by a colonel or a lieutenant colonel. The organization was also quite flexible according to volume, needs and urgency of the works, so brigades could also be formed into division-status units called Einsätze (ES), placed under the command of a brigadier or a colonel. Each Oberbauleitung included several Bauleitungen (BL, Construction Command, roughly of regiment strength), about 3,000 strong, commanded by a major. The BL was divided into several battalions called *Baustellen* (building sites) or *Lager* (camps), which had about 1,000 workers. Building sites and camps could be regrouped to form an Abschnittsbauleitung (ABL, District Command) headed by a captain. These units included company-size *Trupp*s, about 150 men strong, placed under command of a senior NCO. The companies were divided into *Kameradschaften* (platoons) and *Rotten* (sections or squads) headed by junior NCOs.

The Einsatzgruppe West had been formed in late 1941 to carry out works and repairs in France, Belgium and the Nether-

Organisation Todt

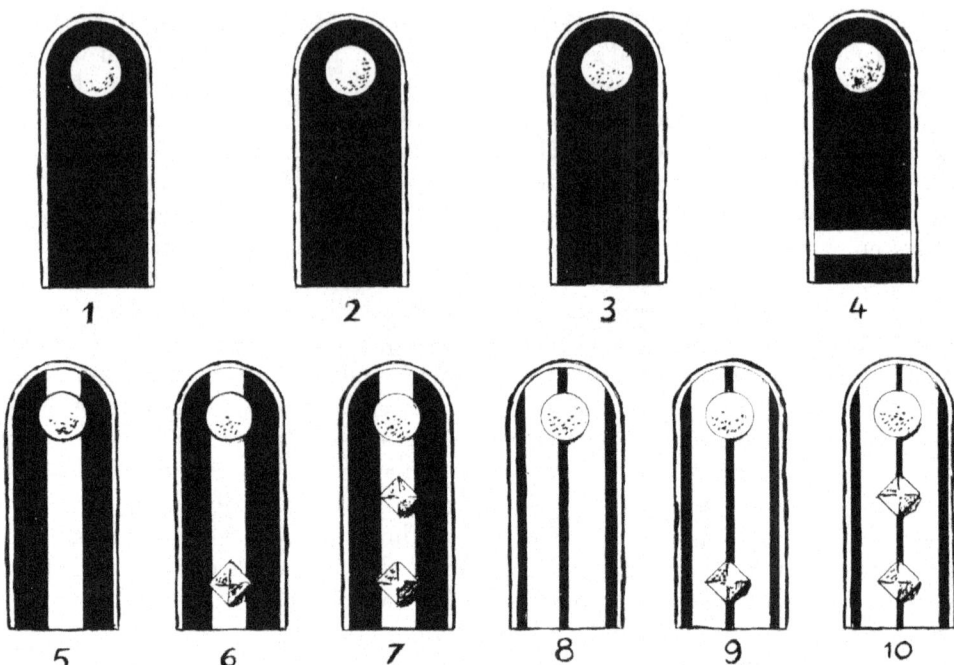

OT ranks (displayed on the shoulder straps):
1: OT-*Arbeiter*
2: OT-*Rottenführer*
3: OT-*Kameraddschaftsführer*
4: OT-*Meister*
5: OT-*Truppführer*
6: OT-*Obertruppführer*
7: OT-*Haupttruppführer*
8: OT-*Frontführer*
9: OT-*Hauptfrontführer*
10: OT-*Gruppenleiter*

Sample collar patches (used after 1943):
1: *Mannschaften*
2: *Truppführer*
3: *Obertruppführer*
4: *Haupttruppführer*
5: *Frontführer/Bauführer*
6: *Oberfrontführer/Oberbauführer*
7: *Hauptfrontführer/Hauptbauführer*
8: *Stabsfrontführer/Bauleiter*
9: *Oberstabsfrontführer/Oberbauleiter*
10: *Oberstfrontführer/Hauptbauleiter*
11: *Einsatzgruppenleiter* II
12: *Einsatzgruppenleiter* I
13: *Amtschef* OT

lands. Its headquarters were established in Paris, at 33/35 Avenue of the Champs Elysées. Its subdivision Einsatz Westküste built submarine pens in Bordeaux, Brest, La Rochelle, Saint-Nazaire and Lorient. Its other subdivision, Einsatz Kanalküste, built a part of the Atlantic Wall. The Einsatz Luftwaffe built airfields in northern France during the Battle of Britain in 1940 and V1 rocket sites in 1943–44. The Einsatzgruppe Wiking, with headquarters established at Oslo, covered Denmark and Norway since 1940 and was charged with the building of coastal defenses and submarine pens at Trontheim and Bergen. The Einsatzgruppe Südost (southeast), formed in early 1941, and the Einsatzgruppe Karpathen, created in July 1944, were active (notably for the exploitation of chrome, iron, bauxite, manganese and asbestos ore) in German-occupied Serbia, Greece, Albania, Croatia, and Hungary, and in Romania for the extraction of oil.

For the purpose of supporting the troops invading the Soviet Union after June 1941, the Einsatzgruppe Jakob was created. This large formation—totaling 50,000 German cadres and some 750,000 foreign workers—was reorganized in February 1942 and divided into four units, each attached to a corresponding army group: OT Einsatzgruppe Nord (north), OT Einsatzgruppe Mitte (middle), OT Einsatzgruppe Süd (south), and OT Einsatzgruppe Kaukasus (Caucasus Mountains, situated between the Black and the Caspian seas).

In June 1943, the OT Einsatzgruppe Italien was formed in Italy to establish several lines of fortifications such as the Gothic Line. The Gothic Line extended from La Spezia, through the mountains north of the Arno River, to the sea south of Rimini. The line was not completed, but sections running through the Apennines were formidable, with narrow mountain passes heavily defended. The defenses consisted of camouflaged, armed concrete pillboxes, concealed artillery emplacements, barbed wire and minefields. To have a clear line of fire, villages were destroyed and trees were cut down. The line made Allied progression slow and costly.

Originally the OT's field of operations was confined to foreign occupied territories, but as the Allies intensified the air bombardments of German towns in 1943, several new OT-Einsatzgruppen were created to clear the damages and rebuild the destroyed installations at home: Einsatzgruppe Tannenberg, EG Rhein-Rhur, EG Kyffhauser, EG Oberrhein, EG Hansa, EG Alpen, and EG Deutschland.

Paradoxically, Nazi Germany was not organized as a totally integrated, mobilized and centrally controlled state. Neither war production, manpower, construction, administration, nor intelligence was rationally centralized. The structure of German politics and administration—instead of being pyramidal—was in fact a confusion of personal empires, private armies and rival intelligence services. The Nazis were obsessed by order, which was illustrated by

Organisation Todt cipher.

OT armband reading, "Is working for the OT."

Badge of French OT volunteers. The badge—worn on the upper right sleeve—consisted of a yellow cogwheel hemming a shield with the French tricolor (blue-white-red) and the inscription "France."

parades, processions and meetings, but actually the system of government was chaotic in order to create zeal and rivalry. Hitler liked to see a good deal of ruthless competition under him, since he assumed that this way was the only road to outstanding achievements. At the head of these private empires Hitler appointed leaders who were both immensely strong and powerful but at the same time were vulnerable, as their position and power depended solely on his will. This Nazi leadership had constantly to be on the qui vive, as there was ferocious rivalry at the top between Hitler's henchmen. The uncertainty of politics, the danger of arbitrary change, and the fear of personal revenge meant that all top henchmen had to protect themselves against surprise. Eager to acquire as much power as possible, they formed clans and cliques with variable alliances, allegiances and loyalty. Bormann, Himmler, Ley and Göring were jealous of Speer's prerogative and influence, and used every opportunity to undermine his position. When Speer fell ill in 1943,

Göring exercised pressure upon OT leader Xaver Dorsch to take control of the building organization, something he had wanted since Fritz Todt's death. When Speer recovered from his illness he had to fight in order to reestablish his influence with Hitler and renewed his subordination of Dorsch at Göring's expense. Albert Speer, however, was incapable of avoiding the growing influence and the expansionist drive of SS Reichsführer Heinrich Himmler. By the end of the war, the SS were a state within the state, an army within the armed forces, and a huge military, economic and political lobby. By that time the only force capable of counterbalancing the SS was the NSDAP, headed by Martin Bormann, Hitler's *éminence grise*.

OT-Militia (OT-SK)

When World War II broke out, following the Reich's tremendous early victories, the OT was called upon for construction work in occupied countries that had been defeated. At the same time, OT workers found themselves in frontline situations. It thus became a necessity to arm German personnel in order to defend working sites and installations against sabotage, thefts and surprise attacks from partisans and resistants. Every German worker received some sort of instruction in the use of small weapons, but soon it became clear that this was not enough, and a full-time police force was needed. The OT-Schützkommando (OT-SK, armed protection squads of the Organisation Tod) were created in early 1942 to impose German law and Nazi order at work sites abroad. Since May 1940, there had already existed security units of the OT known as Stosstrupp der Werkschar OT, which curiously were controlled and equipped by the DAF—the German Labor

OT specialty badges for bricklayer (left) and carpenter (right).

Front (see Chapter 2). An ill-defined and ambiguous relationship existed between the DAF and the OT until February 1942, when Albert Speer took over as OT leader after the death of Fritz Todt. One of Speer's first measures was to sever all connections with the German Labor Front.

The tasks of the armed OT-SK militia were to guard building sites against theft and sabotage, and to be prepared for any surprise attack while working on the building sites. Another task was escorting and protecting German workers, leaders, engineers and high-ranking officers of the corps. In addition, the OT-SK supervised the workers, the forced laborers, the teams of Jewish slave-workers and the Soviet prisoners of war. The total strength of the OT-SK militia seems to have been about 150,000. The protection squads were reinforced by Schutzpolizei (Schupo, in short) Police Regiment 28, which in November 1942 was renamed SS Polizei Regiment Fritz Todt and was headed by Oberstleutnant der Schutzpolizei Fritz Helmut Kosterbeck. Most of the OT-SK men belonged to groups of older men, who were expected to have received military training during World War I. Refresher courses were held, notably at the OT military security training centers at Flossenburg and Frankfurt in Germany, Inowlodz and Posen (Poland), The Hague (the Netherlands), and Pont-Callec and Pontivy in Britanny

(France). Courses and training were supervised by the Sturm Abteilung (SA Storm Troops), and lasted for about one month. Graduates then had a week-long probation in one of the OT-Sonder-kommando units. Equipment, uniforms and weapons, however, were often lacking. Most of the modern arms and regular military clothing went by priority to the Wehrmacht, so the OT militiamen were often forced to make do with whatever captured or obsolete equipment they could lay their hands on. Manpower, too, was scarce, as most physically able German males were already serving in the armed forces. To make up for the shortage of manpower, the OT protection squads had to rely on the recruitment of pro–Nazi foreign volunteers to fill the ranks. Many Dutchmen, Flemings, Walloons and Frenchmen, as well as nationals from Eastern Europe and Russia, volunteered for the armed OT squads. By the end of World War II, the OT-SK men were also employed to guard prisoners of war, criminals and concentration camp inmates. The Germans also encouraged the formation of local foreign police squads composed of reliable, pro–Nazi volunteers. One of these, for example, was a small militia created in January 1943 to guard the OT construction site and the submarine pen of La Pallice–La Rochelle in France. This police formation—called Kriegsmarinewerftpolizei (KMW, War-Navy Shipyard Police)—totaled some 200 armed volunteers and was headed by a French World War I veteran, lieutenant René Lanz. They were recruited from collaborationist and pro–Nazi French parties, notably invalidated, discharged, or disabled ex-servicemen of the Légion des Volontaires Français contre le Bolchévisme (LVF, Legion of French Volunteers Against Bolshevism).

The OT-Schützkom-mandos were also assigned to active combat duties in anti-partisan warfare on the Eastern Front and in the Balkans. In March 1945, all SK companies were disbanded and the best able-bodied men were transferred to the Waffen SS and other German military combat formations, notably the Volkssturm (see Chapter 4).

German Defense Wall Medal (Deutsche Schutzwall Ehrenzeichen). The bronze Medal of Honor for the German Defense Wall was instituted by Hitler in August 1939 and awarded to zealous, energetic and determined workers involved in the construction of defensive positions such as the West Wall and Atlantic Wall. To qualify for the award required, for military personnel, a minimum of three weeks' work; for civilians, a minimum of ten weeks. Some 800,000 medals were awarded during World War II. The reverse carried the inscription "Für Arbeit zum Schutze Deutschlands" (For work on Germany's defense).

RANKS OF THE OT

The OT had become a militarized body and its members were uniformed and given ranks, which were displayed on the shoulder straps and collar patches. The OT was directed by the Chef der OT (chief of the OT), first Fritz Todt and later Xaver Dorsch. The hierarchy of the OT German volunteers and conscripts (OT-Eigenes Personal) was divided into three parts: *Bau* (construction personnel); *Bauwesen* (command supply and equipment); and *Technik* (technical, administrative, signal, and medical personnel). There were also distinctive ranks for the armed OT-SK militiamen. Each branch had different—and somewhat confusing—ranks, as listed below with their approximate equivalents.

Bau

Chef der Frontführung	General
Frontführer	Colonel
Stellvertreter des Frontführer	Lieutenant Colonel
OT-*Haupttruppführer*	Major
OT-*Obertruppführer*	Lieutenant
OT-*Truppführer*	Second Lieutenant
Kameradschaftführer	Sergeant
Rottenführer	Corporal
Frontarbeiter	Private/Worker

Bauwesen

Leiter der OT-Zentrale	General
OT-*Gruppenleiter*	Colonel
OT-*Oberbauleiter*	Lieutenant Colonel
OT-*Bauleiter*	Major
OT-*Haupttruppführer*	Captain
OT-*Obertruppführer*	Lieutenant
OT-*Truppführer*	Second Lieutenant
OT-*Meister*	Sergeant
OT-*Kameradschaftführer*	Sergeant
OT-*Rottenführer*	Corporal
OT-*Frontarbeiter*	Private/Worker

Technik

Chef des Amtes Bau-OT	General
OT-*Einsatzgruppenleiter* I	Lieutenant General
OT-*Einsatzgruppenleiter* II	Major General
OT-*Einsatzleiter*	Brigadier
OT-*Hauptbauleiter*	Colonel
OT-*Oberbauleiter*	Lieutenant Colonel
OT-*Bauleiter*	Major
OT-*Hauptbauführer*	Captain
OT-*Oberbauführer*	Lieutenant
OT-*Bauführer*	Second Lieutenant
OT-*Haupttruppführer*	Sergeant
OT-*Obertruppführer*	Sergeant
OT-*Truppführer*	Sergeant
OT-*Meister*	Corporal
OT-*Vorarbeiter*	Worker 1st class
OT-*Stammarbeiter*	Private/Worker
OT-*Arbeiter*	Worker

OT-Sonderkommando

SK-*Oberstfrontführer*	Colonel
SK-*Oberstabfrontführer*	Lieutenant Colonel
SK-*Einsatzleiter*	Lieutenant Colonel
SK-*Stabfrontführer*	Major
SK-*Hauptfrontführer*	Captain
SK-*Oberfrontführer*	Lieutenant
SK-*Dienstgruppenleiter*	Sergeant
SK-*Stoßtruppführer*	Sergeant
SK-*Kameradschaftführer*	Corporal
SK-*Mann 1.Klasse*	Militiaman 1st class
SK-*Mann*	Militiaman

UNIFORMS AND INSIGNIA

The Organisation Todt, another prime example of Nazi uniformed formations created during Hitler's regime, had no historical precedent. During its period of existence, its rank structure, style of uniforms, and insignia were constantly altered. The OT men wore many kinds of uniforms, based on the army dress, according to rank and specialization. The changing OT uniforms and insignia were regulated by a decree issued in 1940 and reorganized in 1942. Many uniforms worn by the OT and the other auxiliary troops were captured from the occupied European nations and dyed to match the standards of the German forces.

Workers wore a fatigue uniform with an armband bearing a swastika and the abbreviation "ORG. TODT." The *Arbeitsanzug* (working suit) or *Drillichanzug* (fatigue uniform) was widely used. Made of unbleached denim material, it consisted of a shapeless, buttoned jacket with two patch pockets and a turned-down collar. The trousers were made of the same material and were simply cut, with two side pockets.

Organisation Todt

OT Obertruppführer *(lieutenant)*.

Hauptbauleiter in Organisation Todt (colonel in technical service).

Uniforms and Insignia

Drilliganzug (fatigue suit). The depicted man wears a tunic, a collarless, grey pullover shirt, and the army 1936-pattern trousers made from field-grey wool material. The somewhat baggy trousers, often held up by suspenders, had side pockets, a four-button fly front, and a high waist with a higher V cut into the back.

Frontarbeiter Organisation Todt. Workers wore a fatigue uniform with—often—an armband bearing a swastika and the abbreviation "ORG. TODT."

Organisation Todt

SK-Mann, member of an OT-Schutzkommando.

OT-SK *Kameradschaftsführer* (corporal). The depicted OT-SK corporal wears a light brown tunic, the army M1935 steel helmet, the OT armband and the *Streifendienst* (patrol service) gorget when on duty. He is equipped with German infantry items including a Mauser K98 carbine, a gas mask folded in a cylindrical metal container, a hand grenade and ammunition pouches fixed on the duty waist-belt.

The fatigue suit was white or light grey, but colors tended to vary quite considerably, as the bleaching effect of the sun and repeated washing was severe. After some period of service, the fatigue suit color faded and in many cases they ended up as a natural fabric tone. The fatigue suit was easily washable and extensively used for fatigue duty including all kinds of work such as construction, painting, instruction, cleaning and maintenance.

German privates and NCOs wore a uniform that included a service tunic, trousers, and boots or work shoes. The color was *Erdbraun*, halfway between mustard and light brown. The tunic—with or without breast pockets—had piped shoulder straps; the color differed from branch to branch. The color pips were red for *Bauwesen* (construction), yellow for *Verpflegung* (supply and transport) and *Ausrüstung* (equipment), lemon yellow for *Nachrichten* (signal), dark blue for *Sanitätswesen* (medical service), black for *Musikwesen* (musician), green for *Verwaltung* (administration), white for the *OT-Schutzkommando* (protection squads), and brown for the *Propagandastaffeln* (war correspondents).

Uniforms and Insignia

OT *Frontführer* (colonel in construction service).

Eastern Organisation Todt worker wearing fatigue suit, Ost badge on the chest, and OT armband.

Specialists had silver-braid badges on black disks on the right cuff: a trowel for masons, a crossed saw and axe for carpenters, a ladder for scaffolders, a cross spanners for mechanics, a snake on a staff for medics, a light-flash for signalers, a silver-grey lyre for musicians, and a steering wheel for drivers, for example. Foreign volunteers workers wore national shields on the left upper arm: tricolor blue-white-red in a yellow cogwheel for Frenchmen, or a black lion on a yellow shield for the Flemish, for example.

Personnel of the OT-SK armed-protection police squads wore a brown or grey uniform with black shoulder straps piped with white. On duty (and when available) they wore the typical German M 35 steel helmet

Left: OT stylized cloth eagle badge (worn on left sleeve).

Organisation Todt

Organisation Todt officer. The man wears the standard mustard khaki tunic with OT cipher on the collar patches and the inevitable OT swastika armband.

Organisation Todt Engineer.

and the *Streifendienst* (patrol service) gorget consisting of a half-moon-shaped metal plate held by chains.

Senior officers and cadres wore a mustard-khaki uniform similar to that worn by the Nazi Party members. It consisted of a white, light grey or mustard-yellow shirt with a black tie, trousers and tunic with piped shoulder straps that used different colors to signify different branches. On the left upper sleeve the swastika armband was worn below a narrow light grey stripe carrying the letters "ORG. TODT." The collar of the tunic carried rank insignia composed of piped parallelogram-shaped patches, the OT monogram, a gold eagle and a laurel-leaf border. OT personnel sometimes wore a stylized bird in the branch's color on the left sleeve, piped in gold for senior officers, silver for lower ranks, and no piping for contracted workers.

Female auxiliaries were employed for medical, administrative and cleaning functions. They wore a dark blue battledress blouse, skirt and a field cap or sidecap, plus a silver eagle badge on the left upper arm and a specialization cuff badge.

For bad weather, all ranks were issued the standard, long double-breasted *Mantel* (greatcoat).

Headgear included various hats decorated with the Nazi emblem called *Hoheitszeichen*: an eagle holding a swastika in its claws. Headgear included the *Feldmütze* (peakless forage cap), the *Einheitsfeldmütze* (a popular soft cap with a long peak) and—for officers—the *Schirmmütze* (a soft or rigid peaked cap).

As a rule members of the OT were not armed, but senior ranking officers were sometimes allowed to have a small sidearm, generally a Walther PKK pistol. In occupied Europe and particularly in Russia, Balkans and France where guerrilla resistance was encountered, drivers, NCOs and junior leaders could be armed with light weapons, or escorted by armed guards of the OT-SK militiamen when available. They were armed with various—German-made or captured—weapons ranging from pistols to rifles, carbines and submachine guns.

The rounded-up workers, Jews, prisoners of war, Russian "volunteers" and other slave laborers were sometimes issued uniforms, similar to the previously described *Drillichanzug* (fatigue suit) when available. Many of them, though, simply wore civilian clothes, or their original military dress in the case of POWs. Concentration camp inmates wore the typical black and white striped "pajamas," a low-quality fatigue suit made of poor material, including peakless cap, loose-fitting tunic and trousers, and wooden clogs.

CADRES AND SLAVE LABOR

The scope OT used a highly complicated, mechanized production process that relied upon skilled and coordinated teamwork from a large number of specialist companies. The OT personnel and the managerial staff were composed of German volunteers and conscripts (OT-Eigenes Personal), civilian workers (*Zivilarbeiter*), and employees of private firms contracted by the organization. As most young men were drafted into the Wehrmacht, the OT had to accept older recruits, notably aging SA men (Sturm Abteilungen, a paramilitary organization in disgrace since the 1934 purge), functionaries from the Nazi Party (NSDAP, Nationalsozialistische Deutsche Arbeiter Partei) and mature men from other Nazi organizations. In addition, the OT offered "soft jobs" for all who were not eager to enlist or serve in the regular German army. In March 1942, the average age was 35–55; in mid–1943 it was 42–58; and in April 1944, the OT was composed of men aged 45 and above.

As already said, to make up for the lack of personnel, Volksdeutsche ("ethnic Germans" mainly from Romania, Yugoslavia and Hungary) were conscripted. In other occupied European countries, the Germans set up employment agencies whose task it was to recruit volunteers willing to go work in Germany or wherever the OT had building projects. However, given the poor results obtained by the volunteer program, soon systematic rounding-up and compulsion were applied. The lack of volunteers was so great that camp inmates, civilian criminals and political prisoners were drafted, while women were accepted for signals and administrative duties. Foreigners could join the OT (and the German industrial work forces at large) as volunteers, either to obtain the liberation of a relative who was a prisoner of war, or for material and financial reasons, or to avoid deportation to Germany. Dutch, Danish, Flemish and Norwegian people were considered "Germanic" and received pay and relatively decent working and living conditions. German nationals and foreign "Germanic" volunteers worked hard, though, often from 7 a.m. to 7 p.m. except on Sundays, when work stopped around midday. However, the machines were kept running by night shifts as well, as pouring concrete was a 24-hour-a-day job. Other European people—including Russians—received increasingly inferior treatment. The building of large constructions (such as bunkers and air raid shelters) involved highly skilled craftsmen, with heavy machines and sophisticated equipment doing a lot of the backbreaking labor, but equipment was usually in short supply. As a result, manual work was still the mainstay of the building industry and at times, large gangs of navvies had to put in some hard work. In September 1942, Hitler decreed that shovel and muscle jobs, dangerous, difficult and dirty work, and menial tasks such as navvying, digging mine galleries, breaking stones and carrying heavy loads should be done exclusively by foreigners. As a result most German nationals in the OT were in engineering, administrative, logistics and supervisory functions. They were technicians, engineers, supervisors, truck drivers, specialized laborers operating cement mixers, cranes, diggers, pile drivers, cement pumps and other mechanized machines, but some of them were also slave drivers and occasionally murderers. The common OT workers contributing to German building programs everywhere, as well as laborers in German war factories, were not voluntary at all. A large proportion was foreign and an enormous number of them were pressed into German service. The basic elements of the Nazi foreign labor policy consisted of mass deportation and mass enslavement. It was an expedient principle of underfeeding and overworking foreign laborers, of subjecting them to every form of degradation and brutality. It was a course of action that compelled foreign workers and prisoners of war to manufacture armaments and to engage in other operations of war directed against their own countries. In short, it was a policy that constituted a flagrant violation of the laws of war and the laws of humanity. The Organisation Todt maintained contacts with the SS, which hired *Zwangarbeiter* (slave labor) from concentration camps. From all European occupied nations, prisoners of war, political prisoners, convicts, rounded-up unemployed and displaced civilians, and concentration camp inmates (including Jews) were enslaved in forced labor. The use of vast numbers of foreign workers had already been planned before Germany went to war and was an integral part of the policy for waging aggressive war. As early as May 23, 1939, a meeting was held in Hitler's study at the Reich Chancellery to discuss and organize the matter. The arbitrary recruitment was eventually carried out by a special labor mobilization service—called Arbeitseinsatz—directed by the Nazi politician, *Gauleiter* of Thuringia, and honorary SA- and SS-Obergruppenführer Fritz Sauckel (1894–1946). Sauckel had joined the Nazi Party as early as 1923, had worked under Hermann Göring through the Four-Year Plan, and in March 1942 was appointed by Hitler general plenipotentiary for the mobilization of labor. The Arbeitseinsatz was a sub-branch of the Ministry of Labor, headed by Franz Seldte, and therefore had no connection with either the DAF (German Labor Front) or with the Organisation Todt or with the Ministry of Armament, headed by Albert Speer. As an NSDAP *Gauleiter*, Fritz Sauckel answered only to Hitler. Sauckel's service turned out to be the greatest slave trade in history. Tirelessly and efficiently, the ruthless Fritz Sauckel directed a brutal hunt for workers and abducted approximately 6 million men and women from all over Europe (especially from Poland and Soviet Union), during the three years he was active. Sauckel himself admitted that, of that number, at most 200,000 had come of their own free will. Fritz Sauckel was among the 24 high-ranking Nazi personalities accused in the Nuremberg International Military Tribunal. Found guilty of war crimes and crimes against humanity, he was given the death penalty and executed in October 1946.

From the start, a distinction was made by Sauckel's service between workers from Western Europe and laborers from the East. After the invasion of the Soviet Union, the Germans captured thousands of prisoners of war and thousands of Soviet citizens. Known as *Ostarbeiter* (Eastern workers) or

Fremdarbeiter (foreign workers), these populations were driven into forced labor in Germany. The deportation and enslavement of civilians reached unprecedented levels in the Occupied Eastern Territories as a direct result of labor demands. In order to meet these demands, the Nazis made terror, violence, and arson the staple instruments of their policy of enslavement. The SS, but also the German police and occupation army, were directed to participate in the abduction of forced laborers, and in the case of raids on villages or the burning of villages, to turn the entire population over for slave labor in Germany. Husbands were separated from their wives and children from their parents, and inhumane conditions were imposed. The German attitude towards prisoners of war and civilian forced laborers was shaped by the Nazi racist *Untermensch* (sub-human) theory, according to which they were dealing not with human beings like themselves but with a subhuman race. The slave labor program had two purposes. The primary purpose was to satisfy the labor requirements of the Nazi war machine by compelling foreign workers, in effect, to make war against their own countries and their allies. The secondary purpose was to destroy or weaken peoples deemed inferior by the Nazi racists, or deemed potentially hostile by the Nazi planners of world supremacy. The Nazis regarded themselves as a master race and considered the lowest German workers to be racially and biologically a thousand times more valuable than the other populations of Europe. An OKW (Supreme Army Command) directive of September 8, 1941, on the treatment of Russian prisoners of war declared that they had forfeited every claim to be treated as honorable enemies, and that the most ruthless measures were justified in dealing with them. The program of enslavement and its accompanying measures of brutality were not limited to Poland and the occupied Eastern territories, but were gradually extended to Western Europe as well. Frenchmen, Dutchmen, Belgians, and Italians all came to know the Nazi slavemasters. Many prisoners of war, captured resisters and civilians were at the disposal of the Organisation Todt and the German war industry. The use of prisoners of war was in flagrant disregard of the rules of international law, particularly Article 6 of the regulations annexed to Hague Convention Number 4 of 1907, which provides that "the tasks of prisoners-of-war shall have no connection with the operations of war."

Badges for foreign workers were usually worn on the left breast. Left: The Polish Worker badge, introduced in March 1940, was composed of a purple letter P on a yellow background with purple border. Right: The *Ostabzeichen* (East Badge) was worn by all workers, drafted or volunteer, from occupied Eastern Europe. It was compulsory starting in February 1942. The lettering OST and framing was black, and the background was either light blue or white.

Forced workers were treated like prisoners and required to wear a distinctive emblem. This was worn on the breast and consisted of a violet-colored P on a yellow cloth diamond for the Poles (introduced in March 1940), or a white and blue cloth badge with the letters OST for all workers from the occupied East (introduced in February 1942). Forced laborers were not allowed to leave their camps. The use of railroads, buses or other public conveyances was forbidden. There was, of course, no allowance for free time, vacations or leaves, or visits to restaurants, cafés, bars, theaters, motion pictures or other cultural entertainment. Visiting churches, regardless of faith, was not permitted. Sexual intercourse with German women and girls was strictly prohibited, and where it was discovered, was severely punished by death or by transfer to a concentration camp. By day and night, in all weather, laborers worked in difficult, exhausting, and dangerous conditions. When building huge bunkers, for example, there were heavy loads to be carried in makeshift installations, along precarious ladders, staircases, scaffolding, and vertical walls without safety rails, in the midst of sharp, rusty and protruding iron rods, hissing and unpredictable machinery, slippery slopes and quicksand in the form of liquid cement. Forced laborers were surrounded by armed SK guards with dogs, and were subjected to a merciless discipline. Wherever there was sabotage, the slightest protest or resistance, or violations against discipline including work refusal and loafing at work, it was repressed with extreme violence. Sauckel boasted to Hitler concerning the contribution of the forced labor program to the construction of the fortifications of the Atlantic Wall by Dorsch and Speer's Organization Todt. In a letter to Hitler dated May 17, 1943, Sauckel wrote: "In addition to the labor allotted to the total German economy by the Arbeitseinsatz since I took office, the Organisation Todt was supplied with new labor continually. Thus, the Arbeitseinsatz has done everything to help make possible the completion of the Atlantic Wall."

As the war went on, the labor camps became overcrowded, facilities for hygiene grew inadequate, and food rations were lowered while working time increased. For example, in the small island of Alderney (in the British Channel Islands), a concentration camp was established for about 1,000 political prisoners who were engaged as slave laborers upon the construction of the fortifications of the Atlantic Wall. The camp—named KZ Sylt—was staffed by the SS and was a branch of the infamous concentration camp Neuengamme in Germany.

The Nazi authorities insisted that slave laborers, while being deported to Germany or after their arrival, be degraded, beaten, and permitted to die for want of food, clothing, and adequate shelter. Once within Germany, slave laborers were subjected to treatment of an unusually brutal and degrading nature. They were over-exploited with such cruelty and roughness that many of them died from exhaustion, exposure, malnutrition, or bad treatment. Sick and infirm citizens of the occupied countries were taken indiscriminately with the rest. Those who managed to survive the trip into Germany, but who arrived too weak or too sick to work, were put to death or returned like cattle, together with those who fell ill at work, because they were of no further use to the Nazis. The return trip took place under the same conditions as the initial journey, and without any kind of medical supervision. Death came to many, and their corpses were unceremoniously dumped out of the cars with no provision for burial.

The OT also employed work battalions of rounded-up Jews who were treated with the worst ruthlessness. Jews (and Gypsies as well) were considered by the Nazis as the archenemies of the German people. By the Third Reich's definition, they were "non-Aryan," and "culture-tainting inferiors." From the start, the Nazis were determined to organize the destruction of the Jews—a goal put into horrifying practice at an industrial scale in mass extermination camps and forced labor camps. Particularly harsh and brutal treatment was reserved for them, and this was a part of the Nazi program of extermination through work. Measures were adopted to insure that extermination through work was practiced with maximum efficiency. Impressed Jewish workers were underfed, the amount of food in the camps being extremely meager and of very poor quality; food consisted generally of about one-half of a pound of black bread per day and a bowl of watery soup for noon and night, and not always that. They were forced to live in grossly overcrowded camps where they were held as animals and were otherwise denied adequate shelter. They were herded together in wooden barracks not large enough for one-tenth of their number. They were forced to sleep on wooden frames covered with wooden boards in tiers of two, three and even four, sometimes with no covering, sometimes with a bundle of dirty rags serving both as pallet and coverlet. They were denied adequate clothing. They worked and slept in the same clothing in which they had arrived. Virtually none of them had overcoats and were compelled, therefore, to use their blankets as coats in cold and rainy weather. In view of the shortage of shoes, many workers were forced to go to work in their bare feet, even in the winter. Sanitary and medical conditions were exceedingly bad, and as a result, they suffered from many diseases and ailments soon leading to incapacity and death. Owing to the great numbers crowded into small spaces and to the lack of adequate sustenance, lice and vermin multiplied, disease became rampant, and those who did not soon die of disease or torture began the deliberate process of starvation worsened by exhaustion. Slave laborers were generally forced to work long hours up to and beyond the point of exhaustion. There was no limit to working hours. Their duration depended on the kind of working establishments in the camps and the kind of work to be done. These were determined by the camp commander alone. A refusal to work or an infraction of the rules usually meant flogging or other types of torture, and in each case usually ended in death by hanging after extensive suffering. Slave laborers were also beaten and subjected to inhumane indignities for no reason at all.

German army armband (Deutsche Wehrmacht).

An example—among many, many others—is the labor camp Vaihingen/Enz (also called Camp Wiesengrund), which was created in 1944 as one of the approximately 50 auxiliary camps of the base camp Natzweiler-Struthof, located south of the city of Strasburg (France). It was in the proximity of a quarry, in which the Organization Todt was to construct an underground plant for aircraft production. About two weeks after the construction of the Vaihingen camp the first freight train, with approximately 2,200 Polish Jews from Lublin, arrived in August 1944. Because of the advance of the Allied forces to the western border of Germany, Natzweiler-Struthof was evacuated in September 1944. At the end of October the underground plant's construction was stopped. Already, large numbers of the camp's prisoners had been transferred to other auxiliary commands. Further transfers followed in November. At the same time the concentration camp Vaihingen was changed into a *Krankenlager* ("sick persons' camp"). Prisoners suffering from sickness and otherwise unable to work were brought to Vaihingen from the other labor camps of the provinces of Baden and Württemberg. By the end of the year 1944, approximately 2,400 prisoners were in the camp. An infirmary was created in December, and in January 1945 prisoner physicians came into the camp. The actual purpose of the camp was now to facilitate the deaths of the imprisoned humans. Due to the instruction of Heinrich Himmler to let no concentration camp inmates fall in enemy hands, the prisoners able to walk were taken to the Dachau concentration camp on April 4, when the Allied forces neared the camp. Soon after, the 1st French Army reached Vaihingen. There were still seriously ill prisoners in the camp. Completely insufficient nutrition, catastrophic hygienic conditions, and, at the beginning of 1945, an epidemic of the spotted typhus disease took approximately 1,600 human lives in this camp. The corpses had been buried near the camp in mass graves.

It was thus obvious that the Organisation Todt was not merely an innocent civilian conglomerate of building companies. Its members often behaved like colonialists and conquerors. The whole organization was de facto a part of the Nazi racist system of terror, annihilation and extermination.

It must also be said that many forced laborers were killed by Allied air raids.

Fortifications

With the establishment of the West Wall in the late 1930s, the Organisation Todt had ample experience in the construction of fortifications and concrete bunkers. This role was continued and extended during World War II.

As early as 1940, the OT constructed huge gun batteries in the Pas-de-Calais in

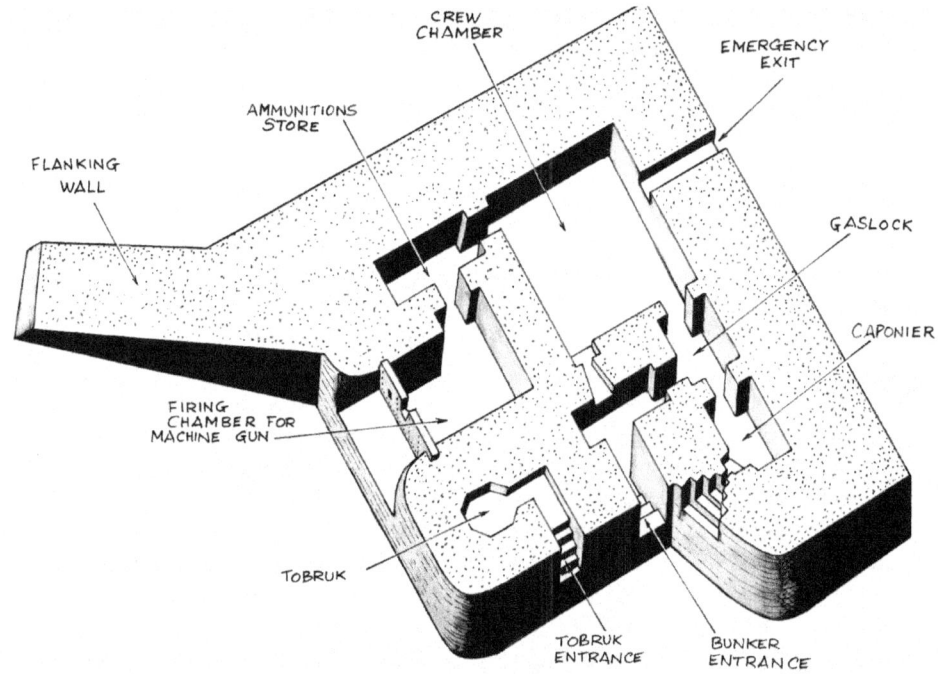

Groundplan, MG casemate type 630. This Regelbau bunker plan, issued in April 1942 for the Atlantic Wall, was intended to house a machine gun served by one NCO and five men. It measured 11.50 m long (flanking shield not included), 9.60 m wide and 5.10 m high. Its construction demanded 610 m³ of concrete, 29 tons of reinforcement rebar and 3.8 tons of metal plates for the ceilings. Observation was effected by means of a periscope.

Fortifications

northern France intended to support the invasion of Britain, the abortive Operation Sealion. These "offensive batteries" became the foundation of a defensive system called the Atlantic Wall, a girdle of strongholds and coastal batteries from Norway to southern France intended to repel British and American landings on the western façade of Hitler's empire, and to prevent the opening of a second front on the European continent. Started in 1940, work on the Atlantic Wall was intensified as a result of the successful British commando raid against Saint-Nazaire in March 1942 and the repulsed Canadian landing in Dieppe on August 19, 1942. Based on armed bunkers made of thick concrete; armed emplacements and batteries covering air, sea and land; minefields, beach-obstacles and anti-tank defenses, the Atlantic Wall was composed of Regelbau (standard) bunkers just like the West Wall. The drawback of standard designs was that they did not always lend themselves to the special demands of a particular sites, and this could result in tactical problems. But owing to a systematic and standardized approach to the problem, the Germans Engineer Corps, and more particularly the Organisation Todt, achieved efficient and astonishingly rapid bunker construction. The Atlantic Wall was strongest around important ports, which were heavily defended and constituted as *Festun-*

View of MG casemate type 630.

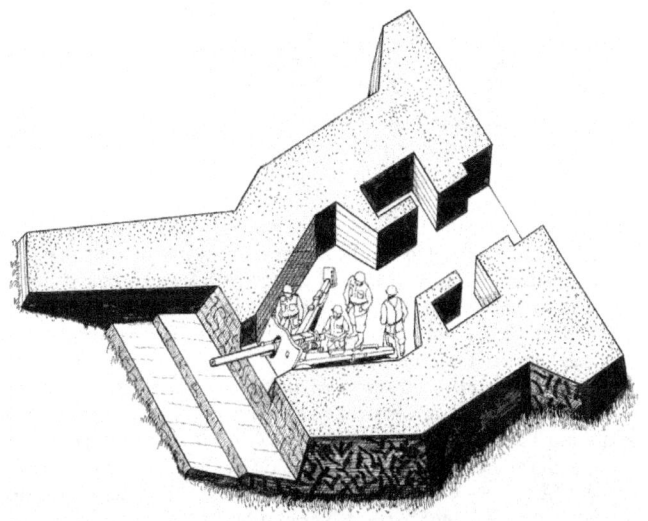

Groundplan, Pak casemate type 612. This plan for a standardized casemate for field and anti-tank artillery type 612 was issued in February 1943 for the Atlantic Wall. It was a very flexible design that could house 16 sorts of army guns and howitzers from caliber 7.5 cm to 10.5 cm owing to its large door placed at the back. Its length was 9 m, its construction demanded 385 m^3 of concrete, 17 tons reinforcement rebar and 4.1 tons of metal plates for ceilings. The embrasure was often closed by thick wooden shutters giving protection from splinters and sand infiltration. Each of the ammunitions-recesses contained from 350 to 500 projectiles, depending on the housed gun. Because of its great capacity, the casemate 612 was widely used for army flanking work as well as for army and navy medium range artillery emplacement (in this case, the flanking shield was omitted). The OT built 645 of them for the Atlantic Wall.

gen (fortresses), and in sectors deemed the most probable for Allied landing. Gradually the coasts between the main ports were filled with emplacements armed with coastal guns, *Widerstandnester* (infantry positions), *Stützpunkte* (fortified strongholds) and *Stützpunktgruppe* (groups of strongholds), which were reinforced and multiplied at the end of 1943 and the beginning of 1944, when an Allied invasion became imminent. Coastal defenses were increased by numerous obstacles, bunkers and mines, while armored reserve forces were stationed inland for a counter-attack role.

The furtherance of the Atlantic Wall was spurred by Field Marshal Erwin Rommel, in his capacity as inspector of fortifications and as commander of Army Group B. On June 6, 1944, the Atlantic Wall was far from completion because of shortages of materials, weapons and forces. Its garrison, composed of second-class divi-

Above, top: Front view, Pak casemate type 612. *Above, bottom:* Front view, casemate type 683, Battery Saint-Marcouf. This plan for the heavy artillery casemate type 683 for a 21-cm gun (Schartenstand für 21 cm Geschütze) was issued in February 1944. It was a huge construction (the roof and walls were 3.5 m thick) necessitating a bulky mass of 2,000 m³ of concrete, 100 tons of reinforcement rebars and 22.6 tons of metal plates for ceilings. The length was 21.80 m and the breadth was 16 m. This bunker was especially designed to house a captured Czech 21-cm Skoda gun (weighing 37 tons and firing about 25 projectiles per hour to a distance of 30 km with a lateral arc of 120°). Only two were built (a third one was in construction) at Crisbecq battery near Saint-Marcouf in Normandy, France. Crisbecq was one of the most powerful German batteries, with the long range guns capable of firing at Saint-Vaast-la-Hougue in the northwest and to the Baie des Veys in the southeast. It opened fire on D-Day (June 6, 1944). The battery was silenced by Allied fire shortly after the landing. *Below:* Cross-section, casemate type 683 at St. Marcouf battery, Normandy, France.

sions, could not repulse the powerful and well-prepared Allied Operation Overlord in Normandy. The Atlantic Wall, which attracted the world's attention because of D-Day, was the most famous fortified line built by the Organisation Todt, but it was not the only one.

The Germans occupied the south of France after the Allied landing in North Africa in November 1942, . From 1943 onwards, the Armeeoberkommando 19 was concerned with the defense of the French Mediterranean coasts—including the island of Corsica.

Front view, casemate type M 271. The navy artillery casemate M271 was issued in April 1943 for the Atlantic Wall. Its construction required 930 m³ of concrete. The gun in the firing chamber was sometimes protected by an additional armored gun-house. Four M271s were built by the Organisation Todt in Navy Battery Tirpitz at Raversijde (armed with 10.5-cm SKC/32 guns placed in gun houses) near Ostend, Belgium.

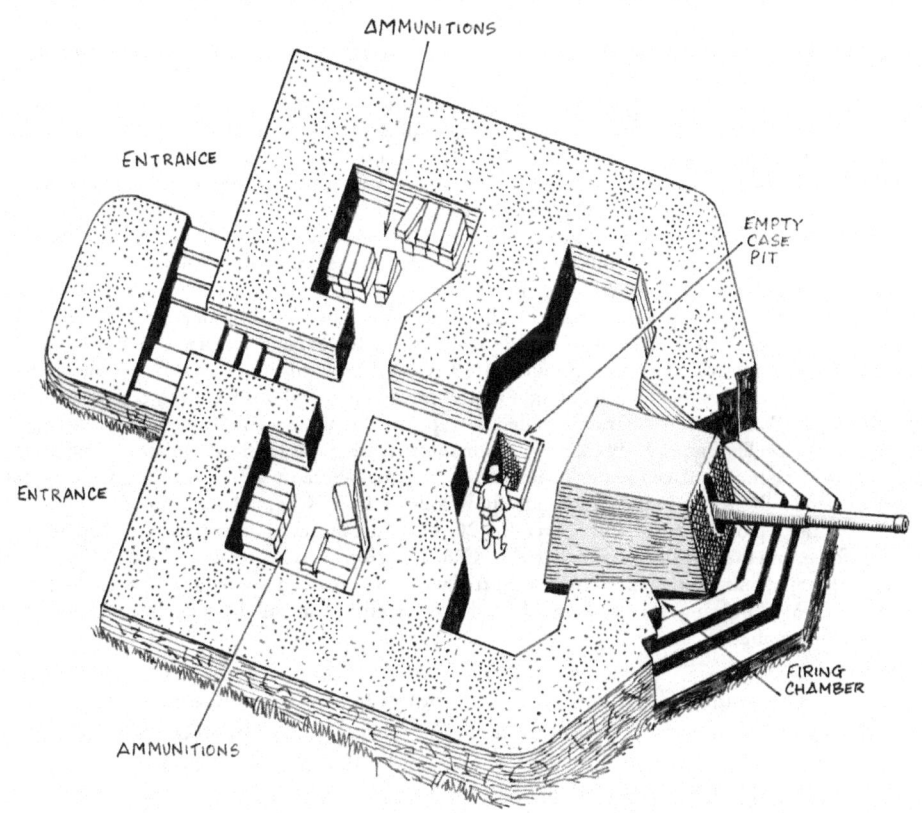

Groundplan, casemate type M271.

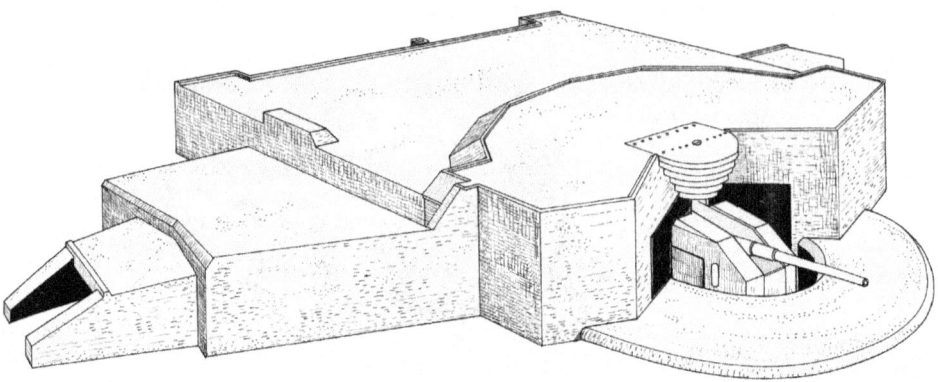

Battery Lindemann Pas de Calais, Northern France. The Lindemann navy coastal battery (also known as MKB 6/244-Stützpunkt Neuß) was positioned near Sangatte on a hill named Les Noires Mottes. Manned by gunners from the 6th Battery of the 244th Navy Artillery Battalion, the MKB 6/244 was one of the most powerful artillery positions in the whole Atlantic Wall. It was armed with three 40.6-cm SK C/34 (L/52) ship guns originally intended for battleships of the projected H-Class. Designed by the Krupp Company in 1934, these guns—nicknamed Adolf in Hitler's honor—were used as coastal weapons and originally placed in the region of Danzig and known as Batterie Schleswig-Holstein. The guns were brought to the Channel in early 1941 and renamed Batterie Grossdeutschland. Finally in 1942 they were renamed Batterie Lindemann (after the captain of the warship *Bismarck*, which had been sunk in May 1941). The huge 40.6-cm guns were extremely powerful; they could fire a 1,024-kg shell to a range of 42 km, or a 594-kg shell to a range up to 56 km, and thus further than Dover. The shockwave was so tremendous that the guns could not be fired at the same time. The guns were housed in massive armored turrets revolving on a ball-race; the turrets were single-level gun-houses on a pedestal, with the rear of the mounting supported on pivoted wheels traveling on a rail track. They were protected by three similar and imposing three-level artillery SK bunkers; these were specially adapted to receive guns and turrets and were called Turm Anton, Turm Bruno and Turm Caesar. The battery also included a fire-leading station (a variant of Type S446) that was fitted with a range-finder (10 m in length, placed in an armored observation turret), and Type Würzburg See-Riese FuMo 214 radar, as well as a computation room, an office for the commanding officer, a radio room, and a power plant; the lower level included crew quarters, rooms for officers, washing facilities, the water supply, a heating room and a filter room. Several additional observation and measuring posts were placed at Cap Blanc-Nez, Cap Gris-Nez, and Fort Lapin near Calais. Each artillery bunker was bordered by an electrified wire fence, minefields, barbed wire, anti-tank ditches, and various obstacles. Secondary and close-range weapons included two captured Russian 7.62-cm guns, two 5-cm anti-tank guns, one captured French 2.5-cm anti-tank gun, three heavy mortars and about 30 machine-gun posts, all protected by concrete bunkers and Tobruk pits. Anti-aircraft defense included six captured French 7.5-cm M30 (f) guns, three 4-cm guns and three 2-cm FlaK guns. In 1943, the garrison totaled three senior officers, 34 non-commissioned officers, and 280 gunners placed under command of Kapitän-Leutnant Werner Lokau. After the June 6, 1944, Allied landings, the battery engaged supply convoys in the Channel, and from September 4 to 15, it shot at the region of Dover. On September 20, 1944, the battery was heavily bombarded by the Allied air force, and the position was assaulted by Canadian troops on September 25 with infantry supported by Sherman tanks and Crabs (Shermans fitted with a flail to open a path in the minefields). After a day and a night of fighting, the garrison rebelled and forced Lokau and his staff to surrender on the morning of September 26.

Named Südwal (South Wall), this region showed strong fortifications around the fortresses of Marseilles and Toulon, as well as groups of strongholds at Agde, Sète, Port Saint-Louis and Port-de-Bouc. On 15 August 1944, the Allies landed in Provence between Hyères and Cannes (Operation Dragoon). Uncompleted, the Südwall was rapidly abandoned, and the German armies retreated back north.

The Organisation Todt also built airfields in northern Norway that were used to

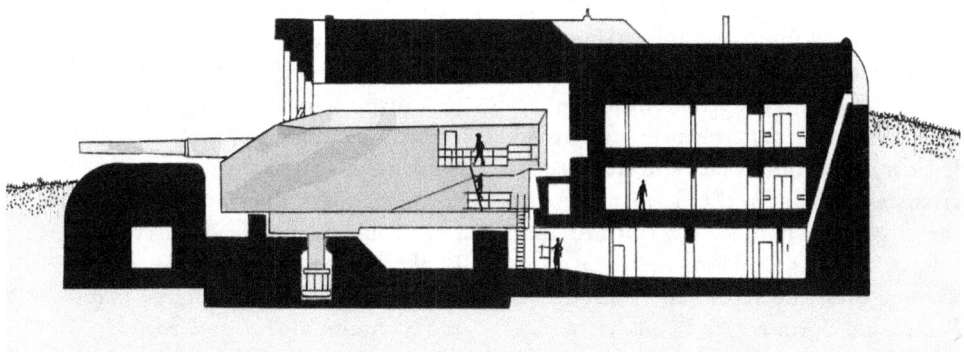

Cross section, casemate battery Lindemann Pas-de-Calais, Northern France. The lower level of each Turm of battery Lindemann included a ventilation room, a power plant and four ammunition stores (two for cartridges and two for shells); the ammunition was delivered by hoists to the rear of the emplacement, from where they were conveyed to the rear of the turret on trolleys and hoisted to the ramming table. The middle level was divided into crew quarters, toilets and washing facilities, supply stores, and a filter room. The upper level comprised officers' and NCOs' quarters, an administration office, an infirmary, a mess, and a kitchen with water and food supply.

attack Allied Artic convoys en route for Murmansk, as well as fortification lines aiming to stop Russian offensives in the East: e.g., the Wotan Line, built at the end of 1943, ran parallel with the Dnieper River from the Black Sea to Kiev. The Panther Line of February 1944 defended Lake Peipus. The Germans planned a continental-scale line of fortification in the East in the event that they won the war. The project of the Eastern Wall was seriously entertained by Hitler. According to the Nazi concept of *Lebensraum* (the essential theory of living space), the Russians were to be chased headlong across the Volga, over the Ural Mountains and deep into Siberia and Asia—their "barbaric home." Intended as another Great Wall of China, the Eastern Wall would have prevented the Russians from ever returning to Nazi-controlled Europe.

In autumn 1943, the Führer ordered a new program of fortifications to stop the Allied progression in Italy. The Gustav Line—established at the end of 1943—was a series of German military fortifications constructed by the Organisation Todt. It ran from just north of where the Garigliano River flows into the Tyrrhenian to the mouth of the Sangro on the Adriatic. As the Germans were forced to retreat north, other defensive lines were hastily built: the Caesar Line in May 1944, the Viterbo Line in June, the Trasimene Line in July, and the Gothic Line in August.

U-Boat Pens

The most impressive of all World War II German bunkers were without doubt the concrete pens for submarines on the Atlantic coast. The OT built enormous concrete bunkers to protect warships, and more particularly U-Boat (submarine) pens in France. In Germany herself the construction of submarine pens had started before the war, at Hamburg for example. Soon after the victory of June 1940, the Germans occupied all the shores of the North Sea, the Channel and the Atlantic Ocean in the areas they controlled. Having control of numerous important harbors, they engaged in a war at sea against Britain and, at the end of 1941, against the United States of America. The Battle of the Atlantic was a long and bitter fight—one of the most decisive campaigns of World War II—to control the vital naval communications between Britain and the USA. On Germany's side, the air force and surface war-

Organisation Todt

ships did not play a major role, and the main German weapon was its submarine fleet. Submarines were especially vulnerable to air strikes when they were alongside quays when resupplying and repairing. Therefore U-Boat installations were protected by concrete shelters built by the German navy and the Organisation Todt. The main Atlantic submarine bases for Germany's naval effort were at Brest, Lorient, Saint-Nazaire, La Pallice and Bordeaux, in France, as well as at Trontheim and Bergen in Norway for the northern Atlantic Ocean. Those harbors were given the status of *Verteidigungsbereich* (fortified zone), then became *Festungen* (fortresses) in 1944. Though incorporated in the system of the Atlantic Wall, U-Boat installations had a completely different role. Instead of being defensive positions they were offensive bases. Each of them included a vast militarized perimeter with ancillary installations and facilities as well as an enormous concrete work—specially designed to shelter submarines—situated in a dock communicating with the open sea. Under this thick carapace various alveoli, docks and quays were built with hoisting devices and installations allowing all supply and refuel operations. Some alveoli were fitted with pumps so that they could be transformed in dry docks where submarines' hulls could be inspected and repaired. The bunker was a large logistical base furnished with facilities such as energy plants, fuel tanks, ammunition and torpedo stores, transformers, various workshops, maintenance installations, ventilators, accumulators, heating rooms, personal accommodations, telephone and radio rooms, headquarters, command posts, administration offices and so on. The bunker was generally crowned with an observation and signal tower equipped with radar and radio, and it was connected to the rest of the harbor by means of railways. Its entrances were defended by machine guns and anti-tank guns placed in close-range casemates integrated into its thick walls. Against aircraft, FlaK guns were placed on the roof.

The German U-Boat pens were indeed remarkable structures, and their construction ultimately consumed more concrete than all other coastal defenses put together. Their amazing thickness proved capable of resisting the Allies' strongest bombs. The roofs, resting on 2.5- to 3.5-m-thick walls, were generally composed of steel beams, armored plates and massive, reinforced concrete slabs; they included three concrete layers and their tops were covered by a so-called *Fangrost* (screen or bomb trap) composed of two rows of concrete beams (each 2 m high and 1.5 m wide); the *Fangrost* framework was intended to explode bombs and dissipate the blasts into the void before they hit the actual roof. Most bunkers constructed by the OT were indestructible, and some are still used today by the French navy. In Bordeaux, La Pallice and Saint-Nazaire, the docks where the U-Boat bunkers were erected, communicated with the sea by means of sluices. To prevent the destruction

OT pin awarded to zealous workers of the German Atlantic submarine bases.

U-Boat Pens

Lorient Keroman III submarine pen.

of those vital passages, the sluices were covered with heavy and thick concrete protective bunkers.

There is no point here in describing in detail all German submarine bases, but a few words about Lorient and La Pallice-La Rochelle might be useful to illustrate the work of the Organisation Todt.

The U-Boat base Lorient was the largest of all submarine pens built by the OT in France. It was the headquarters of admiral Karl Dönitz, who directed his fleets from a

Dom-bunker Lorient (France). Within the Atlantic Wall, the OT built huge "Dom bunkers." These were "cathedral" concrete shelters for heavy railway guns. That of Lorient was intended to protect a submarine for repair. Dom bunkers were generally 70 to 80 m long and 10 m high, they were closed by heavy armored doors and constructed as a bow to resist allied bombs; some are preserved today in Lorient, Hydrequent and Fort Nieulay (France).

villa fitted with a concrete command-bunker. Lorient was the home base to the 2nd U-Flotille Saltzwedel. In January 1940, the 2nd was reinforced by the 10th U-Flotille. The construction of the Keroman U-Boat base in Lorient was made in successive phases. At the beginning of 1941, the Organisation Todt built a huge slipway rolling on rails, making it possible to pull submarines out of the water. Two imposing concrete Dom-bunkers (cathedral shelters, each 81 m long, 16 m wide and 25 m high) were built to protect 250-ton submarines being repaired. In February 1941, a first concrete bunker was erected in Lorient called Keroman I (120 m long, 85 m wide and 18.50 m high), which included five dry docks. A second unit, called Keroman II, was built from May 1941 onwards. Measuring 138 m long and 120 m wide, it sheltered seven dry alveoli equipped with hoisting machines. Keroman I and Keroman II were completed at the end of December 1941. The construction of a third unit, called Keroman III, was undertaken in October 1941. Composed of seven alveoli, Keroman III measured 170 m long, 138 m wide and 20 m high. Its roof (7.4 m thick) could resist heavy, 6-ton Allied bombs. Keroman III was operational in May 1943 and, during the summer of that year, Keroman I and II were enlarged in order to shelter 24 submarines. This extension, called Keroman IV, was never completed. The Lorient U-Boat bunkers cost about 400 million Reichmarks and consumed 571,800 cubic meters of concrete. The protection of Festung (fortress) Lorient was secured by heavy navy gun batteries installed in Plouharnel, in Fort du Talud, in Fort de Locqueltas, in Gâvres, in Kernevel and on Groix Island. Lorient suffered numerous Allied bombardments: 20 in 1940, 16 in 1941, and 12 in the first months of 1942. From November 1942 on, air strikes were continuous; the USAF attacked during the daytime and the RAF at night. On January 15, 1943, the city was completely destroyed but, on the whole, the French civilian deaths and Allied air force casualties were in vain, as the concrete bunker was indestructible. The Quiberon peninsula and Festung Lorient were only liberated at the end of the war, in May 1945. Today, the formidable German installations are still used by the Marine Nationale (National French Navy).

Situated west of La Rochelle, the harbor of La Pallice was the home base to the 3rd U-Flotille Lohs. Construction of the U-Boat bunker La Pallice commenced in April 1941. The vast work (195 m long, 165 m wide and 19 m high) was composed of ten alveoli. The base was operational as early as the autumn of that same year and was enlarged in spring 1942. The basin communicated with the open sea by means of a sluice protected by a huge concrete shelter (162 m long, 25 m wide and 14 m high). The construction of both works demanded about 425,000 cubic meters of concrete. La Rochelle was a powerful *Festung* (fortress), including heavy batteries and defenses installed on Ré and Oléron islands. The Germans only capitulated at the end of the war in May 1945. The intact bunker is still used today by the French navy. It was utilized as a background in the motion picture *Das Boot*, directed by Wolfgang Petersen in 1981.

All along the Atlantic shores, the German navy controlled a broad maritime zone (called "Prachtstraße" in code) serving as a naval communications corridor. To secure this vital and wide zone, the Kriegsmarine operated surface boats: *Schnellboote* (speedboats armed with torpedoes), *Torpedoboote* (also armed with torpedoes) and *Artillerieträgerboote* (gunboats) were designed to practice offensive actions. *Vorpostenboote* were civilian ships transformed into scout units, while *Raümboote* searched and swept mines. The main harbors sheltering those surface units were Den Helder and Ymuiden in the Netherlands; Bruges and Ostend in Belgium; Dunkirk, Boulogne, Dieppe, Le Havre, Fécamp, Ouistreham and Cher-

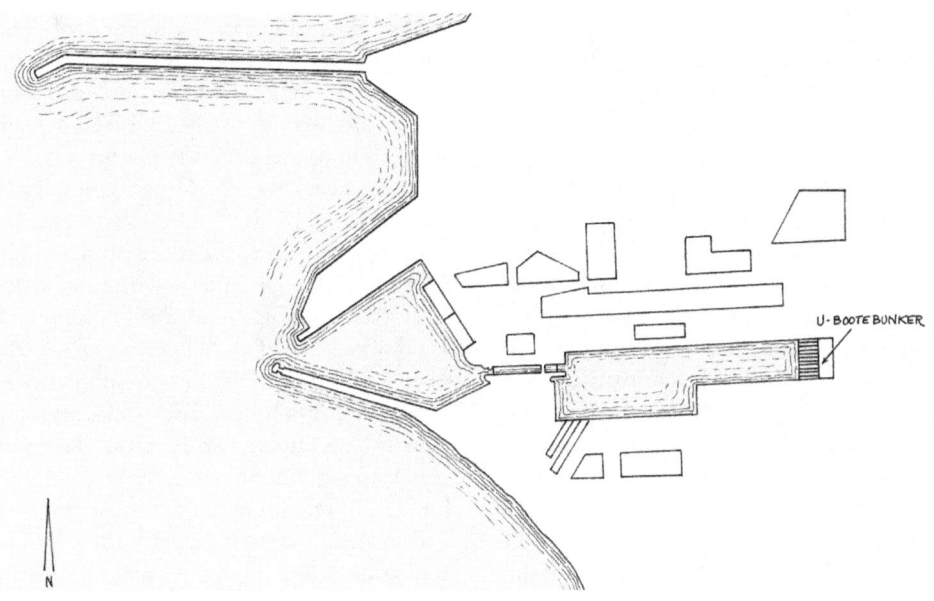

Map, La Pallice harbor, France.

bourg in France; and the British Channel Islands. They were furnished with facilities demanded by maintenance, armament, supplying and refueling. Certain ports were fitted with concrete works sheltering boats from Allied air strikes. In Ostend (Belgium), for example, the German navy commissioned the Organisation Todt with the building of a *Schnellbootebunker* (MTB shelter) with a 2-m-thick roof covering four docks. In the vicinity there were 20 other concrete bunkers protecting logistical installations such as power plants, ammunitions stores, gas and oil tanks, various workshops and stores as well as crew shelters. In Ymuiden near Amsterdam (the Netherlands), the OT erected a *Raümbootebunker* in 1943; measuring 224 m long, the mine-sweepers bunker included 14 alveoli

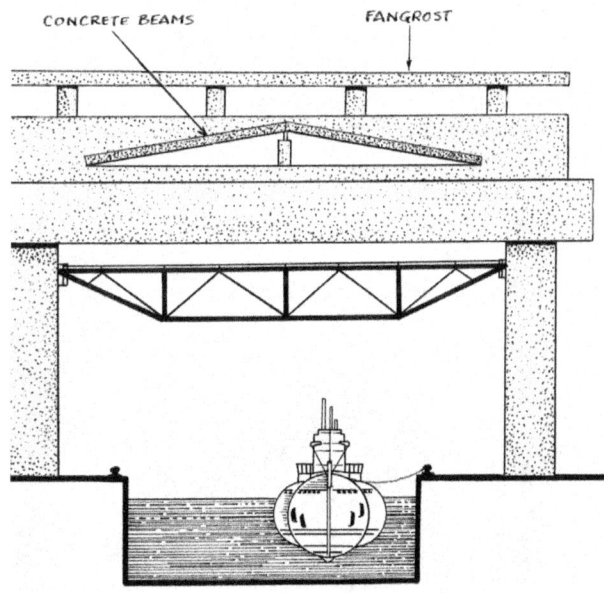

Fangrost at La Pallice-La Rochelle, France. The cross section shows the impressive thickness and the complexity of the roof of the submarine bunker.

and 4 dry docks covered by a 3.5-m-thick concrete roof. Today the Ymuiden bunker is still used for storage and industrial installations.

PROTECTION OF INDUSTRY

Given the increasing bombing activities of the RAF and USAAF, the German authorities responded with dispersal in rural areas and bombproof construction of buildings involved in war industries. The OT and other building companies were commissioned to build gigantic underground installations, industrial shelters, concealed armament factories, and camouflaged concrete assembly/launch sites for *Vergeltungswaffen* (retaliation weapons V1, V2 and V3). The OT constructions for industrial protection were indeed formidable, and were so numerous that to list them all would be prohibitive. Therefore only a few examples will be described below.

One of the Messerschmitt bombproof airplane assembly plants, designated Weingut, was designed and constructed by the Polensky and Zöllner Company in a densely wooded area near Landsberg, east of Munich, Bavaria. Still incomplete in 1944, its bombproof roof rose about 15 m above the ground and dropped about the same distance below; the concrete roof was an arch of 97 m in span, a thickness of 5 m and an intended length of 400 m. The internal structure would have included four stories with workshops, overhead cranes, air conditioning and a railway platform.

In October 1943 the Organisation Todt started to build the U-Bootbunkerwerft. This was a concrete plant for the assembly of type XXI submarines located along the river Weser in a place called Farge, about 25 km downstream of the city of Bremen, Germany. The type XXI electro-submarines, designed in 1943, were a desperate attempt to win back the initiative in the Battle of the Atlantic. They included a streamlined hull, rapid reloading for the torpedo tubes and enlarged battery capacity for a longer stay underwater. They were armed with 23 torpedoes and 4 anti-aircraft guns, and they had a speed of 15.5 knots (surfaced) and 16 knots (submerged). Prefabrication was adopted, and the separate hulls of the submarines, plus the prefabricated and sectionalized components, were produced inland in special bunkers by the Deutsche Schiffs und Maschinenbau AG (Deschimag), Werk Weser AG (U-Bootbunkerwerft, Hornisse, Bremen) and the Blohm und Voss AG (U-Bootbunkerwerft, Wespe, Hamburg). The new submarines were part of Hitler's Wunderwaffen (miracle weapons) and were Admiral Dönitz's last hope to put the Allies back on the defensive. However, production difficulties were never overcome, and only a handful of the revolutionary XXI submarines were ready at the time of the May 1945 surrender. Bunker Valentin was build under the supervision of the Organisation Todt Einsatzgruppe Hansa. The bunker was 426 m (1,398 ft.) in length and 97 m (318 ft.) at its broadest point. The roof had a

Valentin bunker factory at Farge.

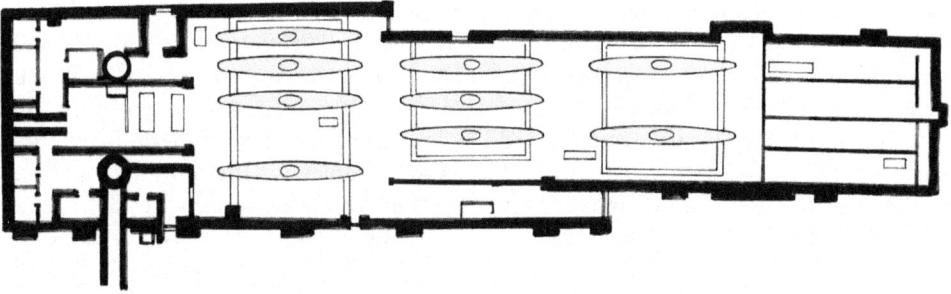

Plan of Valentin bunker.

thickness of 4.5 m (15 ft.), but some parts were as thick as 7 m (23 ft.), and the walls were 4.57 m (15 ft.) thick. The internal room, measuring some 50,000 cubic meters, contained all the equipment and machinery for the assembly of 14 submarines at a time. The construction of the bunker necessitated no less than 500,000 cubic meters (650,000 cubic yd.) of cement reinforced with some 27,000 tons of steel. The total cost was estimated to be 120 million Reichsmarks. For the building large amounts of slave laborers were used, about 10,000 forced workers, prisoners of war, and concentration camp inmates. They were housed in camps in the area around the building site. The conditions in these camps were appallingly bad: work was exhausting, and the food was bad and insufficient, resulting in the death of about 6,000 forced laborers. At the end of the war, about 90 percent of Bunker Valentin was completed, although the building site was bombed several times. On March 27, 1945, it suffered its heaviest attack. A fleet of British Avro Lancasters bombed the bunker with high-explosive, 6,000-kg Tallboy and Grand Slam "earthquake" bombs, and soon the factory was abandoned. After the war the bunker was used by the English and Americans to test bombs. Today, the front part of the bunker is still used as a storage depot for the German navy. A monument in front of the bunker has been erected to commemorate the victims who died during its construction.

REVENGE WEAPONS

Other miracle weapons were the *Vergeltungswaffen* or V-weapons (arms of retaliation), developed at the German research establishment in Peenemünde on the Baltic coast under the supervision of engineer Werner von Braun. Much to the annoyance of Hermann Göring's Luftwaffe, the top-secret V-weapons program was infiltrated and placed under supervision of Himmler's SS. By 1945 the supreme tactical commander of all German secret weapons was SS Brigadeführer (Major General) Dr. Ing. Hans Kammler.

The Fieseler 104, better known as V1, was a fast, jet-propelled, pilotless flying bomb carrying a one-ton warhead moving at a speed of 400 mph. It could travel 600 miles before plummeting to the ground, where it exploded on contact. There was an experimental piloted version of the V1, code-named V4. It was planned for the pilot to be catapulted out of the cockpit about 100 m from the target and to land by parachute—leaving the pilot little chance for survival. This project—which would have brought Japanese Kamikaze tactics to Europe—was cancelled.

The V2 supersonic liquid-fuel rocket was a formidable weapon; carrying a one-ton warhead, it reached a height of 50 miles, and its range was about 200 miles. Plunging down on its target at a speed of over 3,500 mph, the V2 was thus invulnerable to any form of interception. Both V1 and V2 were terrifying weapons, but they were employed too late to bring Hitler victory. Had they been used in great numbers earlier in the war, they might well have changed the final outcome. The German reprisal weapons led eventually to the postwar space programs and the development of cruise missiles and intercontinental ballistic missiles.

For Hitler's V-weapons, the Organisation Todt built several impressive bunkers, known as *Sonderbauten* (special constructions). It should be noted that more prisoners died manufacturing and building the industrial sites for the production of the V1 and V2 weapons than died as a result their use in the war.

In autumn 1942, the Organisation Todt began the construction of a huge factory-bunker in the Eperlecques forest, 15 km northwest of Saint-Omer in northern France. The Eperlecques bunker, cover-named Northwest Power Station, was originally intended for launching V2 rockets. It was built by the OT, employing some 6,000 forced laborers. The bunker was 140 m long, 50 m wide and 22 m high. Its roof was 7 m thick. Its construction required 120,000 cubic meters of concrete and 40,000 tons of steel. A new building method was used in its construction. The heavy concrete roof was put in place first and then shored up during the completion of the walls. This was to protect the work as construction proceeded. The bunker was connected from the main railroad from Calais to Saint-Omer by a loop line; the railway ran through a tunnel down the long side of the bunker, enabling it to distribute components of the missiles to every department. The Eperlecques bunker was spotted in May 1943, heavily bombarded and severely damaged. The Germans repaired it and then installed a plant producing liquid oxygen. Bombed again and again, the wrecked Eperlecques bunker was abandoned in July 1944. Today the work is open to the public and arranged as a World War II museum.

To replace the Eperlecques bunker, the Germans transformed a deserted stone quarry in Wizernes near Saint-Omer in November 1943. Other sites were considered as replacements at Sottevast and Equeurdreville near Cherbourg, but—never completed—they only diverted labor and materials. Important works were carried out by the OT at Wizernes to create a vast, underground manufacturing plant to assemble, store and launch V2 rockets. The subterranean structures—constructed by the edges of the 30-m quarry face—were protected by a gigantic, concrete, one-million-ton dome 5 m thick and 72 m in diameter. Additional workshops, barracks, and a rocket storage were excavated in the chalk from which two tunnels would run into the quarry. A railway was installed right through the hill to facilitate the handling of components. The impressive Wizernes installation was planned to fire 50 V2 missiles per day, which would have been a terrible threat to southern England, and which predictably became one of Hitler's favorite schemes. Fortunately, the site was never completed. Rapidly spotted, it was heavily bombarded from March 1944 onwards by the dropping of 6-ton "earthquake" bombs. The site was made unapproachable and in July 1944, the destruction was so extensive that the Germans had to stop all activities. Today it is difficult to visualize the installations as they once were; the underground structure is completely sealed off, only a few scattered concrete blocks remain, and—unlike Eperlecques—the installation is not open to public.

Another Vergeldungswaffe was the project Fleissiges Leichen Wieze V3, nicknamed Busy Lizzie by the Allies. The secret project V3 was installed in April 1943 in the Mimoyecques forest at Landrethun-le-Nord near Calais in northern France, 152 km (95 miles) from London. Invented by Dr. Cönders of the Röchling Werk Company, project V3 was Hitler's third secret "revenge weapon." It consisted of a long-range, multiple-charge (or high-pressure pump) battery intended to destroy London. It was one of the most outstanding and potentially devastating weapons of the German arsenal, returning to the offensive character of the early 1940s. The battery included 5 shafts each containing 5 guns, thus totaling 25 guns able to fire 300 shells per hour. Each gun included a huge, 127-m-long barrel divided in individual sections, each fitted with a chamber containing an explosive charge that could be ignited automatically and electronically synchronized the moment the missile had passed. The finned, dart-like projectile (2.7 m long) passed successive explosive chambers, each explosion increasing its speed, so that it left the barrel with extreme velocity. The guns were given an angle of 40 to 50 degrees and aimed in direction of London with a range of over 160 km, thus enough to reach Britain's capital. Barrels, facilities and installations were built 67 m underground in galleries excavated by forced labor under OT and SS supervision. The building personnel also included some 430 skilled German mining engineers (from the firms Krupp, Mannesmann, United Steel and Gute-Hoffnungs-Hutte), who were drafted for the tunneling work. The railway loops denoting activity aroused the suspicion of the aerial interpreters of the RAF and the incomplete work site was quickly located. Then the Allied air forces bombed the installations nonstop from November 1943 onwards. In July 1944 an enormous, 6,000-kg Tallboy bomb made a direct hit, destroying a part of the installation and causing the collapse of one of the gun shafts and several galleries. In the end of August 1944 the Germans abandoned the site. On September 11 the Canadians liberated the region of Calais, and Colonel Sandes made a study of the work. The Mimoyecque guns being a great danger threatening London and South England, their total demolition was completed by the British Engineering Corps in May 1945. Today part of the installation can be visited. The site's International Memorial commemorates the victims, and a stone remembers U.S. Air Force Lieutenant Joseph Kennedy (President John F. Kennedy's brother), who was killed in action during a bombing mission over Mimoyecques on August 12, 1944.

Such spectacular constructions as Weingut, Valentin, Eperlecques, Wizernes and Mimoyecques were relatively rare, however, when compared with the numerous underground factories, which were intended to compose a major part of the German bombproof war industry. Tunneled, underground factories were widely used for a variety of production processes. Subterranean industrial complexes were constructed by the OT but were also built by private mining companies under the direction of consultant geologists and employing skilled mine engineers for the design and slave labor for the realization. By 1945, however, a major part of these underground facilities had not been completed.

The largest German underground factory was a site located under the Kohnstein Mountain in the Harz region of central Germany. Planned in October 1943, with floor areas of over 95,000 square meters, this *Mittelwerk* (middle work) was designed to assemble aircraft jet engines and secret rockets. Constructed in atrocious conditions by slave laborers, the work was composed of two main tunnels, slightly S-shaped, running about 2 km and linked by 43 parallel galleries like the rungs of a ladder. It included component-manufacturing and sub-assembly plants linked by an internal, electric railway.

Other important industrial sites were planned in the Harz Mountain, including two Junkers jet-engine factories, a large liquid-oxygen manufacture (named Hydrawerk), an underground synthetic-oil plant, code-named Kuckuck I (cuckoo project), and a Henschel missile factory located nearby Wolffleben. These industrial networks were fortunately overrun by the Allies before completion.

In Thuringia a large underground factory was set up for mass production of the single-motored jet fighter, which Hitler dubbed Volksjäger (people's fighter). The new, one-seat, jet-propelled He-162 A-2 Salamander Volksjäger was one of Hitler's last hopes. In the field of jet aircraft, the Germans were years ahead of the Allies, but the high command, and Hitler first of all, were slow to realize the potential of the revolutionary designs. The old story of too little and too late applied to all German jet aircraft production. The He-162 was never used operationally.

As the Allies gradually advanced in Germany in early 1945, the terrifying V-weapon sites were replaced by a new threat: the Alpenfestung (National Redoubt or Alpine Fortress). Rumors and unconfirmed intelligence indicated the preparation of an impregnable fortress in the Alpine mountains, covering almost 20,000 square miles in upper Bavaria, western Austria and northern Italy. Its core would be the area of Obersalzberg and Berchtesgaden, where Hitler originally intended to retreat and lead a Wagnerian last-ditch battle, the final struggle against the Allies. The fortress would have been composed of concealed combat emplacements ranging from pillboxes to massive, concrete artillery bunkers, camouflaged barracks and headquarters, bombproof factories, caverns for food, and equipment backed by the OT. The redoubt would have been manned by a specially selected, commando-type corps of fanatical young men (mainly SS and Hitler Youth). Known as Werewolves, these underground combatants would also wage guerrilla warfare intended to create havoc among the Allied occupation forces. Ultimately the Alpenfestung was a hoax; however, the threat was taken seriously by the Allies. The possibility of its existence could not be ignored, and several strategic plans were made as in reaction. As Hitler changed his mind in April 1945 and decided to stay in Berlin, the Alpenfestung never existed in reality. It was actually a huge bluff, the last, great masterly lie devised by propaganda minister Josef Göbbels.

HITLER'S HQ BUNKERS

The OT was responsible for the construction of several operational Führerhauptquartiere (Hitler's command headquarters, FHQu in short), whence he directed operations during the war. The senior construction engineer of the FHQu project was the architect Siegfried Schmelcher (1911–1991), a talented technician who had worked with the OT since 1939 in the Motorway program. In August 1940, the OT created the Sondereinsatz Schmelcher, the construction unit specialized in designing and building Hitler's fortified, restricted headquarters.

First of all, Hitler had his personal Führerszug (special command train) used in the period 1939–1941, codenamed "Amerika." The train, comprehensively furnished, was composed of two locomotives, a *Flakwagen* (flat car armed with anti-aircraft guns), a baggage and supply car, a sleeping car for Hitler himself, a *Befehlswagen* (a command car furnished with maps and communications equipment), a *Begleitkommandowagen* (a car for Hitler's SS escort), a restaurant car, two cars for guests, a *Badewagen* (with showers, bath, and washing facilities), two other sleeping cars for personnel, and a second *Flakwagen*.

Throughout the war, Hitler had about 20 permanent command headquarters in which he immured himself. There was no planned program; the headquarters were built according to the fluctuation of the war, and they greatly varied in size and degree of protection. Some were never completed or never used, while others (such as Wolfschanze at Rastenburg, East-Prussia, the Führer's bunker under the Chancellery at Berlin, and Obersalzberg in the Alps) became dwelling places where Hitler spent much time. The most important FHQus were the following:

FHQu Felsennest, located near Rödert (Münstereifel), was occupied by the dictator from May 10 to June 5, 1940.

FHQu Wolfsschlucht (wolf's glen), at Bruly-de-Pesche near Givet at the Franco-Belgian border, was occupied from June 6 to 24, 1940.

FHQu Tannenberg, located on the Kniebis plateau in Schwarzwald (Black Forest), was occupied by Hitler from June 25 to July 6, 1940.

FHQu Wolfschanze (wolf's lair), at Rastenburg, East Prussia, was occupied intermittently from June 1941 to November 1944; from this location, the Führer directed the operations on the Russian front. The July 20, 1944, plot occurred here.

FHQu Werwolf (werewolf), at Vinnitsa in the Ukraine, was occupied from July 16 to November 1, 1942 and February 17 to March 13, 1943, for the direction of the operations in Soviet territories.

FUQu Wolfsschlucht II—built near Soissons (France) in 1943–1944—was never used. It was intended for the supervision of the war in France after the Allied landing.

FHQu Adlershorst (eagle's nest), was located at the village of Wiesental near Bad Nauheim in the Taunus hills, whence Hitler directed the Ardennes offensive in the winter of 1944–1945.

Each of these complexes was placed in an isolated location in the countryside—often on a forested hill. All of them were different, but each was a mixture of fortress, cloister and concentration camp including several guarded, barbed-wire fences, defended entrances, machine-gun posts, anti-aircraft guns and searchlights. The enclosed perimeter usually included a concrete command bunker with a briefing room; telephone and radio exchange; concrete underground residences for the Führer, his close collaborators, adjutants, secretaries, typists, liaison-officers and high-ranking guests; barracks for bodyguards and security troops; supply shelters; kitchen and mess; infirmary; power plant; garages for vehicles; and other facilities, all bunkers and premises being carefully camouflaged. Some headquarters were particularly large (e.g., Wolfschanze, near Rastenburg) and had the appearance of a concrete village, including additional facilities such as teahouses, cinemas, saunas, and even cemeteries. In the vicinity of each FHQu there was a railway station—possibly a tunnel under which Hitler's train could be sheltered—and an airfield or an improvised landing strip. Apart from reports on the situation, very little news from the outer world penetrated into these holies of holies.

Hitler also directed operations intermittently from castle Klessheim near Salzburg, and from the FHQu Berghof, his prewar holiday home at Berchtesgaden (Obersalzberg). In the vicinity of this small town in the southeastern Bavarian Alps, Hitler had bought a house with his own funds acquired from the sales of his book *Mein Kampf*. This isolated house, named Haus Wachenfeld, he used as a retreat and a command and conference center. The Berghof was greatly enlarged, and it grew from a single mountain chalet to an imposing, sophisticated complex reflecting Hitler's megalomaniacal tastes. The house included a large reception room with a huge octagonal table and a large window providing a breathtaking view of the mountain area, a banquet hall, a large sun-terrace, huge rooms with thick carpets and magnificent decorations, guest rooms, kitchens, etc. In the vicinity there were other houses intended for guests, service and facilities as well as an underground network of concrete bunkers and shelters. A special private hairpin-bend road led from Berchtesgaden to the Berghof. Hitler's chalet was protected by fortifications, electrified barbed-wire fences, anti-aircraft batteries and SS Füher Begleit Truppen (SS escort security troops). There was also a special "Eagle's Nest" with a private elevator to the top of the mountain, where the dictator could resign himself to complete solitude. The compound was demolished by the Allies after the war to avoid the creation of a neo–Nazi pilgrimage place.

The Führerbunker (Hitler's bunker) in Berlin, where Hitler resided until the end of his regime, was the most notorious and probably the safest place in the whole of Nazi Germany. The Führerbunker was a subterranean, concrete structure located some 15 meters (50 feet) below the chancellery in Berlin. By the time of the siege and battle of Berlin in April 1945, the monumental Reich Chancellery had become disused. Its huge rooms and impressive corridors with their vast slabs of porphyry and marble, their pompous decorations, their ponderous doors and large candelabra, were bombed out and burnt. The ruined mausoleum of Egyptian scale, which had been designed by Albert Speer and built before the war to house Hitler's megalomania, was in ruins and only manned as a local command post. The garden resembled a battlefield with huge bomb craters, lumps of concrete, smashed statuary and uprooted trees.

Hitler's bunker was roofed with more than 5 meters (16 feet) of concrete, reinforced with grids of steel bars, then topped with 10 meters (90 feet) of earth. It was reached from the chancellery by descending a stairway from the butler's pantry. This stairs led to a narrow tunnel enclosed by three airtight, watertight, thick, armored bulkheads. The first one closed the passage to the pantry, called Kannenberggang (named after Hitler's butler Arthur Kannenberg). The second bulkhead gave way to an outer stair with access to the garden of the Foreign Office. The third—placed in the middle of the passage—led down to the bunker. The bunker comprised two levels. The upper level included a central passage (used as a general dining-place) with 12 small rooms, 6 on each side, for lumber and storage rooms and servants' quarters including the *Diätküche* (kitchen), where Hitler's vegetarian meals were prepared by his cook Fräulein Constance Manziarly. At the end of the central passage a curved stairway led downwards to a still deeper and larger bunker. That was the Führer's bunker proper. This lower level included 18 small, cramped and uncomfortable rooms and a central passage divided in two by a partition. The first part of the passage was used as a general sitting room and gave access to utilitarian offices, lavatories and bathroom, a guardroom, an emergency telephone exchange, and the power plant. The second part of the passage was arranged as a conference room. A door on the left gave access to a suite of 6 rooms reserved for Hitler and his girlfriend, Eva Braun. She had a private bedroom/sitting room, a bathroom and a dressing room. Hitler had a personal bedroom and a study. In addition there was several guest-rooms, an anteroom, a small map and conference room and a narrow room known as the Hundebunker (dog's bunker), used as a break room for the Führerbegleitkommando (SS escort and bodyguards). At the end of the guard room there was a ladder leading to an unfinished concrete observation tower above the ground. At the end of the passage, a door gave access to a small anteroom used as a cloakroom. This led to an emergency exit and a stair leading up into the chancellery garden.

It was in this bunker that Hitler committed suicide on April 30, 1945.

PUBLIC SHELTERS AND ANTI-AIRCRAFT TOWERS

The emergence of bomber aircraft brought a new dimension to warfare. As early as 1917, the German air force had attacked London and had made it clear that their air raids did not differentiate between military and civilian targets. In the interwar period 1918–1939, the threat of air attack was universally recognized and feared, and shelters were designed. In Germany private businessmen—notably the Winkel Company from Duisburg, and Paul Zombeck of Dortmund, Grün and Filbinger, took to building and selling *Schutzräume* (protective buildings). When Allied air raids started, public shelters were in general the responsibility of civilian authorities, but Organisation Todt was also commissioned with the construction of huge concrete shelters for the civilian population. The construction of the air-raid shelters was coordinated by the Reichsluftschutzbund (RLB, Reich Air Defense League), an organization created as early as 1934. The main important cities of Germany were secretly classified into three categories depending on their value for the war economy. A large-scale program of passive aerial defense was established under the auspices of the Reichsluftschutzbund but as passive air defense was not a priority, only a few air-raid shelters were built by 1939. At the beginning of Allied air raids above the Reich, those shelters were not numerous and were reserved for Nazi Party members and for relatives of soldiers who had died at the front. With the beginning of mass bombing in 1942, the Germans were forced to rethink their air strategy and to develop a satisfactory number of shelters. With the intensification and growing violence of the Allied bombardments, the number and capacity of the shelters were considerably increased, with buildings able to hold 500, 1,000, 2,000 or 4,000 people. A few shelters had capacities of up to 12,000 or even 18,000 persons. In fact, large, multi-story buildings were much more economical; the 500-person shelters required a volume of 3 cubic meters of concrete per person, while the 4,000-person shelters required only 1.8 cubic meters. At the end of the war, the air raid shelters—if overcrowded—could probably accommodate up to 75 percent of the urban populations in all principal German cities. Though underground shelters and tunnels were not unknown, the multi-story *Luftschutzraüme* were built above ground and always placed in the middle of a city. They were huge, concrete, rectangular buildings with 2- to 3-m-thick roofs and walls. Though there was neither unity of style nor standardized internal arrangement, the external appearance of the building was always intended to match the architectural character of the neighborhood. They were thus often camouflaged as normal urban buildings, sometimes with tiled roofs and a complete veneer of brick, as well as with false windows painted on the walls. The use of solid foundations varied with subsoil conditions.

Some of the early shelters had the exper-

Radar/FlaK tower in Vienna (Austria). This radar tower, part of the air defense of the capital of Austria, comprised three radar towers and three FlaK towers.

imental shape of a round tower. A few even had a remarkably futuristic rocket shape in order to deflect bombs. Some shelters were decorated in a somewhat "Nazi style" and were also used as propaganda objects. Their monumental construction had often the additional objective of providing the public with some form of psychological and political reassurance. A *Luftschutzraüme* was composed of a vast reception hall, with staircases and elevators leading to many waiting rooms on the upper floors. The building usually included special airtight entries, an independent power plant, an infirmary, water supplies and sewage, separate lavatories and washrooms for each sex, and sometimes luxuries such as telephones, air-conditioning and sleeping facilities.

Another type of building built by the Luftwaffe and the OT in connection with the war in the German skies were the anti-aircraft towers known as *Flaktürme* (FlaK towers).

The German air force had fighters (e.g., Messerschmitt Bf 109 and Focke-Wulf 190) to intercept and destroy enemy bombers, but as World War II proceeded, the German air force collapsed and the emphasis was on the use of FlaK (anti-aircraft) batteries. The anti-aircraft towers—just like the *Luftschutzraüme*—were huge, monolithic bunkers built above ground and camouflaged as normal civilian buildings, but they were fitted with a terrace armed with searchlights, and FlaK guns. As there was no standardization, the overall shape and style of the FlaK towers varied to some extent with time and space, but they all had simple geometrical shapes and many common features. They were mostly a little taller than the normal average urban constructions and vegetation around them so that guns and searchlights could have an unobstructed arc of fire and wide view, and for this reason they could be as high as ten stories. The various floors were arranged as ammunition stores and gunners' quarters. They also housed rescue teams, doctors and

Flaktürme Wilhelmsburgstraße in Hamburg. The tower was armed with four 12.8-cm FlaK guns and could shelter 18,000 civilians.

medical personnel, police squads, firemen, bomb clearance squads, etc. In many cases the towers were not exclusively military. Often there was a large space left for civilian and hospital purposes; the towers were thus often both active and passive defense objects and were an extension of the air-raid-shelter program.

A Flaktürme was always connected to another tower similar in design, the radar-tower housing detection equipment (often radar antennae) and gun-laying installations. These pairs were distributed across the city, equidistant from each other. They were also connected to Luftwaffe command posts, which coordinated and conducted fire.

For example, the air defense of Berlin included six large towers—built in 1941–1942—that rose above the cityscape at Humboldthain, Friedrichshain, and from the grounds of the Berlin zoological park. The twin towers situated in the zoo were called L Turm and G Turm. The first, L-tower, was a radar and communication control center bristling with radio and radar antennae. The second, G-tower, was very large, covering almost the area of a city block. It was designed as a huge, five-story warehouse, 40 m (132 feet) high, with concrete walls 2.4 m (8 feet) thick. The gun battery placed on top of the roof included eight heavy 12.8-cm FlaK guns. The top floor of the tower housed the 100-man military garrison. Ammunitions were brought to the upper terrace by means of a freight elevator. Beneath that was a 95-bed Luftwaffe hospital with X-ray room and two fully equipped operating theaters staffed by 6 doctors, 20 nurses and 30 orderlies. The next floor down was used to safely store treasures from the Berlin museums, including numerous priceless Egyptian, Greek and Roman antiquities, Gobelin tapestries, a vast quantity of paintings and coin collections. The two lower floors were arranged as public air shelters for 15,000 people. The G-tower was entirely self-contained, with water supply, kitchen, food store, emergency services and its own power plant.

Massive as the public shelters and the FlaK towers were, they proved to be of only limited value when the weaponry of aerial bombing changed in late 1942. As the extent and the frequency of Allied bombing increased and its effectiveness grew, a larger part of the German urban population flocked to the public bunkers. These became overcrowded by five to six times their design capacity. Records showed bunkers designed for 18,000 people used in practice by up to 60,000 persons and at times even more. Needless to say, overcrowding made the service provisions inadequate; sanitary arrangements were overstretched, ventilation became ineffective and bunks were in insufficient number. In the case of "fire storms," casualties were astronomically high, and thousands of people died a horrible death inside the public shelters. A fire storm or a fire typhoon was a meteorological phenomenon. It occurred when individual fires caused by widespread and repeated Allied incendiary bombing combined into a major conflagration. The heat generated by the blaze created a giant column of rapidly rising hot air that sucked cool air into the center of an inferno, causing strong winds that fanned and intensified the existing flames. The heat in the fire typhoon was so intense that inside the public bunkers, metal parts melted and what remained of human beings was a thin grey ash. This happened in Hamburg in late July 1943 with an estimate of 42,600 dead and c. 37,000 wounded.

AFTERMATH

The Organisation Todt was a unique conglomerate of state and private firms, which grew monstrously into one of Nazi Germany's most powerful private empires. It became a large paramilitary corps that by 1943 had almost become the fifth formation of the German Wehrmacht—the others four being the Heer (ground forces),

Marine (navy), Luftwaffe (air force), and Waffen SS (private Nazi SS army). By the end of 1944, the Organisation Todt's strength reached its peak with a total of more than a million cadres and workers. It included 44,500 Germans and 12,800 foreign personnel, 4,000 German women, 313,000 Germans and 680,700 foreigners in contracted firms, 165,000 prisoners of war, and 140,000 drafted criminals. By that time, the OT's technical ability was doubtless even as bad as its discipline. Complaints about corruption in the OT and other signs of organizational degeneration dramatically increased in 1944 as Germany retreated on all fronts.

The Organisation Todt was an overtly Nazi organization and, as such, a part of Hitler's system of terror and extermination. After the war, many companies contracted to the OT employing slave labor were expropriated by the Allies Control Commission. Many OT personnel were tried and received penalties ranging from death to imprisonment and fines.

Many of the incredible and indestructible achievements of the building company Organisation Todt are still visible today. The Atlantic, Channel and North Sea coasts of Europe are still bruised by the bunkers of the Atlantic Wall, while submarine pens and some public air-raid shelters in Germany are still in use for both military and civilian purposes.

CHAPTER 2

DEUTSCHE ARBEITSFRONT (DAF) AND REICHSARBEITSDIENST (RAD)— GERMAN LABOR FRONT AND NATIONAL WORK SERVICE

CREATION AND PURPOSES OF THE DAF

Soon after Hitler came to power in January 1933, the Nazis launched a brutal, nationwide campaign to consolidate his dictatorship. A series of events helped solidify their hold on power, including the Reichstag fire and subsequent emergency decree, and the passing of the Enabling Act, which sounded the final death knell for the Weimar Republic. The intent of this process, known as *Gleichschaltung*, was the complete coordination of all political and other activities by the Nazi Party. Every element of German life was gradually integrated by force into a functioning Nazi social machine. The coordination became a national pursuit, with its collection of "fronts." All political parties with differing views and aims were banned. In May 1933 all trade unions and worker organizations were declared illegal, their leaders imprisoned and their wealth confiscated. Hitler chose one of his henchmen, Robert Ley, to set up a Nazi organization in their place. The Deutsche Arbeitsfront (DAF, German Labor Front) was created in May 1933 by Robert Ley as the sole labor organization of the German Reich. The DAF was then one of the components of the NSDAP.

As was typical for the Third Reich, the DAF was totally ad hoc in nature in that Ley initially had no idea of what he would set up to replace trade unions. The ensuing half-year after the DAF had been proclaimed was quite confusing, as a number of concepts vied with one another. Gradually Ley and his staff evolved the idea of a totalitarian mass organization, which both employers and employees would join on an individual basis. By the end of 1933 Ley gained the acceptance of the DAF as the Nazi organization, which would bring together business and labor under his control. The bloody elimination of the SA (the Sturm Abteilung, the assault troops of the Nazi Party) in June 1934 gave him the opportunity to purge his organization of many radicals and to cement his power. In October 1934 Robert Ley could claim "totality" for his DAF, and could go on to give shape to his own agency as an all-embracing empire, which would "educate and take care" of the German people.

The Labor Front comprised the entire intellectual and manual labor world of the Third Reich, including more than 25 million workers. The concept of the DAF was to ensure the political stability and smooth operation of all German industry and commerce.

Its function was to conciliate rather than advance social demands through a combination of carrot-and-stick. The DAF was the major vehicle designed to keep the workers under control, to bring together business and labor, and put an end—by force and coercion—to the class struggle that had bedeviled Germany for decades. The right to protest and to strike was abolished, and wage rates and working conditions were no longer negotiable but dictated by Ley and top businessmen. The organization was intended to carry out *Gleichschaltung*, the complete restructuration of the German society according to Hitler's vision of a modern, prosperous, racially pure *Volksgemeinschaft* (popular community) in which every "Aryan" German might achieve his dream of upward mobility on the backs of subjugated and exploited "inferior" races. With a combination of idealism and fear, the DAF wanted to integrate the workers into the nation and to provide opportunities for progress and social reconciliation, but it also aimed at creating a totalitarian, conflict-free society, which would end the chaos of political pluralism and class antagonism. The ultimate goal was to create a "brown collectivism," halfway between state communism and liberal, capitalist free business, which would embrace every German from cradle to grave and would destroy forever any idea of private life. The purpose of the DAF was that people would work for the good of Germany, willingly subordinating themselves as individuals to the collective will of the nation, which was embodied in Hitler's will. This was expressed by one of the slogans of the DAF: "Every worker must regard himself as a soldier of the economy." To heighten this sense of solidarity and "equality," workers were encouraged to wear identical, uniformized blue working clothes. The DAF, under the leadership of Robert Ley (who had the title of Leiter der Deutschen Arbeitsfront), became a major power and political contender during the Hitler regime, challenging government ministries and industry in its striving to become a Nazi "super agency" in the socio-economic realm.

Robert Ley

Robert Ley was born on February 15, 1890, at Niederbreidenbach in the Rhineland. A rural man in origin, he attended the Faculty of Natural Science at Jena University in 1910 to become a chemist. The outbreak of World War I interrupted his education, and Ley went to war first as an artilleryman and later as an airman. He was decorated with the Iron Cross 2nd Class. In July 1917 he was shot down, severely wounded in his frontal lobes, and captured and imprisoned by the French. After the war, Robert Ley was released from captivity and returned home to Germany in a state of shock. He was deeply affected by the stress of combat, injury, imprisonment and repeated surgical invasion. This perhaps explained his subsequent erratic and unbalanced behavior. He also started to indulge habitually in alcohol. The psychologically labile and socially insecure Ley completed his degree in food chemistry at the University of Münster and started a career as a research chemist with IG Farben in Leverkusen, but was dismissed for habitual drunkenness. He gradually disengaged himself from normal bourgeois life and, in 1924, inspired by Hitler's failed putsch of November 1923, joined the Nazi Party. He

Robert Ley (1890–1945)

became an ardent National-Socialist proselyte, a close henchman of Hitler, and performed social and political tasks. For him National Socialism became a religion and Hitler a messiah. An excellent rabble-rouser, a tireless agitator, and a fanatical Jew baiter, he was elected to the Prussian Landstag in 1928 and in 1930 to the Reichstag. His public verbal excesses landed him in court and jail, while his private life was marked by scandals due to over-consumption of alcohol. From 1931 to 1934 he was NSDAP *Gauleiter* in the Rhineland district and *Reichsorganisationsleiter* (ROL, the Nazi Party's director of organization). In May 1933, after the seizure of power, Ley rose in importance when he took over the control of trade unions and when Hitler appointed him as head of what was to become the German Labor Front. The reason Hitler chose Ley for this role was obvious: Ley was a fanatical Nazi with complete loyalty; he had had a profession that would tend to predispose him to favor business over labor; and as Nazi Party's director of organization, he had the skills and experience to cope with the transformation of trade unions into obedient organizations along Nazi guidelines. Like other top Nazi leaders, Robert Ley collected many jurisdictions to augment his growing bureaucratic empire, notably the *Ordensburgen* (Order Castles), which were elite Nazi training schools. Created in 1936, the Ordensburgen included four castles (Crössingen, Sonthofen, Vogelsang and Marienburg), which were the highest residential academies, a kind of Party university, an institutional core of Nazi brothers united in racist mysticism. The graduates were expected to enter the highest echelons of Nazi Party leadership.

Unshakably loyal to Hitler, Ley was an unstable personality and an erratic, inept administrator with restless ambition. He had an inferiority complex and wanted to "become somebody." He only became an official criminal, a corrupt loser whose crackpot theories and ludicrous public statements did not prevent him from making a scandalous personal fortune under the cover of Nazi activities. The humorous mannerisms of the Nazi Party's director of organization and DAF leader were a source of amusement even to his supreme lord and master. Hitler loved to hear stories of how Ley used to turn up at the offices of Munich's urban planning department, elegant in a white summer suit, white gloves and straw hat, with his smartly attired wife in tow. Ley's grandiose ambitions and dreams of power were mirrored in his princely lifestyle. He had a model farm where he raised hogs; he claimed that this was a top priority since his experimental pigsty was of great importance for future food production. Like Hermann Göring, he had access to virtually unlimited public funds; he owned a number of villas and estates throughout Germany—notably a sumptuous demesne near Cologne, which he named Rottland. When he traveled Ley had the choice of several expensive modern automobiles or his own train. He was always luxuriously dressed, smoked the best cigars and drank without moderation the finest liquors. He was also a libertine who treated his wife so outrageously and cruelly that she committed suicide. The widower quickly consoled himself with a cuddly, young Estonian girl. A plebeian and radical Nazi, a violent and bitter anti–Semite, a notorious and incorrigible drunk fond of vulgar ostentation, Ley exemplified the coarse, corrupt and criminal face of Hitler's regime.

For many Germans, humor was the best tonic for coping with everyday frustrations, and poking fun at ranking Nazis became a popular pastime. The mockery included verbal shorthand in which abbreviations had special meanings. A "Gör" (for Hermann Göring) was the most medals a man could pin to his chest without falling on his face; a "Ley" (for the DAF's leader) was the longest a person could talk gibberish nonstop. Although Hitler was a strict teetotaler with a sick and obsessional aversion to meat, tobacco and liquor, alcoholism was widely recognized as a form of Nazi self-indulgence, and many Nazi leaders were dipsomaniacs. There was an inordinate amount of drinking at annual celebrations of the *Alte Kämpfer* (old fighters, stalwarts of the old guard of early NSDAP members honored for their role in the rise of the Nazi movement). Ley shared his title of Reichstrunkenbold (national drunkard in chief) with Heinrich Hoffmann, Hitler's official photographer, publisher and art expert.

Despite—or perhaps because of—his addiction to alcohol, Robert Ley was a person of great verve and huge enthusiasm who threw himself into his job with great energy. Ley's popularity and the DAF's dynamism peaked in 1938, but during the war his power was gradually reduced. Ley was one of those Nazis who never quite made it to the top ranks of the NSDAP but whose noxious activities had a major impact on the German people. Until his last breath, he had a quasi-religious commitment to National Socialism, never gave up his faith in ultimate victory, did all he could to foster the cult of his charismatic Führer. By the end of World War II Robert Ley had not forsaken his vaulting ambition but was eclipsed by other top Nazi leaders, notably Albert Speer, Heinrich Himmdler, Joseph Göbbels, and even Fritz Sauckel, the man entrusted by Hitler with mobilizing labor for Germany's war effort. After Martin Bormann became Hitler's personal secretary in April 1943, Ley found his previously easy access to the Führer increasingly barred. Despite his wide range of power, his relative importance within the party leadership greatly declined. When Hitler's regime started to collapse, Ley was only a marginal figure in the Nazi hierarchy. By then he had become a pathetic madman and a pitiful boozer, but he was still a highly dangerous criminal completely disconnected from reality. In the autumn of 1944, he urged Hitler to use tabun (a poisonous nerve gas) against the Russians. By profession a chemist, he wanted to design new deadly poisonous substances. He went on with speculating that the western Allies would accept gas warfare against the Russians because at this stage of the war the British and American governments had an interest in stopping the Soviet progression in Eastern Europe. When the enemy approached, Ley advanced the following crackpot theory: According to him, should the Russians overrun Germany from the East, the torrent of refugees would be so heavy that it would press upon the West like a migration of the nations, break through, flood the West and then take possession. In all seriousness, he asserted that the war still could be won in early 1945, as he had documentation to produce a decisive miracle weapon consisting of death rays generated by electricity, which he intended to experiment with on rabbits. The true Nazi believer urged Hitler to form fanatic combat units to further the final victory. Even Hitler mocked the absurd initiatives concocted by his delirious and drunk Labor Service leader, but he held him in some form of affection until the end. During the last period of the war the dictator liked to have his Alte Kämpfer ("old companion of the first hour") close at hand. In April 1945 Robert Ley fled southward in an attempt to save his skin instead of sharing death with Hitler in Berlin. He was captured by the Americans near Berchtesgaden in Bavaria. Indicted by the International Military Tribunal in Nuremberg, he remained an implacable, religious-spirited Nazi who embodied the worst of Hitler's henchman. He committed suicide on October 25, 1945, by hanging himself in his cell before being tried as a war criminal.

Organization of the DAF

Like a metastasizing cancer, the DAF continually grew, changed shape and encroached on the jurisdictional turf of national government, private business, and the Nazi Party. It quickly became a huge and dynamic bureaucratic body with over 44,000 paid functionaries, several hundred thousand part-timers, and millions of dues-paying members. Membership in the DAF was voluntary, but any person who was a worker in any area of German industry or commerce was more or less a member by default. Refusing to join the DAF was regarded as a manifestation of hostility against Hitler's regime and could have dramatic consequences, e.g., warning and harassment, fines, loss of job, or even imprisonment. Obviously, given the racist character of the Nazi regime, Jews and "non–Aryans" were not allowed to be members of the DAF.

With its millions of dues-paying members (each worker had to pay 1½ percent of his monthly wages as dues) Ley's organization was bloated with wealth, which enabled it to become both a politically powerful Nazi Party affiliate and an enormous business conglomerate with holdings in banking, publishing, insurance, construction, automobiles, retailing and leisure travel.

The DAF was composed of the following departments:

Emblem of the Deutsche Arbeitsfront (DAF, German Labor Front).

- The Nationalsozialistische Betriebszellen-Organization (NSBO), or National Socialist Factory Organization, had been created by the Nazis as early as 1927 in Berlin to form propaganda units in factories to gain workers' support and votes. Originally intended to replace the eliminated trade unions and continued their role of organization of Nazi industrial propaganda formations in factories, the NSBO was responsible for the political work and guidance of the DAF. It was concerned with the party and political interests of the workers, while the larger DAF represented their economic interests. According to a contemporary joke, the initials NSBO stood for "*Noch sind die Bozen oben* [The Party favorites are still on top]." After the seizure of power in January 1933, NSBO activities declined drastically. In June 1934 their influence was further reduced after the SA purge, the murder of the cum-

DAF senior work leader (left); RAD workman (right).

DAF and RAD

Emblem of the NSBO.

Emblem of the NS-Hago.

Emblem of the Reichsnährstand (RNS).

bersome Ernst Röhm and the anticapitalist Gregor Strasser, and the arrest and imprisonment of several left-wing, Strasser-minded NSBO leaders. The final blow came in 1935 when the NSBO was disbanded and merged with the DAF.

- The Nationalsozialistische Handels und Gewerbeorganisation (NS-Hago, National Socialist Trade and Industry Organization) fulfilled the same role as the NSBO—to replace the forbidden labor unions—in the trade and craft branches. Just like the NSBO, the NS-Hago could not resist the growth of the DAF, and the organization lost all significance after 1934.
- The Reichsnährstand (RNS, Food Estate) was set up in September 1933, when all previous agricultural associations and organizations were disbanded. It was headed from 1933 to 1942 by the Nazi ideologist, honorary SS *Obergruppenführer* and *Reichsbauernführer* (National Farmers' Leader) Richard Walther Darré (1895–1953). The RNS focused on Darré's *Blut und Boden* (Blubo, Blood and Homeland)—a hazy ideology according to which the peasantry was the pure life source of the Germanic Nordic race. The essence of the crackpot *Blubo* theory involved the mutual and long-term relationship between a people and the land that it occupies and cultivates. To preserve a healthy stock of that precious peasant blood, Darré demanded the restoration of the ancient traditions, as well as serious efforts to restore the purity of Nordic blood, including exterminating the sick and "impure." As a result, the German agricultural world, markets, prices and ownership of land had to be strictly controlled and regu-

Organization of the DAF

NSBO man c. 1937. Left: The NSBO uniform was composed of an SA kepi-style cap, replaced in 1934 by a brown or dark blue peaked cap (or a visorless field cap); a brown, SA-like *Dienstbluse* (actually more a blouse than a shirt) with two breast pockets; a black tie; on the left arm a red NSDAP armband with a black swastika in a white circle; black riding trousers or breeches; and black riding boots. Top right: The National Sovereignty emblem (*Hoheitszeichen*) in metal form existed in several variants, and was worn at the front of headgear. Bottom right: The black cloth rhombus with NSBO membership emblem was worn on the upper left arm. Under it there was a black machine-embroidered or machine-woven *Verdienstabzeichen* (stripe displaying the wearer's year of entry in the organization), which was discontinued by the end of 1935.

lated along Nazi racial lines. Agricultural production aimed at self-sufficiency.
- The Association of National-Socialist German Jurists.
- The 13 Treuhänder der Arbeits (Trustees of Labor), corresponding to the 13 economic regions of Germany.
- The leaders of the 12 groups of the Reichstand der Industrie.
- The Organization of German Industrialists.

To these, several important sub-organizations were added, and will be described below.

- Schönheit der Arbeit (Beauty of Work)—a program for improving working conditions.
- The organization Kraft durch Freude (Strength Through Joy), providing organized leisure for the German work force.
- The Reichsarbeitsdienst (RAD, National Labor Service), the official state and Nazi Party labor service.

Ley's empire, a grandiose enterprise presented as the summit of Nazi ideals, was in fact an organization marred by corruption, criminality and oppression. The bureaucratic structure and the large budget provided plenty of opportunities for officials to make money for themselves by putting their hands in the till. Robert Ley himself made a fortune by directing funds into his own pocket.

The DAF was one of the Angeschlossene Verbände (Affiliated Groups) of the Nazi Party and was militarily organized. The struc-

DAF-RNS pin. This pin was issued by the RNS in commemoration of National Farmers' Day at Goslar in 1935. The bronze-plated steel badge (35 mm in diameter) was manufactured by the Deschler and Sohn Company from Munich.

ture of the DAF was copied from that of the Nazi Party, so that one same man could be both NSDAP and DAF official. When this was not the case there was rivalry between the Party and the DAF, and this was typical of Hitler's rule. Indeed there was never a clear command structure but instead an incoherent and inextricable system based on the old Roman principle *divide et impera* ("divide and rule"), instilled by Hitler himself, who was incapable of sharing power. Hitler's rule was based on the suppression of political opposition by terror, and on the support of an overwhelming majority of Germans. Over and above this, it was also built on the rivalries between the prominent leaders of the Third Reich and the institutions they represented. Formal positions of power grew to personal empires, but they were always imprecisely defined and often overlapped with the authorities of others. The permanent conflict between the senior leaders of the Nazi system made it possible for Hitler to play his role as a universally accepted unifying figure and final authority. Added to this was his own specific conception of the role of leader and his highly contradictory personality: the indisputably final arbiter often avoided making decisions, and once decided, things could be changed or delayed or nullified at any time.

The DAF's structure was based on that of the NSDAP. The smallest unit was the *Block* (block), which consisted of about 15 members, headed by a *Blockwalter* (block warden). Two to six blocks formed a *Zellen* (cell), which was led by a *Zellenwalter* (cell warden). Each commerce or industrial organization that had at least 10 employees was considered a *Betriebsgemeinschaft* (plant community) under the leadership of a *Betriebsführer* (plant leader) and under the control of a *Betriebswalter* (plant warden). Several small industrial or commerce businesses that each had less than 10 workers were grouped together in communities based on the street they were located on. Plant communities and the individual members of the plant communities within the jurisdiction of a local party group of the NSDAP formed an *Ortsgruppe* (local group) of the DAF under the leadership of an *Ortsgruppenwalter* (local group warden). The local groups within a NSDAP *Kreis* (circle) comprised a DAF *Kreis* (circle) under the leadership of a *Kreiswalter* (circle warden). The DAF *Kreise* (circles) were organized into *Gaue* (regions) under command of a *Gauwart* (region warden). The largest organizations of the DAF were the DAF *Bezirke* (districts), which were headed by *Bezirkwalter* (district wardens). There were 13 DAF *Bezirke* in 1935. At the top there was the Zentralbüro (central office) with Robert Ley as *Leiter der Deutsche Arbeitsfront* (leader of the German Labor Front).

The military structure of the DAF was mirrored in the wearing of a uniform. Members wore a black or brown uniform with red swastika armband, khaki shirt, black tie, and side cap. Pale blue piping edged the epaulets and hats. The symbolic insignia of the DAF was a swastika standing on its point, placed inside a disc in the shape of a 14-toothed cogwheel. The DAF belt buckle featured a swastika within a cogwheel, while leaders had this design within a wreath.

The DAF was a lucrative business. It developed a number of fruitful publication, printing, promotion and distribution companies, with about 110 newspapers and periodicals. The organization also included a paper factory. The official journal for the millions of DAF members was *Arbeitertum* (*Labor World*), a heavily illustrated, bi-weekly propaganda magazine. The DAF also published nonfiction thematic almanacs, calendars, photo albums, art books, poetry booklets, children's books, catalogs, postcards, posters and an extensive list of culture-related books and novels loaned by book clubs such as Büchergilde Gutenberg and Deutsche Hausbücherei. The independence and freedom of the publishing directors and editorial departments were, of course, eliminated by a censorship office, and a unified Nazi political orientation was imposed.

Initially, when World War II began, the DAF went to great lengths to insure that the majority of its members in areas deemed vital would be exempt from the draft and subsequent service in the Wehrmacht. This was the case until about 1942, when the increasingly heavy strain of war forced all but the most important workers to be eligible for the draft and military service. Another impact the turning tide of World War II had on the DAF was in the formation of independently organized anti-aircraft artillery units, staffed with men of specific industries and businesses, and put into action on a as-needed basis, literally either on the roof of the business in question, or close by it on the ground outside of it. These units were pulled together from men inside the factory itself and were called up whenever an attack was imminent or taking place. As these units were very ad hoc in nature, they did not receive a great deal of training if any at all, and they were equipped with only light, anti-aircraft FlaK guns of 2-cm or 3.7-cm caliber. They also lacked fire control equipment, so they functioned mainly to provide barrage fire, sending as much fire into the air as possible in the path of oncoming Allied aircraft. They served much better against lower-flying aircraft because of this. It is not known exactly how many of these units were formed during World War II, or how well they performed in general. It can only be assumed that their services were lacking the punch and training to have been as effective as had been hoped.

DAF *WERKSCHAREN*

Werkscharen were formations intended to act as DAF political shock troops. Robert Ley pressed to create such units in all workplaces and industrial plants. *Werkscharen* were to total from 15 to 93 men according to the size of the manufacture. Large *Scharen* were subdivided into *Rotten* (squads) and *Trupps* (platoons), typically, in SA fashion. There were three components of a work brigade: (1) the *Stammanschaft* (original team) including existing NSBO members aged over 30 and DAF officials; (2) the *Stoßtrupp* (assault troop), comprising fit men under 30 who had

DAF *Werkschar* member, c. 1937. The uniform was dark/navy blue and included a peakless side cap with DAF emblem at the front or a visored cap for officers; a light blue poplin shirt with black neck tie; a short jacket with two breast pockets and a swastika armband worn on the upper left arm; a black leather waist belt and a belt cross strap; breeches of the same fabric and color as the jacket; and black riding boots. For wet weather there was a double-breasted raincoat, and there was a similar thick overcoat for winter wear.

completed their compulsory two years' military service; and (3) the *Jungmanschaft* (young men's team), including all able-bodied young workers under 20 who had not yet performed the obligatory military service. Members of the *Werkscharen* wore a sort of SA-like uniform (but dark blue in color instead of SA brown), and owing to an agreement reached with the SA chief of staff Viktor Lutze, were trained and formed by the SA. With the *Werkscharen*, Ley hoped and intended to form his own private DAF militia, but because of suspicion, rivalry and pressure from other top Nazi leaders, this never happened. Hitler was persuaded to limit the size and functions of Ley's militia and never allowed them to carry small arms. As already said in Chapter 1, *Werkscharen* of the DAF were also present in the Organisation Todt until early 1942, when the OT created its own armed militia known as OT-Schützkommando. Robert Ley also tried to form his own young apprentices'/workers' movement called DAF-Jugend (DAFJ, DAF Youth) but this met with scant success. In October 1933, the encroaching DAFJ was incorporated into the Hitler Jugend (Hitler Youth), headed by Baldur von Schirach.

Schönheit der Arbeit

In order to integrate the workers into the Nazi system, there were several sub-organizations directed by the DAF.

The Schönheit der Arbeit (Beauty of Work, headed, interestingly, by Hitler's architect Albert Speer) was a program that made some efforts to improve the milieu where workers performed their jobs, e.g., by reducing noise, increasing safety, and providing better lighting and ventilation. The improvements lauded by the program were in many cases only theoretical though. Shabby factories were given a lick of paint, potted plants were installed on window-sills and yards were embellished with patches of grass and a few benches on which workers were permitted to indulge in sun-drenched relaxation during the short lunch break. The activities of the program provided a favorite subject for illustration in the propaganda booklets and brochures issued by the DAF. The whole scheme was an attempt to win labor over to the Nazi cause, and the program Schönheit der Arbeit clearly aimed at convincing still more people of the "Beauty of Labor." On the whole it was merely a self-justification of increasing the hard daily toil—particularly when World War II broke out.

Other activities of the DAF included educational and competition programs to improve productivity as well as provide opportunities for advancement and upward mobility to individual workers. The organization also distributed emergency funds for unemployed, sick and injured workers. Nazi Germany was a nation awash with posters and badges. These invariably portrayed idealized visions of life under Nazi rule and were used to exhort the public and recognize individual participation in activities strictly sanctioned by the state. There were thus various awards for labor such as the *Ehrenzeichen Pionier der Arbeit* (Pioneer of Labor Award), instituted in 1940 for the highest efforts in the economic and social sphere; this award was bestowed twice annually—on Labor Day and during the Nazi Party Rally at Nuremberg. Awards and commemorative badges had the dual effect of making the official events seem important and bonding the participants into a united front.

Kraft durch Freude (KdF)

The most popular DAF sub-organization was without doubt the leisure-providing Kraft durch Freude (Strength Through Joy, KdF in short). The hugely successful and popular Nazi KdF scheme was an imitation of the Italian Fascist workers' pleasure organization known as *Dopo Lavoro* (After Work). Originally called Nach der Arbeit (After Work), the German scheme was renamed NS-Gemeinschaft Kraft durch Freude (National Socialist Organization Strength Through Joy). All members of the Deutsche Arbeitsfront were automatically members of the Kraft durch Freude organization. Created in November 1933,

Kraft durch Freude was essentially designed for the purpose of providing organized leisure for the German work force. Interestingly enough, the populist and cunning leadership of the DAF had calculated that the work year contained 8,760 hours, of which only 2,100 were spent working and 2,920 were spent sleeping, leaving 3,740 hours of free time. Thus the driving concept behind KdF was organized relaxation for the collection of strength for more work. The citizens of the Third Reich were to be kept physically fit and strong-nerved enough to serve as chips in Hitler's geopolitical poker game. The KdF strived to achieve this goal by providing leisure activities of enforced conformity for German workers. These events were specifically directed towards the working class, and it was through the KdF that the NSDAP hoped to bring to the "common man" the pleasures once reserved only for the wealthy. By opening the door for the working class to easily and affordably take part in such activities, it was believed that the labor force could be lulled into being more flexible and productive.

There were many aspects of the KdF mass program, including wildly popular and comparatively affordable international cruises provided by an extensive fleet of KdF liners and pleasure vessels for smaller waterways. Trips were organized to the coasts of Norway, Spain, and Italy, as well as to destinations on the Baltic Sea and the German and Danish coasts (these luxury cruises were, however, reserved for Nazi Party members and never widely available for common Germans). The KdF also sponsored and organized a wide variety of other cut-price group activities, including skiing trips, fitness centers, tennis lessons, retreats, day trips, excursions, hikes, tours, concerts and musicals, theater, cabaret, opera and operetta performances, art exhibits, and other cultural and historical displays and events, all of which were cheap and supposedly designed to aid average Germans in enjoying their free time more. It was hoped that this would create a healthier, more educated and more productive workforce.

Emblem of the KdF (NS-Gemeinschaft Kraft durch Freude).

Commemorative badge for a KdF cruise to Italy.

Another aspect of the KdF organization was the provision for workers to have a right to vacation and proper paid holidays, a concept unique to the period in nearly all nations of the world. Moreover, Ley, the DAF and the

Commemorative badge for a KdF ski tour in Franconia.

KdF put pressure on employers and businessmen to provide higher wages, longer vacations, better working conditions, longer notice of termination periods and many other benefits for their personnel. The KdF leisure programs had gratifying economic side effects and were a good spur for the tourism business, restaurants and rural hotel owners as well as for the transport and travel companies, notably the state railway system.

Forest sign. The Nazis encouraged love for nature and the KdF organized hiking tours, but not for all citizens. The sign reads: "Jews are not welcome in our German forests."

The effective aim of KdF activities was to iron out class differences, for the whole vast scheme naturally had an ideological purpose: maintaining the individual's capacity for work and returning him to his place of employment invigorated and re-equipped, just like the engine of a motor vehicle has to be overhauled after it has done a certain number of kilometers. The KdF was also a formidable propaganda weapon that sought to attract tourists from abroad, a task performed by Hermann Esser, one of the Ministry of Public Enlightenment and Propaganda's secretaries. A series of multilingual and colorful brochures were published and distributed in Europe advertising Nazi Germany as a peaceful, idyllic, modern and progressive country, even portraying Nazi leaders as benefactors of the German people. The Nazi regime did its utmost to impress foreign visitors with the grandeur and success of its ideas.

Another major aspect of KdF was the ambitious attempt to make the automobile a reality for as many Germans as possible. Private car ownership in the 1930s in Germany was the prerogative of the rich; only one in fifty Germans owned an automobile. To democratize individual car ownership, the world famous Volkswagen Kever ("Beetle") or the People's Car, originally called KdF Wagen, was created. An extensive system was set up to allow nearly anyone to purchase and own one for the sum of 997 Reichmarks. The DAF sponsored the project, and a huge production complex was developed at Wolfsburg near Hannover. For marketing the car, Ley devised a scheme by which the customer paid 5 Reichsmarks weekly and received a stamp to paste in a saving book. When the sum of 997 RM was saved, the purchaser became eligible to receive his KdF-Volkswagen. Some 336,668 Germans started buying their vehicles on the installment plan, paying some 280 million Marks ($112 million), but the buyers were destined to disappointment. By September 1939, war broke out and the KdF-Volkswagen project was postponed. The existing Volkswagen cars were allocated to party officials and state agencies. The People's Car automotive facilities at Wolfsburg were transformed and militarized. The civilian VW design was modified as an all-purpose military vehicle, known as Kübelwagen (a kind of Jeep), plying the roads of all World War II fronts. In 1946, a new—de-Nazified—Volkswagen company was constituted that honored the old saving stamps, and at last the world-famous VW Kever began cruising the civilian roads. The ultimate Volkswagen Beetle was manufactured in July 2003 in Mexico. Production in Germany had already stopped in 1978. In 1998 a new "retro" VW Beetle was produced with a look inspired by the legendary Kever but with modern technology based on the VW Golf design.

The popularity of Ley's KdF peaked in 1938, the last full peacetime year. The KdF was an immensely successful Nazi organization of inestimable propaganda value to Hitler's regime. In 1938 Kraft durch Freude provided 58,813 popular entertainments, 12,407 operatic performances, 19,523 theatrical events, 10,989 evening variety shows, and 7,921 cabaret shows at a cost of 32 million DM and with an audience of over 54 million. KdF represented about 10 percent of the total DAF budget. There is no doubt that by that time, German workers (at least those of "pure blood") had never had it so good; but when World War II began in 1939, things radically changed. There were no longer funds or time for fun, and the organization's activi-

ties were drastically reduced. One of the most important functions the KdF helped perform was in the provision of the majority of its fleet of ships for use by the German Kriegsmarine. The largest and most famous KdF ship, the *Wilhelm Gustloff*, served initially as a hospital ship during World War II, later as a troop transport vessel. She was sunk in January of 1945 with a loss of 9,343 lives, one of the largest single naval losses in history. The KdF also helped set up and staff rest homes for German troops, provided concerts and films for soldiers at the front, and helped distribute amenities to traveling and returning men at railway stations and other major points in Germany and abroad. This was often done in conjunction with other German social welfare and help organizations, such as the Deutsches Rotes Kreuz (DRK, German Red Cross) and the National-Sozialistische Volkswohlfahrt (NSV, Nazi Popular Welfare).

The KdF was never in any way a paramilitary organization like many of the other auxiliary groups of the period. It existed solely to provide pleasure and relaxation, initially to German workers and later to Wehrmacht troops as well. Its overall goal was to create and mold a controllable work force, but as a

KdF Volkswagen "Beetle" Type 92. The Volkswagen, the cheap "people's car," the famous "Käfer" (Beetle), was designed by professor Ferdinand Porsche in 1936. It was a brilliant, tiny, beetle-shaped vehicle with an air-cooled engine placed in the rear. Hitler ordered Porsche to modify the VW as an all-purpose military vehicle known as the Kübelwagen, which was widely used during the Second World War.

result it also provided millions of Germans with pleasures and rights never before experienced by the average person. The Nazis' economic recovery of the 1930s brought down unemployment. More jobs, stable wages, restored prestige and KdF welfare politics made Hitler's regime appealing after the turbulences of the late 1920s. While minorities (e.g., Jews, homosexuals and political opponents) endured discrimination, terror, repression, humiliation and later murder, ordinary Germans often ignored or excused the concentration camps, and regarded the period 1933–1939 as a sort of golden age with order, calm, full employment, prosperity and an economic boom. The social benefits provided by the Nazi regime, however, were short-lived, as Hitler was gearing the economy for a future war to satisfy his megalomaniacal aims. For a time the DAF and KdF attracted the working class, but they found it difficult to hide the harsh fact of dictatorship. The benefits the Nazi regime brought to the working class were many: full employment with (low) wages; a welfare state with subsidized housing and elaborate recreational schemes; the highest degree of social mobility ever experienced in Germany; a sense of false unity, and national purpose. But these benefits had a huge price, as its cost their freedom. Not all workers swallowed the bait. There were also people who opposed the regime by acts of industrial sabotage and who attempted in building up underground opposition networks. It must be kept in mind that if KdF was a remarkable social experiment, it represented the velvet glove that covered the iron fist. Ley's DAF had close ties with Himmler's repression organization, the SS, which punished with harshness laziness, absenteeism, deviation, sabotage or the slightest protest. An order from Hermann Göring in June 1933 enjoined the Gestapo service to report to the DAF delegates any worker whose political attitude appeared suspect. The whole system of the DAF called for workers and employers to pull together for the common good, but it was a paternalist and feudalistic system with courts and councils run by pliant Nazis who typically found disputes in favor of the employer. The "liberation" of the working class was only apparent in the "golden period" from 1933 to 1939. What all the DAF nonsense and attractive KdF stuffs meant in plain terms was that German workers had to do what they were told. It was the DAF's officials who decided who could be employed and where, who was to be promoted or dismissed, and what they were to be paid. Choice of jobs for workers was restricted, the free

Arbeitsbuch. The labor book was a personal work record of the owner. It was re-introduced in February 1935. The cover displayed the inevitable Nazi eagle with swastika and Fraktur-style letter type.

movement of workers was curtailed, and strict control was paramount. All workers needed an *Arbeitsbuch* (work book), a personal document imposed in February 1935 onward on all German employees. The workbook was actually reintroduced, as it was an ancient, unpopular practice that had been abolished in the 1840s. While it proved impossible to repeal the old labor laws (the pride of German legislation in the 1880s), industrial disputes were outlawed by being declared inimical to the "German concept of social conscience and honor." The workbook was kept by the employer during the time of the work contract, and in it he noted how the worker behaved and performed. It contained details of qualifications and employment history. Without it no worker could secure gainful employment. Forgery and loss of the workbook were punished by fine and even imprisonment.

As for the Jews, they were not permitted membership in the DAF, and never benefited from the KdF's activities, but they were not excluded from the German work force. The DAF fought hard to keep its skilled Jewish workers, but by mid–1942 the Labor Front had to surrender them to the insistent demands of the SS. Their fate was then sealed: extermination in death camps.

Kraft durch Freude armband. It had a white print on a blue field with white borders. It was worn by officials, marshals or stewards who guided or supervised large parties or crowds at public events. The word Ordnerdienst (Order Service) was sometimes added.

REICHSARBEITSDIENST (RAD)

On October 24, 1929, panic struck Wall Street, the New York Stock Exchange, and this crash was the clearest indication of the economic crisis soon affecting the whole world. The crisis did not spare the vulnerable German Republic of Weimar supported by the American Dawes Plan adopted in August 1924. Foreign credit, capital and investments were withdrawn from Germany, resulting in economic upheaval. Commercial and industrial activity went into decline, banks closed, many firms went bankrupt and many people were ruined overnight. Stringent deflationary measures were taken; salaries, wages and rates of interest were reduced; prices dropped; the general standard of living was lowered; and the number of unemployed quickly rose into the millions. The political world seemed to be incapable of finding solutions that would provide a means of overcoming the difficulties of everyday life. Despair and discontent strengthened social unrest, extremism and nationalism, and the crisis allowed extreme political parties to draw strong public attention, notably Hitler's NSDAP. During the early 1930s—a time of great economic hardship in Germany—many political, clerical and civic groups organized independent work camps to help provide some form of employment for the many ex-servicemen and the huge numbers of unemployed workers. On June 5, 1931, Chancellor Heinrich Brüning gave the authorization to create a temporary, state-sponsored national work service in order to supply labor for various civic and agricultural construction duties throughout Germany, first of all to help relieve the strain of high unemployment. Soon the Stahlhelm (a World War I veterans' association) created a national work organization along military lines called the Freiwilliger Arbeitsdienst (FAD, Voluntary Labor Service), and Hitler's NSDAP proceeded to form in 1931 and 1932 a number of rudimentary *Arbeitslagern* (work camps) under the direction of Konstantin

DAF and RAD

Hierl. Hierl (1875–1955) was a professional soldier with a 30-year career, and a veteran of World War I. He had been director of the War Academy in Berlin, had set up his own *Freikorps* in the troubled post–World War I years, and had a pronounced sympathy for the Nazi Party. Interestingly, Konstantin Hierl once had been Hitler's superior. In 1919 Hierl was major in the political department of the Reichswehr in Munich, and it is probably he who ordered Corporal Adolf Hitler to infiltrate and spy on ultra-nationalist parties, among which was the DAP (the future Nazi Party, NSDAP). Ironically, the German army had helped launch Hitler's political career. Hierl, a Nazi activist since 1927, later became a high-ranking member of the NSDAP, at the time being in charge of what was known as Organization Department II of the party. Soon after the formation of the FAD, Hierl began to absorb the many independent work camps that had been formed earlier in a process of centralizing state control over the area of national labor. In August of 1933, six months after the seizure of power by Hitler, the national Veterans' Voluntary Labor Service, Frei-

FAD/NSAD "walking-out" uniform. A precursor of the RAD uniform, the FAD "walking-out" dress was earth brown and included a soft-visored cap, a single-breasted tunic, a swastika armband, and matching trousers. The collar patch indicated the rank, here that of *Vormann* (private first class, red bar bordered in white on a black background). Left: Emblem of the FAD der Stahlhelm, worn on the upper sleeve of the tunic. The central emblem (steel helmet, spade and pick) was white on black and the bar at the top of the shield was yellow and white.

Reichsarbeitsführer Konstantin Hierl (1875–1955).

williger Arbeitdienst, was renamed Nationalsozialistische Arbeitdienst (NSAD, National Socialist Labor Service). There was some confusion about the name of the Labor Service in 1933. It was sometimes called the FAD, sometimes the Nationalsozialistische Arbeitsdienst (NSAD) and sometimes the Arbeitsdienst.

Hitler appointed Hierl secretary of state

for the Labor Service and a member of the Reich Labor Ministry. He continued in his command of the NSAD, and would go on to control it with the title of Reichsarbeitsführer (Reich Labor Leader) until the very end of World War II. Hierl was also appointed Reichsleiter in 1936 and Reichsminister in 1943. Hierl survived World War II, was tried as a major offender by the Nuremberg tribunal in 1946, and spent five years in prison. Hierl was released soon after and died in 1955.

In the early period of the Third Reich, service in the FAD/NSAD was still voluntary, but it was soon made a requirement for those wishing to study at a university or make a career in the NSDAP and its various organizations. Thus by the middle of 1934, the voluntary labor service was only partially voluntary. At the same time there were foreign protests against the German Labor Service, which was regarded as performing clandestine military conscription. Hierl's control over the FAD/NSAD was imperiled when Minister of Labor Franz Seldte (Hierl's immediate superior) agreed with the SA leader Ernst Röhm to merge the FAD with the SA. This takeover never occurred, though, as the purge in June 1934—known as the Night of the Long Knives—totally destroyed the power of the SA. The SA purge greatly strengthened Hierl's position and on June 26, 1935, the Reich's Labor Service Law (RGBI-I 769) was passed. The labor service FAD/NSAD was renamed

Early unit flag of FAD/NSAD.

FAD officer. The early FAD uniform, later continued in the RAD, was basically brown with dark brown facings and piping (colors that obviously were associated with soil). FAD ranks were indicated by a simple system of silver stripes displayed on the collar patch.

DAF and RAD

a final time as the Reichsarbeitsdienst (RAD, State Labor Service). The new RAD was released from subordination to the Ministry of Labor and became a part of Robert Ley's DAF (German Labor Front)—and thus a part of one of the NSDAP Angeschlossene Verbände (Nazi-associated formations). Hierl, as *Reichsarbeitsführer*, became a member of the Reichsleitung (leadership of the NSDAP) and secretary of state. Henceforth service in the Reichsarbeitdienst for a period of six months was made compulsory and nationwide for all German young men aged 17–25 years. Jews, "non–Aryans," German persons married with Jews and "non–Aryans," invalids and the unable, as well as "asocial," "hereditary ill" and other "enemies of the regime" and individuals condemned or excluded from the German community for crimes or "dishonoring actions," were not submitted to the RAD.

Previous to the Reich Labor Service Law of June 1935, another law had been passed in which military service was also made compulsory. Together, the two laws created a central-

FAD lapel badge. The FAD *Goldene Ehrennadel* (Golden Honor Pin) was 28 mm by 21 mm.

Member of the RAD. "Present spade!"

ized, national and compulsory system in which all males of the ages 18–25 would first enter labor service for a period of six months, and upon completion, enter service for two years in one of the branches of the Wehrmacht (German Armed Forces). After the Anschluss (annexation) of Austria in March 1938, compulsory RAD service was imposed in that country in August of the same year. A year later the annexation of Bohemia and Moravia (parts of Czechoslovakia) saw the creation of RAD districts in these new territorial acquisitions.

Hitler regarded the RAD as a necessary and convenient step to rearmament; the young men who shouldered shovels were soon to shoulder rifles. However, contrary to one common assumption, the RAD was not a part of the German armed forces but, as was said earlier, a sub-organization of the DAF. The confusion regarding the RAD resulted largely from a move in 1938 in which the Reichsarbeitdienst and the previously discussed Organisation Todt were directed to support the Wehrmacht in various auxiliary tasks, notably the construction of the bunkers of the West Wall—a task they would perform throughout World War II. The Reichsarbeitdienst later became a Wehrmachtsgefolge (armed forces auxiliary). Then the RAD was deemed an auxiliary organization important to the smooth operations of the regular armed forces, and its members—if captured—became eligible for the status of prisoners-of-war according to the Geneva Convention. Although later in World War II the young men of the RAD were even allowed to carry weapons, they were thus never actually a part of the official Wehrmacht (national armed forces), a status reserved exclusively for the Heer (ground force), Luftwaffe (air force) and Kriegsmarine (navy), and tactically, the Waffen SS.

WOMEN'S LABOR SERVICE

The female version of the male RAD was established in February 1933 and was known as the Freiwilliger Frauenarbeitsdienst (Voluntary Women's Labor Service, also known as the Deutscher Frauenarbeitsdienst and Weibliche Freiwilliger Arbeitsdienst). It was originally a subsection of the Nationalsozialistisches Frauenschaft (NSF, National-Socialist Women's Association). In April 1936 the female labor service was removed from the NS Frauen-

Young RAD man at work.

DAF and RAD

schaft and incorporated into the RAD as the Reichsarbeitsdienst der weiblichen Jugend (RAD/wJ), the female branch of the RAD. The male branch was technically known as the RAD/M, but it was always referred to simply as the RAD. It was yet another indication that no NSDAP agency of any importance could be left in the hands of women. For women RAD service was voluntary, although the pressure to join was intense; but the number of volunteers failed to meet the level of demand, hence the recourse to conscription. In January 1939 the voluntary scheme was dropped and six months' national labor service was declared compulsory for all women from 18 to 25 years of age, with an average of 30,000 annual draftees. Officially they were to be trained in "womanly duties," but since all Germans were expected to work for the common good, RAD/wJ women also supplied agricultural and household labor, particularly for overworked farmers' wives and mothers of large families in urban areas.

Structure of the RAD

At the same time that the RAD was officially established in July 1934, it was also divided into two separate sections for males and for females, as already mentioned. The Reichsarbeitdienst Manner, or RAD/M, was set up for men, and the Reichsarbeitdienst der weibliche Jugend, or RAD/wJ, for women.

The young women of the RAD/wJ entered the organization at the age of 18 after having been "educated" to Nazi values in the two female branches of the Hitler Jugend (Hitler

RAD/wJ sleeve badge. The machine-woven insignia was approximately 75 mm × 95 mm, featuring a black swastika over two ears of wheat in a white, circular field. Below it was the Bezirksnummer (unit number) in roman numerals. The main body of the insignia was dark brown with a white and black border.

RAD/wJ brooch. The nickel-plated steel brooch was 44 mm in diameter.

Emblem of the Reichsarbeitsdienst (RAD Labor Service) badge for men.

Struture of the RAD

Youth): the Junge Mädel (JM, Young Girls' Association, 10–14 years old) and the Bund Deutsche Mädel (BdM, League of German Girls, 14–18 years old). The labor service for women was born simply of economic necessity, hence the recourse to conscription when the number of volunteers (only 40,000 in 1938) failed to meet the level of demand. The RAD/wJ was thus made compulsory for young women aged 18–25 by decree of January 1939. In 1940 the Reichsarbeitdienst der weibliche Jugend was organized into 25 *Bezirke* (regimental districts), each divided into 5 or 6 battalion-size *Lagergruppen* (groups of camps). These in turn were composed of about 15 *Lagern* (companies or camps); there were about 2,000 camps. The smallest RAD/wJ unit was a *Kameradschaft* (section or squad) comprising 6 to 12 young women.

Similarly, the young men entered the RAD/M after their time in the Hitler Jugend (Hitler Youth), first in the Deutsches Jungvolk (DJ, Young German Boys, 10–14 years) and the Hitler Jugend proper (14–18 years). Those wishing to perform their service before embarking on an apprenticeship or training could join at the age of 16.

The male RAD/M was organized into 40 *Arbeitsgaue* (labor regions) headed by a brigadier, each being numbered with a Roman numeral from I to XXXX.

In addition there were other units at disposal: Reichsarbeitsdienst-Division z.b.V.1/Infanterie-Division Albert Leo Schlageter; Reichsarbeitsdienst-Division z.b.V.2/Infanterie-Division Friedrich Ludwig Jahn; Reichsarbeitsdienst-Division z.b.V.3/Infanterie-Division Theodor Körner; and Reichsarbeitsdienst-Division z.b.V.4/Infanterie-Division Güstrow.

An *Arbeitsgau* was headed by an officer with a staff, headquarters and a *Wachabteilung* (bodyguard company) numbered according to the *Arbeitsgau* it was located in. Around eight battalion-sized units, known as *Arbeitsgruppen* and consisting of 1,200 to 1,800 men each, were also grouped under each *Arbeitsgau*. Several *Arbeitsgruppe* could be assembled together into a regimental-sized unit known as a *Bereich*, headed by a colonel, while an *Arbeitsgruppe* itself consisted of six company-sized formations

RAD Arbeitsgau XXI Niederrhein (21, Lower Rhine) pin badge. The RAD was divided into *Arbeitsgaue* (divisional regions) each numbered with a Roman numeral from I to XXXX (1 to 40).

Arbeits Dank badge.

known as *Abteilungen*. The company-sized RAD *Abteilung* (not to be confused with the unit of the same name in the Wehrmacht, which had the size of a battalion) was headed by a captain. It formed the core group around which the functions of the Reichsarbeitsdienst revolved. The pre-war RAD *Abteilung* was based at a specific camp location from which its members would train, drill, practice, and take part in the various labor projects their unit was assigned to. Each camp and its *Abteilung* were indicated by a number designation listed along with its higher *Arbeitsgruppen* number. These two numbers were displayed together on the ubiquitous RAD *Dienststellenabzeichen*—a cloth badge in the shape of a downward-pointing shovel blade worn on the upper left shoulder of all uniforms and greatcoats worn by all personnel. An RAD *Abteilung* consisted of about 300 men grouped together in a 6-man staff and 4 platoon-sized units called *Züge*, each of about 50 men, under the leadership of a sergeant. Each *Zug* was in turn made up of three 17-man, section-sized units known as *Trupp*, headed by a corporal.

RAD officers and leaders were enjoined to adopt a comradely attitude towards their troops, although never at the cost of discipline or respect of hierarchy. For example, they were encouraged to share their midday meal with them and behave in general in such a manner as to break down social barriers.

As in most armed German forces and Nazi organizations, the RAD had musicians. Each *Abteilung* was expected to have a fife-and-drum band and every *Arbeitsgruppe* a marching band or fanfare trumpeters. Musicians were distinguished by traditional items of German dress decoration. A lyre was displayed in woven form on badge and shoulder straps. Removable *Schwalbennester* ("swallows'

RAD trumpeter. The musician wears *Schwalbennester* (swallows' nests, shoulder ornaments), a lyre badge (left) and a swastika armband on the left sleeve. The fringed banner was attached to the instrument by means of three straps.

nests")—roundish cloth attachments—were fixed to the shoulder seam. They featured seven vertical stripes in a red-white-black pattern and were only worn when the musicians were employed as bandsmen during meetings, rallies, commemorations, ceremonies and other celebrations. Normal day-to-day service did not require them to wear the swallows' nests.

The RAD also had a large administrative branch (*Verwaltung*, made up of qualified doctors, lawyers, administrators, treasurers, and other specialized professions) in which the emphasis was obviously on bureaucracy rather than practical work. There was a welfare organization, known as Arbeits Dank (labor thanks), as a form of insurance for FAD/NSAD/RAD members who during their service sustained illness or injury attributable to their labor. The Arbeits Dank also assisted poorer members to acquire education they needed but could not afford in order to obtain a job after leaving the RAD. All members and former members of the National Labor Service were required to belong and, of course, to contribute to the welfare of Arbeits Dank.

Prewar Tasks of the RAD

Officially the RAD's task was to train German youth physically and educate them in Nazi political values. Young men and girls aged 18 were subjected to manual labor and strict discipline. The initiation of a young labor corps was born simply of economic necessity, and the service had far-reaching economic benefits. But there was more. Ley and Hierl's long-term vision went far beyond the need to contain unemployment. The Labor Service was to be a major cornerstone in building, consolidating and maintaining the Nazi regime. Their concept was that manual work provided the means of molding the character of the young Germans and reviving interest in the dignity of hard work. This view was illustrated by the RAD motto: "*Arbeit adelt* [work ennobles]." If the young people of the RAD formed a huge manpower resource that did not need paying, at the same time they learned devotion to Nazi ideals. The work service was a means of dissolving the traditional authoritarian structure of the German family and neutralizing the equally authoritarian influence of the official Catholic and Protestant churches. The organization was established as a form of honorary service to the national community, its object being to train young people in a strict, disciplined "true approach to work." The reward was the health of community life, the betterment of the Fatherland, and the right to march in mass formations with their spades glinting like rifles at rallies. The young men and women of the RAD always took part in the major Nazi parades and demonstrations, notably the Nazi Party Rally Day held every year at Nuremberg before the war.

The uniformed RAD was also designed to break down social and professional barriers. No distinction was made as to social background, occupation and education. University and high-school graduates, craftsmen, peasants, and workers alike were subjected to the same menial tasks as part of Nazi policy to inculcate an "appropriate respect for manual and hard labor"; at least, that was the theory. In the practice, however, the Nazis could never—by only a simple, arbitrary decree—put an end to social and class differences. Total leveling of the nation through hard work always remained a utopian ideal, and the cleavage between rich and poor, between educated and non- or less-educated, stayed the same. Service in the RAD was unpopular and dreaded by many young Germans, both males and females, particularly those from the upper-middle and upper classes. Despite Nazi propaganda, rich and educated youth resented to have to waste six months of their lives with other young Germans they considered to be their social and intellectual inferiors.

Additionally, and perhaps the most important, the RAD had a strongly military spirit and system of discipline, thus providing an excellent introduction to eventual military service. The RAD had a huge number of unpaid, conscripted young men and women who were organized in virtually military, uniformed, disciplined battalions. The regimental training and rugged conditions were intended to prepare the youth for war. The qualifications, achievements and (eventually) punishments that occurred during service in the RAD were noted in the *Arbeitsbuch* (labor book) and followed the holder during his whole professional career.

The RAD was widely used by Josef Göbbels's Propaganda Ministry. First of all, the Labor Service had the advantage of considerably—although artificially—lowering the unemployment statistics, an important point that increased Hitler's popularity in a country burdened for years by unemployment. Second, the RAD was conveniently used to present the new face of Germany, a modern country made up of supposedly equal citizens working together for their future.

Hard work and preparation for war, which were actually the purpose of the RAD, were focal points of Nazi life, but this had to be done joyfully. RAD units marched in disciplined ranks at all-important Nazi gatherings, feasts, rallies and meetings, shouldering their spades like rifles and chanting like Greek choruses. Propaganda materials showed nothing but smiling faces; radiant and virile expressions; determination; freshness of spirit; tanned, happy members; and youthfully joyous; healthy vigor. Needless to say, reality was more prosaic.

The girls of the RAD/wJ were trained and used in womanly domestic duties. Actually, they were employed for public utility, as farm auxiliaries, domestics and servants for mothers of large families, and hospital or factory workers. The few of them having professional skills could become secretaries, office supervisors, nurses, social or medical assistants, for example.

Before World War II, the young men of the RAD/M were taken to various land, forestry and water related projects demanding hard physical labor. One of Hitler's aims was to make Germany an independent and economically self-sufficient country by means of autarky. More land had to be cultivated for food production, and new roads and canals were to be built for facilitating its exploitation. The prewar task of the RAD was the attainment of these goals. With a lot of marching and singing, RAD young people took part in labor projects all in the interest of the expansion of arable land, the reclamation of marshland for cultivation, the construction of roads, canals and dykes, drainage improvement work, tree removal operations, conservation of soil, reclamation of fallow or wasted land, and so forth. RAD units were instrumental in the construction of canals, paths, roads and Fritz Todt's famous prewar autobahns. For example, one of the work projects completed by the Reichsarbeitsdienst in the 1930s was the Hochrhönstraße (road through the Rhön Highlands) in northern Bavaria, near the border with Hessen and Thüringia. The road, with a length of 25 km, connects Bischofsheim-an-der-Rhön to Fladungen. It still exists today and has become a tourist highlight through a pleasant landscape.

Young RAD workers were housed in tent camps, discarded barracks, requisitioned buildings and hastily erected hutments. Hierl had ordered the design of a standard *Lager-*

RAD private trousers. The RAD earth-brown trousers were army-style. They had a four-button fly front, high waist, and two pockets, and were held by suspenders or a belt.

holzhaus (prefabricated wooden camp hut) capable of being transported by truck wherever needed. For example, the road through the Rhön Highlands required the construction of several camps to house the RAD workers. The largest of these was built at the northern edge of the Schwarzes Moor area near Fladungen. This camp, for RAD battalions 5/283 and 6/283 (later 1/288 and 2/288), was called the Dr. Hellmuth-Lager, for the *Gauleiter* of Main-Franconia, Dr. Otto Hellmuth, who was in charge of plans and construction in this area. The camp consisted of a double row of wooden barracks with a refectory hall at one end and a large training and exercise hall at the other, the whole being surrounded by a high earthen berm. The camp was entered through an archway made of natural basalt stones, native to this area, built into the front of the exercise hall. This basalt archway is the only part of the camp still standing today. During World War II the Hellmuth camp housed prisoners of war, who worked in the nearby fields. After the war the buildings housed displaced persons, and the camp was later decommissioned and dismantled.

The results and achievements of land reclamation, in spite of Göbbels's optimistic annual reports, were rather limited. Land was actually reclaimed but often used for other purposes than farming (e.g., military installa-

Entrance to RAD camp at Fladungen. The basalt stone archway of RAD camp Dr. Hellmuth at Fladungen still exists today on the highway through the Rhön Highlands.

Hitler Gruß. Members of the DAF and RAD, and all others members of Nazi associations, were required to greet each other with the Hitler Gruß (Hitler salute)—an adaptation of the ancient Roman salute. It was done while at attention, with the right arm raised a little higher than the shoulder, and saying enthusiastically, "Heil Hitler!" while clicking the heels.

tions, compounds, army training grounds and ranges, and airfields). Besides, there were too few peasants available to tend the newly created farms.

In addition to land and road development projects, RAD units were also involved in emergency responses including fire fighting, flood control, repair of storm damage, and removal of snow blocking roads in winter. They could also be engaged to help with harvesting, or to supplement the work force of Organisation Todt in the realization of Hitler's sumptuous and megalomaniacal architectural projects designed by Albert Speer, notably in Berlin and Nuremberg.

The RAD-men's life was often grim, and was strictly supervised, with uniform bedmaking, locker and kit inspection, camp discipline and indoctrination classes. They were expected to work efficiently and joyfully. Their workday could be 9 hours, and was frequently even as long as 13 hours with a 5-minute break each hour. Sundays were "free," but were often dedicated to indoctrination courses, political education, Nazi-oriented cultural activities, and organized excursions, as well as sport, physical exercises, and paramilitary training. The subjection to authoritarian rule and the exploitation of cheap youth labor were justified by the National-Socialist leadership with the claim that "everyone's welfare was at stake." Concern for the individual's needs was regarded as synonymous with irresponsibility.

In a role the RAD/M would come to know well, it supported the Wehrmacht during the occupation of Austria in March 1938, the occupation of the Sudetenland in October 1938, and the occupation of Czechoslovakia in March 1939. During the summer of 1938 and until the war began, 300 RAD/M units helped in the construction of the West Wall fortification line along the western German boarder, while in the east, another 100 RAD formations aided in the construction of the Ostwall—a fortification line established along the eastern German border. As war drew nearer, in August of 1939, 115 RAD units served in eastern Prussia helping with harvest work, and other RAD units served in Danzig in eastern Prussia at various development projects of general public utility.

THE RAD AT WAR

General mobilization was declared in Germany on August 26, 1939, and Robert Ley's grandiose social schemes had to be temporary shelved. Ironically, the exigencies of war undermined much of what Robert Ley had struggled for and achieved during the peacetime years. The grassroots dynamic of the DAF waned, as its younger functionaries and leaders were drafted en masse into the army. Labor advocacy gave way to draconian controls as the war made increasing demands on German industry. The same DAF that once had fought for a shorter work week now found itself enforcing 72-hour work weeks in 1943. Emphasis on leisure gave way to efforts to raise productivity. KdF cruise ships became floating hospitals. The civilian KdF Volkswagen became a military vehicle. The NS Ordensburgen (schools developed for elite Nazi military and administrative echelons) were gradually placed under the control of SS-Reichsführer Heinrich Himmler. The war that started with Russia in 1941 reinvigorated Ley's quasi-religious commitment to National Socialism. Now the real enemy was clearly designated. The great struggle against the hated Bolshevism and Jewish plutocracy could be engaged on a global basis. The tireless Robert Ley gladly accepted all the burdens that the war pressure laid on him, and his quest for even more jurisdictions went on unabated. Hitler appointed him *Reichswohnungskomissar*, to control housing in Germany. These victories turned out to be pyrrhic, while Ley's defeats were real. A combination of economic bottlenecks, mounting destruction by Allied bombing, rivalry and administrative ineptness led to his failure to restore any more than a tiny fraction of the housing Germans were losing.

During the war Robert Ley suffered another major defeat. To sustain its massive war effort, Germany needed a huge labor force, and to meet this demand, Hitler appointed Fritz Sauckel as plenipotentiary for labor mobilization in 1942. This came as an embarrassing blow, an immense disappointment and a humiliating rebuff to Robert Ley, the man who for years had the monopoly on dealing with German workers. As previously said (in Chapter 1, Organisation Todt), Sauckel was given full responsibility by Hitler for the mobilization of labor to support Albert Speer's armaments and ammunitions programs.

At the beginning of World War II, the RAD lost over half of its men and 60 percent of its leadership to the armed forces, and it was suggested that the service should be disbanded until the war was over. However, Ley and Hierl managed to remain in their positions by proposing that the RAD could serve as an auxiliary to the Wehrmacht and work with the engineers of the Heer (the ground force), and to a smaller extent the Luftwaffe (air force). To aid the call to arms, 1,050 individual Reichsarbeitsdienst units were transferred in full to the Wehrmacht, specifically to the Heer, to form the basis of the new Bautruppen—the construction troops that would build roads, clear obstacles, strengthen bridges, construct field kitchens and facilities, dig trenches, create barriers and fortifications, and take part in all manner of other military construction duties. The RAD *Abteilungen* were transferred directly to the Heer and expanded to 401 men each through the addition of older, untrained army reservists. They were formed into a series of 55 regiment-sized units known as *Abschnittsbaustäbe*, which were numbered in the 1-to-111 series. Each *Abschnittsbaustäbe* consisted of four 2,000-man *Bau-Bataillone* in the 1-to-335 number series. Each of these was in turn made up of four of the ex–RAD *Abteilungen*, now expanded to 400 men each. At this time, 18 heavy and 12 light motorized road construction battalions were also formed from the RAD units transferred to the Wehrmacht. About 60 percent of the newly formed *Bautruppen* units spent the majority of their time during the Polish campaign clearing roads so that supplies and combatants could continue to reach the front. They also collected and sorted captured equipment and weapons, guarded prisoners, and helped with the Polish harvest. The victorious Polish campaign had justified the usefulness of the RAD, and the organization was not dissolved.

After the campaign in Poland (September 1939) the RAD reverted to its original form and continued to carry out its duties under its own commanders, under RAD rules and administration. The Labor Service was removed from Wehrmacht control and resumed its prewar work, but following the invasion of Denmark in the spring of 1940, it was once again placed under military control. The Wehrmacht kept the *Bautruppen* units that had been formed from the RAD and in their place was formed a new contingent of 900 RAD Abteilungen that would take up the previous duties of the Reichsarbeitdienst.

Throughout World War II the RAD played an important part in Germany's war effort. The RAD continued to serve its originally established purpose of training young men prior to their service in the Wehrmacht by providing construction and agricultural work for the nation. But the RAD increasingly took part in more militarized roles. During the Norwegian campaign and the war in the West in 1940, hundreds of RAD units took part in supporting the troops by helping to ensure that supplies continued to reach the front over cleared roadways. Again they helped repair damaged roads and bridges, built and repaired airstrips, constructed coastal fortifications, loaded and unloaded supplies and ammunition, laid minefields, manned fortifications, and even helped guard vital locations and prisoners of war.

The RAD was originally created as a purely German agricultural development agency and was exclusively for training German youth, but as the war progressed the rules were relaxed, and the work service became a permanent, auxiliary branch of the army. And since many Germans were drafted in the armed forces, the RAD was gradually opened to foreign enlistment—though on a much smaller scale than were the Organisation Todt and the NSKK (Drivers' Corps; see Chapter 3). In 1942, there was a small unit of 180 Danes, and a Dutch battalion—comprising 300 volunteers—called Gruppe Niederlande. In late 1943, new foreign RAD units were formed with volunteers from the Baltic lands, mainly young Estonians. In February 1943, RAD young men aged 18 were recruited to form the 19th Waffen SS Panzer Division Hohenstaufen.

Pro-Nazi Foreign Labor Services

Although they are not the focus of this book it is important to note that national labor services, modeled on the German RAD, were created in most countries occupied by the Nazis in Europe. These included the Land Arbejds Tjenesten in Denmark; the Arbeidsjensten in Norway; the Nederlandsche Arbeit Dienst in the Netherlands; the Vrijwilligen Arbeidsdienst voor Vlaanderen in Belgian Flanders; the Service Volontaire du Travail pour la Wallonie in Belgian Wallony; the German-led Sonderdienst in Poland; the Chantiers de la Jeunesse Française in France; and various similar organizations in Serbia, Romania, and Croatia. For example, the Drzavna Radna Sluzba (DRS, Croatian State Labor Service) was founded on August 20, 1941, and modeled on the German RAD. All physically fit males from 19 to 25 were obliged to serve in the DRS for 12 months, prior to a call-up for service in the armed forces. There were also regular cadre personnel. By the summer of 1942, more than 90,000 men served in the DRS, under the command of General Palcic. Over and above their work service, the DRS also acted as combat engineers in emergency situations.

Another example is the French Service du Travail Obligatoire (STO). In February 1943, the French Vichy state, headed by Marshal Philippe Pétain and Minister Pierre Laval, ordered the creation of the STO, by which men aged 18 to 25 were to be deported to Ger-

Belgian VAVV volunteer. The Vrijwilligen Arbeidsdienst voor Vlaanderen (VAVV, Voluntary Work Service for Flanders) was the Belgian counterpart of the German RAD. It was a paramilitary organization opened for at least six months to volunteering "Aryan" young men aged 18 to 25. The Voluntary Work Service for Flanders was headed by René van Thillo, a high-ranking official of the pro–Nazi Party Vlaams Nationaal Verbond (VNV, Flemish National League, created in 1933, and headed by Gustave "Staf" de Clerq). The members of the VAVV wore a green uniform and were employed in various public works. They were also indoctrinated and progressively integrated in the pro-Nazi collaboration, and involved in politics. Some of the most radical members enlisted in the German armed forces and Waffen SS to fight on the Russian front.

Badge of the Nederlansdsche Arbeidsdienst (NAD, Dutch Labor Service). The emblem of the wartime Dutch Labor Service was directly copied from the Nazi German RAD (a spade and two corn ears) with the addition of a small scroll reading "*Ick Dien* [I serve]."

many for compulsory industrial work. The German government promised that for every three French workers sent over, they would release one French prisoner of war, a clause that proved to be a lie, as very few prisoners of war were released.

Nazi Germany used the foreign labor services to compensate for its loss of manpower as it enlisted more and more soldiers for the Eastern Front. The various foreign labor services provided several units, which supported the German air force and the army engineer corps, particularly on the Eastern Front.

Militarization of the RAD

RAD units served on all fronts during World War II, from Norway to the Mediterranean Sea, and from France in the West (e.g., to help the Organisation Todt in building the Atlantic Wall and the submarine pens) to the far reaches of Russia in the East. Units served in Albania, Greece, and the former Yugoslavia. In the Soviet Union, they supported the Wehrmacht in its massive drives towards Moscow in 1941, and into the Caucasus region in 1942. The war with Russia provided the RAD's greatest challenge. In many instances, RAD units found themselves in areas that became part of the front, and some of them were forced to form improvised combat units. In 1942, there were at least 427 RAD formations serving on the Eastern Front. Originally the RAD members did not train in the use of weapons, but wartime pressure forced a change to that situation. Increasingly in the fighting on the Eastern Front, RAD units were issued helmets, military equipment and light weapons, and they took up arms to fight off elusive partisans who disturbed supply lines and constantly provoked them. Some units were drafted directly into military service on the spot for occupation and surveillance duties. The repression brought by the German security forces against the partisans' guerrillas was particularly brutal, and the fighting was marked by atrocities on both sides. The partisans knew the terrain better than the Germans, they had the (forced or willing) support of the local populations, and—as they had no front line to hold—they could make surprise attacks on their enemy's weakest point whenever and wherever they chose, after which they vanished in the countryside and hid in deep, impenetrable forests and swamps. In response the Germans were obliged to guard all key positions and communication lines. Security operations became thus one of the common duties of the RAD units. The German security forces also arrested or shot Jews, rounded up populations accused of support, shot hostages, looted and burned villages, and executed prisoners in a terrible spiral of violence that only made matters worse.

By 1943, the days of victory were gone, and Germany had begun to overstretch herself. The grimness of the wartime conditions and the very high civilian and military casualty rate made Kraft durch Freude an organization of the past, put the German Labor Front under increasing strain, and caused the total mobilization and militarization of the National Labor Service. Before the war, girls of the RAD/wJ had normally been released after the compulsory six-month period of service. Under the wartime emergency conditions they were forced to remained in service for the duration of the war, and were obliged to work as auxiliaries to the agricultural labor force and as workers in armament factories, in hospitals and schools, in public utilities and in transportation systems. Fritz Sauckel (the plenipotentiary general for the mobilization of labor) ordered that only a certificate of pregnancy could exempt a young woman from employment. The products of this directive were popularly known as "Sauckel children."

RAD young men still performed pick-and-shovel work, fought fires, cleared bomb damage and built temporary quarters for the bombed-out, but an increasing number of recruits were fully armed. By the end of 1943 military instruction became an important part of RAD training. The service was no longer limited to the multitude of combat support roles listed above. Recruits, who could now enter the Labor Service at the age of 16½, were instructed to handle rifles, grenades and anti-tank weapons. Two RAD battalions fought in the battle of Arnhem in September 1944. The ever-increasing bombing offensive on Germany resulted in RAD involvement in anti-aircraft artillery. Hundreds of RAD units were trained and used as FlaK (anti-aircraft artillery) units under the control of the Luftwaffe. Many saw service along the Western Front in the form of RAD FlaK batteries, while others also saw service in the East as ground combat units against the advancing Soviet armies. In October of 1944, at least 60,000 RAD troops are known to have served in Luftwaffe FlaK batteries. When serving in FlaK Batteries, the troops were known as Luftwaffe-Flakhelfer (air force auxiliary artillerymen). RAD troops were but a small fraction of the hundreds of thousands that served in such a role during World War II. After 1943, young women of the RAD/wJ were also militarized. They served in the Luftwaffe in the Flugmeldedienst (air warning service) and as RAD-Flakwaffenhelferinnen (anti-aircraft auxiliaries) in medical and administrative roles but also in combat functions, e.g., searchlight operators and occasionally gunners.

As the war reached its end in early 1945, conditions within Germany had worsened to such an extent that it was necessary for the RAD men to be employed as full-time soldiers, usually to fight as infantrymen. Service in the RAD was reduced to six to eight weeks' time, while training was limited exclusively to infantry and anti-tank tactics. Again Hierl was able to avoid a move to integrate the RAD within the German Volkssturm (the People's Army; see Chapter 4), thus officially maintaining the independence of the RAD till the very end of World War II. But he could not prevent conscription into the frontlines as the war neared its conclusion. Some RAD units were incorporated into last-ditch combat groups and Volkssturm battalions. A few took part in the last battle of Berlin in April 1945.

Six major frontline units consisting of RAD troops were formed in the last months of World War II, three of which are known to have seen limited but fierce action. The six units of mainly RAD troops known to have been formed were as follows. (Note that "z.b.V." is short for *"zur besonderen Verwendung* or *zur besonderen Verfügung,"* which means "for special employment" or "for a special mission.")

- RAD-Division z.b.V.1-Infanterie-Division Albert Leo Schlageter
- RAD-Division z.b.V.2-Infanterie-Division Friedrich Ludwig Jahn
- RAD-Division z.b.V.3-Infanterie-Division Theodor Körner
- RAD-Division z.b.V.4-Infanterie-Division Güstrow
- Gebirgsjäger (Mountain) Brigade Steiermark
- Gebirgsjäger (Mountain) Brigade Enns

The RAD was disbanded after the defeat of the Third Reich on May 8, 1945.

Ranks of the RAD

Young men wishing to enlist as RAD officer candidates could join at the age of 17, but only with written parental agreement. Enlistment was for at least ten years and applicants had to produce a certificate of an unblemished character, issued by their local police office. Most important, they had to produce evidence of "pure Aryan descent," that is, non-Jewish. Wishing to serve as a permanent RAD officer did not exempt a person from the two-year period of obligatory military service. Three sorts of career were offered: senior NCO, lower commissioned officer, and higher commissioned leader. An RAD career started with a whole year in the ranks; then it was possible to apply for courses and training. When successfully completed, this led to promotion, graduation and specialization depending on character, skills and leadership ability. RAD careers were interrupted when World War II broke out in September 1939, when some 60 percent of the leadership was called to service in the Wehrmacht. Officially drafted officers remained RAD members so that no seniority was lost because of war service.

Ranks and rank insignia of the RAD changed three times from 1936 to 1945. The rank configurations were composed of various words such as *Führer* (leader), *Führerin* (female leader), and *Meister* (master), combined with such prefixes as *ober* or *haupt* (upper), *oberst* (supreme), *älteste* (senior), and *unter* (junior).

The ranks of the RAD/M for males included the following, with the approximate equivalent:

Officers

Reichsarbeitsführer	Marshall
Generaloberstarbeitsführer	General
Reichsarbeitsführer	Lieutenant General
Oberstarbeitsführer	Colonel
Oberarbeitsführer	Lieutenant Colonel
Arbeitsführer	Major
Oberstfeldmeister	Captain
Oberfeldmeister	Lieutenant
Feldmeister	2nd lieutenant

NCOs

Unterfeldmeister	Sergeant
Obertruppführer	Sergeant
Truppführer	Corporal
Untertruppführer	Candidate Corporal
Hauptvormann	no equivalent
Vormann	Private (volunteer)
Arbeitsmann	Private (conscript)

According to the Nazi "macho" attitude, ranks for women were rather honorific and did not include real commanding authority. Women's ranks were intended to instill militarization, respect of hierarchy, and obedience to the leader. The ranks of the RAD/wJ (females) included the following.

Officers

Stabshauptführerin	Colonel
Stabsoberführerin	Lieutenant-Colonel
Stabsführerin	Major
Maidenhauptführerin	Captain
Maidenoberführerin	Lieutenant
Maidenführerin	2nd Lieutenant

NCOs

Maidenunterführerin	Sergeant
Jungführerin	Sergeant
Kameradschaftsälteste	Corporal
Arbeitsmaid	Private (conscript)

Rank insignia were displayed on both the uniform collar and shoulder straps.

In the period 1936–1940, the collar patches were black with braid and pips indicating ranks, reflecting a Nazi Party organization.

In the period 1940–1942 patterns were slightly altered, reflecting the increased militarization of the RAD. Collar patches were simplified and brown shoulder straps were

DAF and RAD

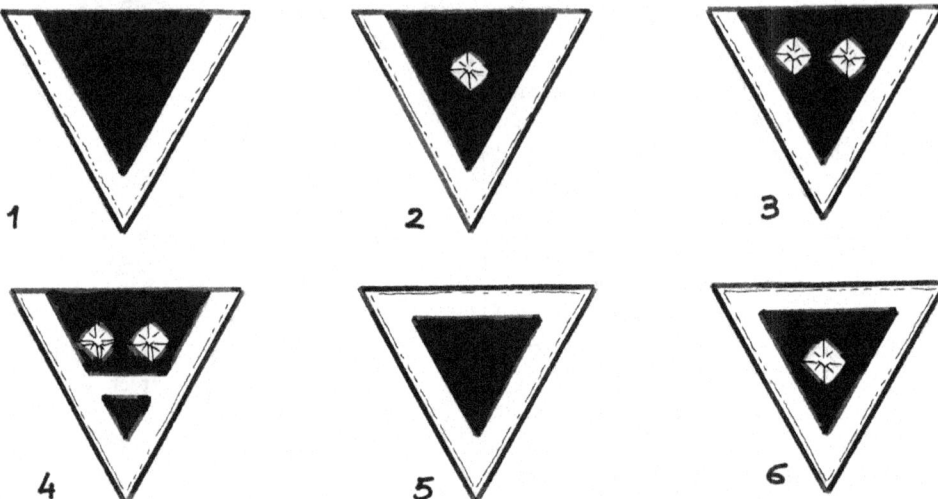

RAD rank chevrons for wear on the fatigue suit. Issued in 1942, this brown and silver insignia only concerned the ranks between *Vormann* (lance corporal) and *Obertruppführer* (senior sergeant), as officers did not wear the working suits. *Arbeitsmänner* (privates) wore no insignia at all. (1) *Vormann* (Lance-Corporal), braid chevron; (2) *Obervormann* (senior lance corporal), braid chevron with single silver pip; (3) *Hauptvormann* (upper senior lance corporal), braid chevron with two silver pips; (4) Untertruppführer (lance corporal NCO candidate), chevron with two silver pips and bar; (5) *Truppführer* (sergeant) aluminum braid triangle; (6) *Obertruppführer* (senior sergeant) aluminum braid triangle with one silver pip.

On the right lower sleeve, RAD members wore Armelstreifen (cuff titles). With an average width of 33 mm, these came in four distinct groups:
- Errinerungsband were commemorative honor cuff titles;
- Kriegserrinerungsband were World War I honor cuff titles commemorating service during the war of 1914–1918;
- Formation cuff titles were worn by elite or specialized units;
- Campaign cuff titles indicated a period of active service in a specific theater of war.

RAD cuff titles. *Top:* Emsland cuff title. This cuff title was worn by units assigned to the Emsland project, a reclamation operation for marshy land in northwest Germany. The numeral indicated the *Gruppe* (group). *Middle:* West cuff title (W). This commemorative cuff title was worn by units having worked on the fortifications of the West Wall (Siefried Line) in 1938. *Bottom:* This specialty cuff title was worn by bodyguards of Reichsarbeitsführer (RAF) Konstantin Hierl (head of the RAD).

RAD Anhalt sleeve band. By a law of April 1935, Hitler permitted the RAD members of Arbeitsgau XIII and all personnel of Group 135 to wear on their tunic sleeve the special Anhalt cuff title. The reason was that the small state of Anhalt (located between the Harz Mountains and the river Elbe in central Germany) was the first of the German provinces to make the voluntary labor service official and state-funded. The sleeve band (but also various badges, flags and awards) was intended to recognize the state of Anhalt as the birthplace of the Nazi RAD. The state colors of Anhalt (red, green and white) were reflected in the cuff title. The silk band was green with red border top and bottom, and white or grayish lettering.

introduced for low ranks. Wehrmacht aluminum braids were also issued. In 1942 rank insignia were introduced for wear on the working fatigue suit by NCOs and low ranks. These were in the form of pips on chevrons pointing downwards, worn on the upper right sleeve.

In the period 1943–1945, rank insignia became more in line with insignia worn by the Wehrmacht with aluminum braid and piping.

Uniforms of the RAD

RAD Men's Uniform

In the early period of Nazism, a period of economic recession, members of the FAD did not have a regular uniform. Before 1933 dark or light brown tunics and trousers, unstiffened visor caps, and swastika armbands dominated. After the Nazi seizure of power a formal uniform was introduced. Throughout its existence, the uniform of the RAD symbolized its initial connection with both working the land and military service. Members of the RAD wore a wide variety of uniforms ranging from fatigue suits to German army–like field uniforms.

The service dress for all ranks consisted of an earth-brown tunic with a dark brown,

RAD Obervormann (conscript-private 1st class). The uniform for privates and NCOs consisted of a brown, four-pocket tunic with dark brown collar showing a five-sided braid, brown trousers, black leather boots or work shoes and brown cap. All ranks wore the "spade" upper-sleeve badge on a black cloth shield displaying the battalion and company numbers.

stand-and-fall collar and shoulder straps (both with rank insignia as described above). The tunic had two pleated, patch breast pockets with three points, two internal skirt pockets with rounded flaps, five buttons down the

DAF and RAD

Left: RAD *Arbeitsmann*, 1943. Right: RAD worker wearing fatigue suit with the standard M35 steel helmet and gas mask.

front closure and exposed buttons on all four pockets. All ranks wore on the left upper sleeve a *Kampfbinde* (red armband with a black swastika in a white disc) indicating a Nazi organization; this was hastily removed if taken prisoner to avoid serious problems, particularly on the Eastern Front or in the Balkans, where any Nazi affiliation often meant direct execution. When the RAD member was operating under army control, an armband with the line "*Im Dienst der Deutschen Wehrmacht* [in service of the German army]" was worn as identification. Above the armband was sewn the *Dienststellenabzeichen*, the Spaten (spade) unit badge. This consisted of a black cloth with a white downturned spade; on the spade were displayed red numerals indicating units. Those serving on divisional staffs wore Roman numerals from I to XXXX; staff officers in the battalions wore their battalion numbers alone, which ran from 10 to 501; and officers and lower ranks within the battalion had a small company number, from 1 to 12, below the battalion number.

The earth-brown trousers were army-style with a four-button fly front and high waist and were held by suspenders or a belt. The earth-brown color of the uniform was to prove a curse for RAD men serving on the Russian Front. Since the color was almost the same as the Red Army uniform's tone, captured RAD men could be accused of being partisans trying to disguise themselves as Soviet soldiers, and immediately shot.

Footwear included the standard army marching boots. As an economy measure, these were gradually replaced with heavy, ankle-length, laced work shoes, plus short anklets, leather puttees or gaiters. Officers wore similar uniforms but of better quality. They often wore flared riding breeches and black riding boots.

For fatigue duties NCOs and privates wore the standard Drillichanzug (dungarees). This denim fatigue suit included a hard-wearing, off-white or light brown linen or calico casual jacket and trousers in varying styles. When working in hot weather, RAD men were allowed to strip to the waist. In cold conditions they were permitted a warm woolen pullover and an overcoat. The overcoat was a brown, double-breasted, mid-calf-length greatcoat with a large, dark brown falling collar, belts and other black leather fittings in the paramilitary style. On the Russian front, during the terrible first winter of 1941–1942 winter dress included improvised protective clothing such as civilian coats, captured Russian quilted jackets, fur waistcoats and the like, until regular German winter dress was introduced in winter 1942–1943.

RAD young men serving as Luftwaffe-Flakhelfer (air force auxiliary gunners) wore the light grey-blue air force uniform including steel helmet, *Fliegerbluse* (short tunic with "diving" Luftwaffe eagle-and-swastika

RAD decal worn on left side of helmet.

RAD armed private. The man wears the RAD uniform with an additional armband reading "*Im Dienst der Deutschen Wehrmacht* [In service of the German armed force]." He is armed with a Mauser Karabiner 98K rifle and wears standard German infantry equipment.

Left: RAD *Haupttruppführer*. *Right:* RAD private with overcoat.

emblem), greatcoat, trousers, laced boots and gaiters.

Collar patches, badges, and shoulder straps with different piping indicating ranks and units were sewn on tunics, blouses, jackets, greatcoats and winter suits. Specialty badges were worn on the left upper arm and indicated a specialized trade by means of various symbols (e.g., telephone operator, FlaK gunner, and searchlight operator).

Sports played an important role in RAD training, and members were issued a Sportanzug (sports kit). This consisted of a white cotton sleeveless shirt (decorated with the distinctive spade, laurel wreath and swastika RAD shield), black shorts, low running shoes (very often worn without socks), and a brown swimsuit. Regular staff members and sports trainers were issued a dark blue, two-piece tracksuit comprising a warm fold-over collar pullover and matching baggy trousers.

The most distinctive RAD headgear was the *Tuchmütze* (cloth cap), a curious, soft-peaked kepi-like cap halfway between the traditional German farmer's work cap and the huntsman's hat. It was commonly called *Kaffeebohnemütze* (coffee bean cap) by the Germans, and today is referred to as a "Robin Hood hat" by collectors. The hat, designed by Konstantin Hierl, was introduced in 1934. It had flaps with grommet air vents on both sides and was deeply pleated along the top; a dark

Uniforms of the RAD

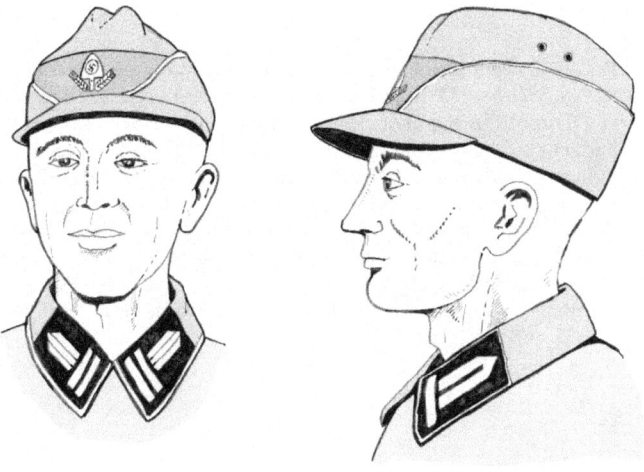

RAD cap (front and side views). This cap was the so-called *Tuchmütze* (aka "coffee bean cap" or "Robin Hood hat").

brown band was sewn around the crown, on which was displayed the RAD badge (an upturned spade and corn sheaves) at the front. Officers' caps were piped silver on the flaps and peak. For work detail the parade cap was often replaced with the peakless *Feldmütze* (field cap) or the standardized *Einheitsfeldmütze* (field peaked cap). Another typical RAD headgear item was the "porkpie" type of peakless work cap.

Left: RAD field cap (Feldmütze). *Right:* RAD porkpie peakless work cap.

RAD unit badge (*Dienststellenabzeichen*). This "spade" unit badge, worn on the upper left sleeve, indicated a member of 6th Company of 356 Battalion.

RAD T-S spade unit badge. On this machine-woven RAD *Dienststellenabzeichen*, "T-S" indicated that the wearer had taken a course at a Truppführerschule (troop leader school). Other assignment badges could carry the following letters: BSF, for Bezirkschule Führung (leadership staff of a regional school); LV, Lehr-und Versuchslager (training and research camp); RS, Reichsschule (staff of the national training school); LA + number, Lehrabteilung (training squad); M, Meldämter (communications department). There were also functional insignias worn on the lower left sleeve for administrative personnel, health service workers, planning staff, legal personnel, and musicians.

RAD patrol service gorget. The *Streifendienst* (patrol service) was the equivalent of the *Feldgendarmerie* (military police) in the armed forces. The *Streifendienst* was composed of volunteers who were responsible for policing daily-life in RAD camps as well as meetings, ceremonies and rallies in the prewar period. Later during the Second World War they also assisted the police by forming auxiliary squads. In service the men of the *RAD Streifendienst* had police powers and were distinguished by a crescent-shaped polished aluminum gorget (9 cm high and 18 cm wide) suspended on the upper part of the chest by a chain passing around the neck. The gorget displayed the RAD emblem (spade, laurel wreath and swastika) and a scroll bearing the word *Streifendienst*.

RAD Obertruppführer (senior sergeant).

In combat zones, the standard, heavy-steel army helmet M35 was widely used by all ranks. The M38 three-piece Luftschutz (civil defense) helmet was also issued. RAD units on active service in the summer in warm lands such as southern France, Italy or southern Russia were sometimes issued a tropical pith helmet.

RAD men were also issued backpacks, water bottles, mess tins, blankets, tents, camping and cooking gear. This made sense since RAD men were often deployed on construc-

Left to right: RAD *Arbeitsführer* (major), sport kit and track suit.

tion or working tasks outdoor in rural areas and needed to be reasonably self-sufficient.

RAD Women's Uniform

Young women of the RAD/wJ wore uniforms in the same earth-brown color with dark brown collar as were in use in the rest of the RAD (but NCOs had their collars piped in white thread in a similar fashion to their male counterparts). The RAD/wJ service dress had many similarities to the uniform of the Nationalsozialistische Frauenschaft (NSF, National Socialist Women's Organization). It included a single-breasted tunic with five brown buttons down the front closure, and two internal skirt pockets with pointed flaps closed with brown buttons. On the left upper sleeve was sewn a distinctive RAD/wJ cloth badge; this was black, brown or brown-green depending on the manufacturer. It consisted of a white circle with a swastika and two ears of wheat; below the circle was a Roman numeral which indicated the wearer's *Bezirke* (district), numbered from I to XXV; the numbers and borders of the badge were in white for lower ranks and silver for senior ranks. The tunic was worn with a white or grey shirt with a gold throat brooch bearing the RAD/wJ emblem, consisting of a swastika set between two ears of wheat. The service uniform was completed with a straight-cut, knee-length skirt with single pleat in the back, and with black hose and shoes. Headgear consisted of a felt fedora; on the left side, the hat carried a silver version of the RAD/wJ emblem. The casual working "uniform" was a practical civilian dress adapted to domestic work; it included a blue dress, a blue blouse, a white apron, and often a red kerchief replacing the soft felt hat.

DAF and RAD

Left: RAD/wJ service uniform. The silver piping around the collar indicated rank, here *Maidenhauptführerin* (approximately captain). *Right:* RAD/wJ working dress. The working dress included a blue dress, white apron, and often a red kerchief replacing the soft felt hat.

By the end of the war, those RAD women serving as air force auxiliaries wore typical Luftwaffe uniforms. The basic uniform of all branches of the women air force auxiliaries was blue-grey. It included a two-pocket, single-breasted jacket fastened by three black buttons; a light blue shirt with black tie; a straight, knee-length skirt with single pleat; blue-grey stockings and black shoes. Headgear consisted of the *Feldmütze* (peakless field cap).

Women serving in the FlaK artillery were

Uniforms of the RAD

Left: RAD/wJ working smock. The smock was issued in a number of colors, usually dark blue, gray or white. The white collar was removable for washing. The display of emblem, rank insignia and other badges was optional. *Right:* RAD/wJ FlaK uniform. The gray-blue uniform worn by young women serving in the Luftwaffe FlaK artillery was functional. It included a steel helmet, a three-quarter-length jacket with large pockets, long, loose ski-trousers, and ankle boots.

Left: FlaK crew badge (RAD/wJ).

issued more practical Luftwaffe grey-blue outdoor uniforms including short jackets, trousers, greatcoats, heavy shoes, *Einheitsfeltmütze* (peaked caps) and steel army helmets, worn only in action. On all Luftwaffe uniforms, the standard "diving" Luftwaffe eagle-and-swastika emblem was displayed on the right breast of the jacket and at the front of headgear. As with the men's uniforms, trade badges were worn on the left upper arm and

DAF and RAD

FlaK Helferin, c. 1944.

Luftwaffe trade badge (signal personnel). The specialty badge was dark blue with a single, thick jagged bolt.

Luftwaffe trade badge (direction-finder operator). The badge was dark blue with eight jagged bolts with a Gothic letter P underneath.

indicated a specialty by means of various symbols (e.g., flight reporter, telephone or teletype operator, air signaler, gunner, and searchlight operator).

Insignia, Flags and Dagger of the RAD

The emblem of the RAD represented a blade of a spade supported by wheat seed-bearing ears. The spade symbolized labor and closeness to the German soil. The wheat ears symbolized the fruit of labor, the crop that grows through hard work. The swastika in the spade (angled at 45 degrees) represented the commitment to Hitler's National Socialism. The spade emblem was worn in the form of a black cloth badge on the left upper sleeve, and in metal form on headgear.

Of the 40 *Arbeitsgaue*, 17 were authorized

Insignia, Flags and Dagger

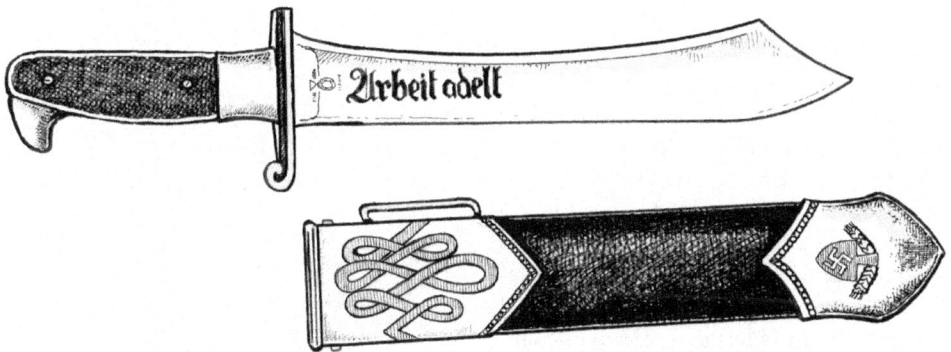

RAD hewing knife with metal scabbard. The blade carries the slogan "*Arbeit adelt* [Work ennobles]."

to wear a traditional cap badge called *Traditions Mützenabzeichen*. These were stamped metal badges, some with colorful enamel, worn on the left side of the *Tuchmütze*.

Rank was displayed on the tunic collars and reflected the nature of the RAD's work with motifs such as ears of wheat and the shovel.

A standard swastika armband was worn on the left arm—but only by male members.

The flag of the RAD was composed of a red cloth; set centrally on the field there was a large black swastika, and overlying the center of the swastika there was the emblem of the RAD: two stylized black wheat ears and the blade of a spade.

There were various RAD medals. The Dienstauszeichnung fur den Reicharbeitsdienst (Long Service Award of the RAD) was instituted by Hitler and awarded in four classes with different configurations for men and women: a gilt medal with a gilt eagle on the ribbon for 25 years of service; a silver medal with silver eagle on the ribbon for 18 years; a silver medal for 12 years; and a bronze medal for 4 years. Given the 12-year lifespan of Hitler's Thousand-Year Reich, presumably only the bronze four-year medal and the silver twelve-year medal were awarded. The women's medal was worn as a brooch hanging from a bow and featured a swastika supported by two ears of wheat. The men's was a medal with the shovel-and-wheat motif.

Hitler was keenly interested in regalia and eager to support the world-renowned German

RAD officer with hewing knife.

DAF and RAD

blade-makers' cartel in Solingen. He encouraged the creation of daggers, knives and swords for all branches of the uniform-conscious civil servants of the Nazi Party. The designs were created by students and masters at the state trade schools, and the Führer himself approved many of the designs. Once a pattern had been selected, it was submitted to the Reichszeugmeisterei (RZM, the central ordnance office of the NSDAP) for final approval and production. Only then could organization members purchase and display their new side arms. There was a profusion of gleaming blades in Hitler's Germany. The Reich Labor Service's sidearm was a kind of hewing knife with a total length of 403 mm. The grip was made of horn and its pommel had the shape of an eagle's head. The broad, slightly curved and sharp blade was 251 mm

A member of the RAD "presenting spade." As the German defenses were devastated, more and more RAD men were committed to combat, and by the end of World War II, the spade was often replaced with the rifle. Several RAD units performed anti-aircraft duty, and during the final months of the war RAD men formed several frontline combat units.

RAD belt buckle.

Traditional cap badges. *Left:* Arbeitsgau I East Prussia, introduced in April 1938; *right:* Arbeitsgau XVIII Saxony-East.

long with the heraldic device "*Arbeit adelt* [work ennobles]" carved in it. The RAD knife was carried in a metal sheath painted black and worn from the waist belt. Originally the robust weapon was issued to all members of the RAD and could be used as a hewing tool in the field, but gradually the knife was awarded only to qualified members who had achieved a set of minimum standards and passed tests of knowledge of Nazi arcana. The knife was an important part of the uniform. Receiving a knife or a dagger was a prestigious moment in a soldier's life in the Third Reich.

Uniforms, equipment and regalia were designed, manufactured, controlled, distributed, and sold by the Reichszeugmeisterei (RZM, the central ordnance office of the NSDAP). The name Reichszeugmeisterei meant, literally, the National Material Control Office, and it can be thought of in the same sense as any government procurement office.

CHAPTER 3

NATIONALSOZIALISTISCHES KRAFTFAHR KORPS (NSKK)

ORIGINS OF THE MOTORIZED CORPS

The National Socialist Motorized Corps (Nationalsozialistisch Kraftfahr Korps, or NSKK) was a paramilitary motorized formation overseeing the transport of supplies and the training of recruits for the German army's motorized and armored units. Its origins can be traced to two main motorized forces.

From the very start in 1919, wealthy Nazi members were encouraged to lend their vehicles when needed for varying lengths of time in order to facilitate the mobility of the nascent Nazi Party. Heinrich Himmler, for example, who later became chief of the SS, started his Nazi career by transporting dispatches and messages on his motorbike. During the 1920s Nazi transport was totally improvised, until April 1930 when the Nationalsozialistisches Automobil Korps, or NSAK (National Socialist Automobile Corps) was founded by order of Martin Bormann. This association was created to organize all NSDAP members who owned a truck, a van, a car or a motorcycle into a single nationwide unit. The NSAK included about 3,000 wealthy automobile owners who sympathized with the Nazis and put themselves at the party's disposal in their free time. The association originally formed a group of mechanics, drivers and vehicles to transport Nazi Party formations, officials and leaders. Albert Speer, owner of a BMW sports car in 1930, reported in his book *Erinnerungen* (*Memoirs*), published in 1969, that his first commitment with the Nazi Party was his membership in the NSAK in the Wannsee section, a suburb of Berlin.

The Sturm Abteilung had their own transport service. Starting in 1928 the SA had *Kraftfahrstaffeln* (motorized teams), a rather ill-organized, small fleet of motorcycles, private cars and lorries, which the Nazis had acquired as early as 1922 and which—under command of leader Christian Weber—were employed to transport the SA shock troops and materials. The SA motorized teams were reorganized in May 1932 and officially renamed Motor Sturm Abteilung (MSA). Both the MSA and the NSAK were inspired by Mussolini's Squadristi, a fascist militia also known as Black Shirts, and both played a significant role during the troubled period from 1919 to 1933 before the Nazis took over power in Germany, known to the Nazis as Kampfzeit (the combat period).

There were close and somewhat confused links between the two Nazi motorized corps. Members of Motor-SA were automatically members of the NSAK, but not the reverse. All commanders of the NSAK were SA officers, but most of the regular members were not. In 1930, SA-Gruppenführer Adolf Hühnlein was made commander of the NSAK and suggested renaming it the Nationalsozialistisches Kraftfahrkorps (National Socialist Motorized Corps), or NSKK. This was also envisaged by SA leader Ernst Röhm, who was in the process of reorganizing the SA militia.

Adolf Hühnlein (1881–1942) had served as a professional officer in the German Imperial Army during World War I and in the Reichswehr until 1924. A Nazi of the first hour, he joined the NSDAP and the SA. He was an "Old Fighter" as he had taken part in the failed Munich Beer Hall Putsch in 1923. Afterwards he was imprisoned with Hitler and Rudolf Hess in Landsberg prison. Highly regarded by Hitler, he seemed to have been hated by other prominent Nazi leaders. Although general inspector of the armored troops, Heinz Guderian admitted Hühnlein was honest and could fruitfully collaborate with him. Ferdinand Porsche, however, found that Hühnlein was not the right man to work with. Nevertheless, Hühnlein, owing to Hitler's backing, made a remarkable career. He became a member of the Reichstag, was appointed *Generalmajor*, and was an honorary member of several organizations linked with sport, transportation, and Hitler Youth.

Hühnlein was awarded prestigious decorations such as the Kriegsverdienstkreuz (War Merit Cross) First and Second Class, and the Blutorden (Order of Blood, the most prestigious Nazi Party decoration) after his death in June 1942.

Interestingly, the Nazi Hühnlein is still remembered to this day as honorary citizen of the cities of Bayreuth (northern Bavaria) and Ahrweiler (Rhineland-Palatinate). The reason is quite unclear. According to the Dutch historian and NSKK specialist Alex Dekker, the reason may be that it is an old story from long ago; possibly many people do not remember who Hühnlein was, and those who know think he was a minor Nazi never condemned for crimes; and due to the inactivity of local politics, things just stay how they are.

The NSKK was officially created in April 1930. When Adolf Hitler became chancellor in January 1933, the NSKK expanded rapidly to 30,000 members. The nationwide campaign of *Gleichschaltung* (coordination of all political and other activities by the Nazi Party) did not spare the German motorized world. Consequently, in September 1933, the NSKK took over all German motor clubs and civilian motoring organizations. By then the corps was militarily reorganized and expanded to 350,000 members, forming 4 divisions, 19 brigades and about 90 regiments. After the elimination of the SA—when Hitler's rival Ernst Röhm and the SA leadership were murdered during the Night of Long Knives (June 29–30, 1934)—the Motor SA was merged with the NSKK. The motorized corps was then made a *Gliederung* of the NSDAP (an independent organization, a separate branch of the Nazi Party, NSDAP) directly placed under Hitler's authority.

It should be noted that in the period 1933–1938, Der Deutsche Automobil Club (DDAC, German Automobile Club) and the Allgemeiner Deutscher Automobil-Club (ADAC, German Motoring Association) still existed, but neither organization escaped Nazi *Gleichschaltung*. The ADAC was obliged to merge with the DDAC, which in fact became merely

Adolf Hühnlein (1881–1942).

a sub-branch of the NSKK, as DDAC members were strongly encouraged and pressured to join the Nazi motorized corps. After Austria was made a part of the Reich in March 1938, all Austrian motor clubs and army transports were swallowed up by the NSKK, which then greatly expanded its membership. Finally in 1938, the DDAC was officially dissolved and all its members were forced to join the NSKK. In January 1939 Hitler could proudly declare in public that henceforth the NSKK enjoyed a complete monopoly over anything pertaining to automobiles in Germany.

Metal badge for a Motor SA/NSKK recruiting week in Hamburg in 1933.

Early NSKK biker (1933). The uniform of this NSKK *Obertruppführer* (sergeant) reflects the close links that existed between the SA and the NSKK. The *Obertruppführer* wears the Motor SA uniform consisting of a brown blouse, black breeches, high leather boots, and a typical ribbed leather crash helmet, worn when driving. *Top left:* insignia of the Motor Hitler Youth.

Hitler was keen on cars and planes, and from the start, the Nazi Party gave a great deal of attention to modern means of transportation. After the seizure of power in January 1933, as we saw in Chapter 1, a wide network of motorways was launched and carried out by the engineer Fritz Todt. In addition, Hitler ordered Doctor Engineer Ferdinand Porsche to design a cheap car for the masses, the previously discussed Volkswagen. It seems that the elitist NSKK leader Hühnlein had his doubt about the cheap car, which was intended to be mass produced. He thought that too many cars driving on the German roads would result in chaos and a terrible increase of deadly accidents.

In March 1935 in direct contravention of the Versailles treaty, Hitler reintroduced compulsory military service and undertook a wide program of rearmament. Because of their size and their

Emblem of the DDAC.

complexity, the reborn German armies depended heavily on conscript manpower for their effectiveness, but fighting units found themselves helpless if transport and communications broke down. So there was a huge logistical infrastructure composed of motor-mechanics, radio-operators, waitresses, cooks and administrative personnel who were servicing and supplying; driving, repairing and maintaining vehicles, weapons, and communication systems; and ensuring that the whole army was administered, supplied, fed, taken care of, paid, and transported.

In January 1939 the NSKK was made responsible for the training of drivers for the army in the NSKK Motor Sport Schools. The politically involved NSKK allowed Hitler to have a grip on limiting the autonomy and independence of the Wehrmacht logistical service. The greater part of the army transports were entrusted to the NSKK. The result was that the army had a limited capacity in transport and drivers, and thus was incapable of ensuring adequate supplies on its own account. Cunningly, the Nazi Party had retained an easy method of controlling the German armed forces.

Haupttruppführer (warrant officer), Motor SA.

STRUCTURE OF THE NSKK

The Nationalsozialistisch Kraftfahr Korps was militarily organized following the example of the SA. It was divided into five geographic *Obergruppen* (regions), North, East, South, West and Middle. Each *Obergruppe* was divided into four or five *Motorgruppen* (motorized divisions). Each *Motorgruppe* in turn was composed of five to six *Motorbrigaden* (regiments). Each regiment was divided into three to six *Motorstaffeln* (motorized battalions). Every *Motorstaffel* included six *Motorstürme* (motorized companies). Each *Motorsturm* was divided into transport *Truppen* (platoons), which were composed of three to four *Scharen* (squads) counting from 8 to 16 men. In 1938 the corps totaled 28 divisions and 100 regiments.

Membership in the Nationalsozialistisch Kraftfahr Korps was voluntary. It was part-time and unpaid for low ranks, but professional, paid and permanent for senior ranks. Members were recruited among the motor-minded Nazi Party members, former Motor-SA men, teenagers from the Hitler Youth and men rejected from military service for medical reasons. Members were not required to have any particular knowledge about mechanics and cars, and the corps accepted persons for membership without driver's licenses. It was thought that training and practice would make up for any previous lack of experience. For this purpose the NSKK gradually opened some 30 Motorsportschulen (Motorized Sport Schools). After 1940, the NSKK created additional instruction centers in the occupied countries at Drammen in Norway; at Diest, Vilvoorde and Geraardsbergen in Belgium; at Zeist, The Hague (1943), Almelo (in 1944) and the "Niederlande" School in Heibloem in the Netherlands.

After the reorganization of 1934, the NSKK counted 350,000 members, and by the end of 1938 this had grown to 500,000. With the bloodless territorial expansion of the 1938–1939 period, new units were raised with members from occupied Austria, Czechoslovakia and East Prussia.

The success of the Nationalsozialistisch Kraftfahr Korps cannot be explained simply by Nazi ideological attraction. One must remember the popularity of motor vehicles in the 1930s when only a few lucky wealthy drivers and only a few professionals possessed cars, motorcycles, vans or trucks. To become a member of the corps meant having access to these modern, glamorous and exciting machines. The NSKK was, however, not an innocent club of well-intentioned and technically minded drivers and mechanics. The corps members adhered to the Nazi racist doctrine. Jews were forbidden to join, and members were screened for "Aryan" qualities, pure blood, and pure German racial background. Hühnlein saw the training of NSKK members as part of the resurrection of Germany, whereby the training was seen as a "struggle for Germany." Members were not members, they were "soldiers of the NSKK."

Prewar Tasks of the NSKK

The original task of Nazi NSAK and MSA drivers was to transport personnel, leaders and material, and eventually to fight against political opponents. With the establishment of the Nazi regime after 1933, political fighting, street rioting, and agitation for voting campaigns and meetings were no longer needed. So the mission of the NSKK took another direction with the emphasis on mobility, propaganda and training. In the 1930s members of the NSKK served as a roadside assistance association: NSKK-Verkehrshilfsdienst (Traffic Aid Service), comparable to the modern-day American Automobile Association or the British Automobile Association.

Another sub-branch called the NSKK-Verkehrserziehungsdienst (Traffic Instruction Service) issued all driving licenses. At the same time many members of the NSKK were employed in duties supporting the local Ordnungspolizei (Order Police) in cities where traffic control was needed.

Another important task was the control and the promotion of all motoring activities in Germany. The corps was designed to teach Nazi ideology, propagate racism and anti–Semitism, channel enthusiasm and passion for motor vehicles, and promote a general understanding of vehicle use and mechanics with an eye for eventual military application of the knowledge. The NSKK organized car exhibitions, promoted tourism by automobile, and managed racing car and motorcycle events. These events were intended as propaganda shows but were also meant to keep members busy. Just to name a few examples: On October 14 and 15, 1933, the NSKK organized a night race at Brunswick known as the Nachtorienterungsfahrt (Night Orientation Tour), and on May 8, 1938, a car race at Hamburg known as the Hamburger Stadtparkrennen. In the period 1936–1939, there was the annual Eiffelrennen (Eiffel Mountains Race). Germany was also represented at international racing events. Of course all these events were accompanied by parades, music, shows and speeches, often presented and attended by important Nazi leaders. Hitler did not practice any sports but he had a friendly disposition towards sports of any kind, cars in particular. Before he became chancellor, he had announced that Germany must compete again on the world's racetracks and circuits in order to demonstrate her national prestige and technological might. When Hitler came to power in 1933, Germany had been absent from international motor racing, and soon the new government directed funds and ordered two companies, Mercedes-Benz from Stuttgart and Auto-Union from Chemnitz, to design Grand Prix racing cars. This resulted in prestigious and outstanding vehicles designed by talented engineers such as Rudolf Uhlenhaut, Alfred Neubauer and Ferdinand Porsche. At the same time a generation of famous and distinguished racing car drivers appeared, such as Rudolf Caracciola, Manfred von Brauchitsch and Hans Stuck. In 1934, German motor racing was organized on Nazi lines and placed under the leadership of Sportskorpsführer Adolf Hühnlein, who was also NSKK Führer. In July 1934, the Germans were unsuccessful at the French Montlhèry Grand Prix but in 1935, Mercedes-Benz's

Auto Union racing car. This car was driven by the famous Hans Stuck at Shelsley Walsh Grand Prix in June 1936.

Member of the Motor-HJ. This young man of the Motor-HJ wears a leather crash helmet. On the left sleeve of his tunic are displayed the triangular district badge, the white/red Hitler Youth diamond with black swastika, and the round, black driving badge.

driver Rudolf Caracciola was acclaimed European champion. In 1936, Auto-Union's driver Bernd Rosemeyer was acclaimed European champion. In 1937, Mercedes-Benz regained its dominance with the powerful W125 car, driven by champion Rudolf Caracciola again. In 1938 Mercedes-Benz's position was under challenge from Hermann Lang driving for Auto-Union and from the British driver Richard Seaman, who won the 1938 German Grand Prix—much to the embarrassment of Hitler and Hühnlein. The same year, the British Donnington Grand Prix was won by the Italian Tazio Nuvolari, driving for Germany. In 1939 the Yugoslavian Belgrade Grand Prix was won by Nuvolari, driving for Auto-Union. A famous German car and motorcycle racing champion of this period was Ernst Jakob Henne (1904–2005), who in 1926 was German 500-cc champion, in 1927 was German 750-cc champion, and in 1928 was winner of the Targa Florio (an open-road endurance race created in 1906 and held in the mountains of Sicily near Palermo). Between 1928 and 1937 Henne achieved a total of 76 land-speed records. The last in 1937 was on a full aerodynamic fairing 500-cc supercharged BMW with a top speed of 279.5 km/h (173.1 mph). This record stood for 14 years. Others famous motorbike cham-

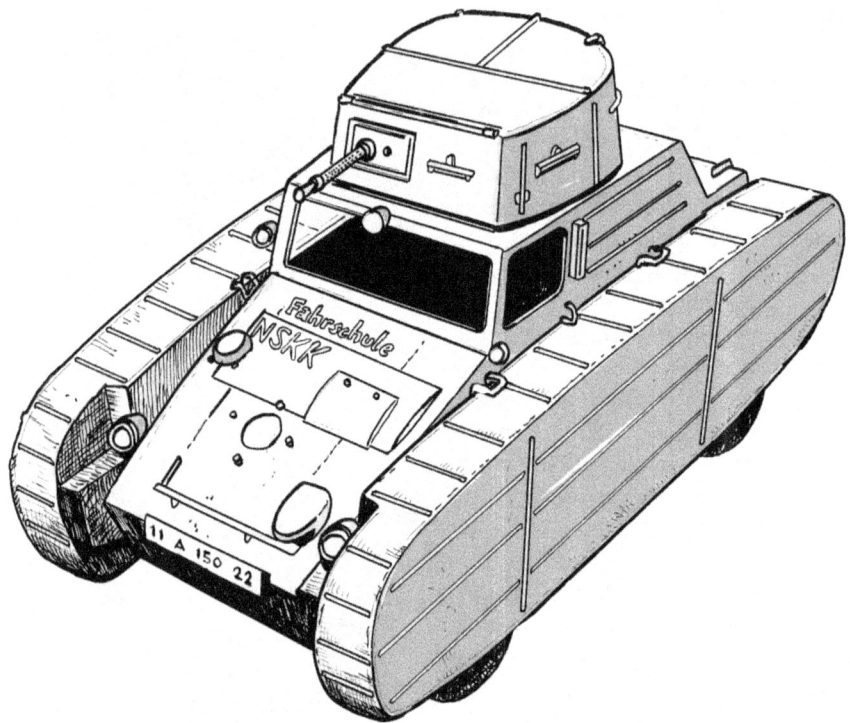

Porsche Typ 82/3 NSKK Fahrschule 1942 "*Attrappe*" (dummy). The training car Porsche 82/3 was a derivate of the Volkswagen Kübelwagen, fitted for the purpose of tank training with phony tracks on the sides and an imitation turret on top, armed with a fake gun. The car was designed by the manufacturer Porsche from Stuttgart. The type 82/3 was the continuation of a line of training vehicles, such as bicycles with canvas structures introduced in 1925, the Hanomag 10 from 1927, the Adler Standard 6 from 1930 and the Opel P4 from 1935. At the start, these models were developed because the Treaty of Versailles from prevented Germany from having armored vehicles. When open rearmament began again under the regime of Hitler, the utilization of phony training tanks was continued—even during World War II, as it was convenient and cheap. The depicted training car was *Panzergrau* (dark blue/gray) and carried the marks of the *Fahrschule* (training school) of the NSKK.

pions were Fritz Linhardt, Joseph Forstner, Karl Gall, Joseph Stelzer, Ludwig Kraus, Otto Ley (winner of the Swedish 500-cc Grand Prix in 1936), and Georg Meier (winner of the Isle of Man Senior TT on a BMW in 1939). Hermann Paul Müller won the 1939 edition of the FIA French Grand Prix held in Reims, France. The winner of that season's European championship was never officially announced due to the outbreak of World War II in September 1939, which brought the curtain down on international motor racing for six years.

German racing cars and motorbike drivers were obviously required to be members of the NSKK, and they were made national heroes as racing successes were so important to the international image of Nazi Germany. In 1932 Hans Stuck married the famous tennis player Paula von Reznicek, whose grandfather was a Jew. He was attacked by the anti–Semite Adolf Hühnlein, but his personal relationship with Hitler, Himmler and Bouhler saved him from serious trouble. Rudolf Caracciola was promoted to NSKK-Staffelführer (the equivalent of squadron leader), and Himmler granted Bernd Rosemeyer an honorary rank in the Allgemeine-SS, an "honor" he would have been unwise to refuse. Rosemeyer died in a car crash in 1938, and even in death his celebrity was used for Nazi propaganda purposes: his coffin was carried by SS men at his grandiose funeral.

Closely connected to the Nazi Party, the members of the Nationalsozialistisch Kraftfahr Korps were politically active and were also charged with the indoctrination of the public in Nazi values. The NSK-Korps had an illustrated magazine named *Deutsche Kraftfahrt* (*German Motor*). There were many magazines, brochures and manuals published in Nazi Germany concerning cars, motorcycles, aircraft, buses and trains, but none of them were as beautiful, informative, well done and successful as *Motor Schau* (*The Motor Show*). *Motor Schau* was a big, oversized 10 × 13¾-inch trade and consumer magazine that concentrated on every aspect of the motor business not only in Germany, but also all around the world. Its emphasis was Germany and German equipment, and every big issue was packed with features, news and advertising related to the motor trades. Unlike the other German motoring magazines, every issue of *Motor Schau* had a striking, full-color industry-related cover and usually lots of color inside. The magazine was published by Motorschau Verlag Dr. Georg Elsner and Co. in Berlin on a monthly basis in the beginning

NSKK school instructor.

in 1937, and as a quarterly by mid–1943. *Motor Schau* was founded by Adolf Hitler's good friend Jakob Werlin, who not only advised Hitler on the purchase of automobiles but also often accompanied him to the annual Automobil-Ausstellung Berlin (Auto Exhibition Show in Berlin) and other motor-related events. Jakob Werlin was one of the five directors of Daimler-Benz and described himself in *Motor Schau* as a "Führer's collaborator in the question of the motorization of Germany."

NSKK members participated in party rallies, meetings, feasts and ceremonies. They dispensed lectures on Nazi ideology, and organized visits to factories for propaganda aims. They still had a logistical role, driving, repairing and maintaining the vehicles of the NSDAP, but gradually their structure was adapted so that the corps could provide technological specialists in military and mechanical matters. Members of the motorized corps had close contacts with the army, notably with the Panzerwaffe (armored forces created in 1935), headed by General Heinz Guderian. They gave mechanical advice and driving lessons to Wehrmacht candidate drivers for operating motorcycles, cars, vans, trucks, armored

NSKK medal. This medal was intended to commemorate a motorcycle race held at Osnabrück in 1934.

vehicles, halftracks and tanks. The technical efficiency of the motor corps was a major trump, considering the formation of armored vehicle crews and the development of Blitzkrieg (lightning war), giving Germany tremendous victories in the period 1939–1941. Candidates were trained by the NSKK in various *Attrappen* (phony vehicles), which were ordinary cars furnished with fake tracks,

NSKK Fahrschulewagen PzKpfw I. The light tank PzKpfw I had a crew of two and was armed with two machine guns. It was designed in 1933 and saw action in the Spanish Civil War and during the early stages of World War II. Before the war, it was also used as a propaganda vehicle in parades, military displays and mock battles that did much to bolster the illusion of German strength both at home and abroad. For training of tank drivers, some PzKpfw I were converted as NSKK *Fahrschulewagen* (training cars) with the armored turrets removed.

Captured Dutch armored truck DAF M-36 in service of the German Ordnung Polizei. The Germans employed captured armored cars, notably those of the defeated Dutch army after May 1940. The Dutch Company van Doorne's Aanhangwagen Fabriek (DAF van Doorne's trailer factory) from Eindhoven was created by the brothers Hubert and Willem van Doorne in 1932. In 1936, DAF began to be involved in military vehicles. The results were various armored cars used by the Dutch army in the pre–World War II period. The six-wheeled M-36 armored car was introduced in 1936; it had a Daimler-Benz 80 hp petrol engine, a crew of five, a total length of 5.85 m, a width of 2.10 m, a height of 2.50 m and a weight of 6,100 kg. The truck was heavily armed with a light Bofors 3.7 cm caliber gun placed in the rotating top turret, and three M-20 7.9 cm caliber machine guns; one was coaxially placed in the turret, another at the front and the third at the back of the hull. In 1938, the M-36 was improved with a Büssing-Nag engine; this variant was known as the DAF M-38 type. After the defeat and occupation of the Netherlands, all war materials were taken over by the Germans, but as the Dutch vehicles were poor combat machines, they were mainly used as NSKK training trucks. Some were converted into command or radio cars. Others were allocated to the Ordnungpolizei (Order Police) for maintaining the Nazi order in and out of the Reich.

phony turrets and wooden guns. The NSKK instructors also had numerous German-made light tanks, which were discarded from service. After 1940, they used many captured armored cars and light tanks from the defeated nations: Poland, the Netherlands, Belgium and France.

The members of the NSKK also gave driving and mechanical lessons to the motor-minded boys of the Motor-Hitler-Jugend, the motorized branch of the Hitler Youth movement (HJ in short). It was no coincidence that Adolf Hühnlein was both NSKK-Führer (chief of the motorized corps) and Ehren-*führer* (honorary leader) of the Motor-HJ. The Motor-HJ served to train young men and teenagers in the disciplines of vehicle use and maintenance as a precursor to military service. This branch was very popular and counted 18,000 members in 1935. In 1938, this had increased to 90,000 members who were later incorporated in the NSKK, in the army transport units, and in the army and Waffen-SS motorized combat formations when the Second World War started. For training purpose, the NSKK had 24 centers and *Fahrschulen* (driving schools) specially intended for youth.

For the very young, there was the HJ-

NSKK *Verkehrsspiel* (traffic board game) designed to teach traffic regulation and rules with playing cards, wooden vehicles and figures, dice, and a board. This educational and political game, designed by Walther Blachetta, was published by Bildgut-Verlag from Essen in 1939, and could be played by two to eight players.

Marine-NSKK

The NSKK covered not only roads but waterways, and a part of the corps, known as Marine-NSKK (Naval NSKK), handled transport on inland water. A branch was specialized in assisting the River Police and in training the German army (and more particularly the combat engineers) with the operating of small landing and assault watercraft. Soon the Marine-NSKK counted four *Motorbootstandarten* (waterway and river regiments) including Berlin, Rhine, Stettin, and Bodensee (Lake Constance). Originally they were called Kraftbooteinheiten (Motorized Boat Units, with the abbreviation Kb on the collar patch). In 1939 they were renamed Motorbooteinheiten (Mb on the collar patch). Members wore a navy uniform, and the emblem or badge displayed a gold embroidered wreath over two crossed anchors, with a swastika in black in the center. Members had a dagger, which was the standard chained SA/NSKK weapon with the inscription "*Alles für Deutschland* [Everything for Germany]," some with gold-plated fittings.

Marine-NSKK officer.

Emblem of the Marine-NSKK.

NSKK and Organisation Todt

Hitler was a one-time artist and would-be architect. He had megalomaniacal plans regarding architecture and intended to rebuild the main towns of Germany and Austria including Berlin, Linz, and medieval Nuremberg—the ideal and symbolic site of prestigious Nazi mass rallies. Most of all, Berlin would be renamed Germania and would become the capital of the "Thousand Years' Reich." As already said, the chief designer was his young and talented architect Albert Speer, who based his design on classical models but on a scale that was unprecedented. The major buildings would indeed have dwarfed the greatest monuments of ancient Egypt and Rome. For these gigantic constructions, NSKK units were put at the disposal of Hitler's architect. These units were named NSKK Baustab Speer (Speer Construction Staff). They were widely expanded to regiment size and renamed NSKK Transportstandarte Speer in May 1940. By that time, Adolf Hühnlein's health was declining. The NSKK chief had cancer, could no longer maintain his grip on the Drivers' Corps, and could not challenge the growing power and youthful dynamism of Albert Speer.

In the period 1938–1940, the Organisation Todt, which had too few cars and trucks, employed NSKK personnel and vehicles to help build the fortifications, bunkers and obstacles of the West Wall on the western border of the Reich. For this purpose, NSKK *Verkehrkompanien* (traffic companies) were formed in order to transport workers, materials and machineries with 15,000 trucks and 5,000 buses.

At the start of World War II in September 1939, these units expanded to regiment size and were re-named NSKK Transportstandarte Todt. In May 1940 the units reached brigade strength and were redesignated NSKK Transportbrigade Todt.

The NSKK at War

When the Second World War started in September 1939, the Nationalsozialistisch Kraftfahr Korps assumed new responsibilities. By that time, the NSKK had become a major asset for the Nazi Party within Germany and throughout all European occupied countries.

The corps ran motorway patrols to assist the police in enforcing traffic regulations. Soon the drivers' corps replaced many of the traffic policemen who had been drafted in the army. For that purpose, a new police branch was created for traffic control. This service would help to mark roads for the motorcades, work out schedules, flag on convoys, and regulate circulation. The NSKK would also be used for inspection of cargo on wartime motor transport, and for this purpose another branch was created known as NSKK-Kontrollen des motorisierten Transportes der Kriegswirtschaften (control service of war goods transported by road). The bulk of the NSKK continued to train truck, half-track and tank drivers, but an increasingly large part of it was engaged to support the German army on the field and at the rear echelon. Many NSKK units operated right behind the front and functioned as transportation and logistical personnel bringing troops, ammunitions and supplies directly to the front lines.

There was, however, a great rivalry within the Nazi leadership. Hühnlein's power was contested by the Organisation Todt, by Speer, and also by Hermann Göring's Luftwaffe. The battle of Britain, which began in summer 1940, saw the creation of another NSKK branch. Air force command had to be reorganized, and squadrons retrained and refitted. Before the air offensive against Britain could be launched, substantial ground installations, technical services and stocks of fuel, ammunitions and bombs had to be moved from the Reich. By that time French, Dutch and Belgian airfields had been extended, improved and made suitable for German bombers and fighters. Before and during the battle, large quantities of equipment, fuel and supplies had to be delivered to the forward airfields in northern France and Belgium. For this purpose a special branch of the NSKK was created, known as the NSKK Transportregiment Luftwaffe (air force transport regiment). Due to his worsening illness, Hühnlein could not keep this unit from being incorporated into Göring's Luftwaffe. The NSKK Transportregiment Luftwaffe soon grew to brigade and divisional strength and in July 1943 was redesignated NSKK Transportgruppe Luftwaffe (air force transport division), placed under the leadership of Obergruppenführer (Lieutenant General) Graf von Bayer-Ehrenberg. Later in the war, the NSKK Transportgruppe Luftwaffe was expanded and deployed on all World War II fronts to supply airfields.

At the start of the war, the NSKK was granted the status of Wehrmachtsgefolge (army auxiliary unit) instead of Wehrmachtsangehörige (army affiliated). This measure allowed members to benefit from the Geneva Convention regarding prisoners of war. NSKK members were not part of the Wehrmacht, though all rules and laws of war were to be applied to them. The corps became more and more militarized, as reflected in the progressive change of designation of the units intended to fit closely to those of the army. Each brigade was divided into three *Regimenten* or *Standarten* (regiments). The regiments included two or three *Abteilungen* (battalions). The battalions were divided into three *Kompanien* (companies). The companies contained several *Hauptkolonnen* (main columns), which were composed of three *Züge* (platoons) or *Kolonnen* (columns). For ad hoc missions, *Sonderkolonnen* (special columns) could be temporarily formed according to operational requirements and tactical needs.

All through the war and on all fronts, drivers and mechanics of the NSKK worked under increasingly difficult conditions and under increasing pressure to keep the German army mobile and supplied. Showing endurance, skill and patience, they supported the Wehrmacht, from the windy Atlantic coasts to the frozen steppes of Russia, and from the snowy mountains of Norway to the hot deserts of Northern Africa. In field workshops they maintained and repaired vehicles, half-tracks and tanks. In all weather and often in difficult conditions—sometimes even under enemy fire—they transported salvage, captured and raw materials; they carried dispatches and delivered mail; they transported troops; and they stockpiled, loaded, drove and unloaded ammunitions, fuel, food, water and other supplies to the front. On the way back they sometimes evacuated casualties and—when ambushed—were obliged to take arms against partisans. If taken prisoner, notably on the Russian front, as members of a Nazi organization, NSKK men were often shot on the spot or badly treated, or put to work as forced laborers.

One of Adolf Hühnlein's ambitions was to incorporate the Organisation Todt (OT) into the NSKK, and when Fritz Todt died in an air crash in February 1942, he put himself forward as OT chief. This was rejected by Hitler because Hühnlein was by then a very sick man. Instead Hitler appointed Albert Speer as minister of armament and head of the OT.

As there can be no construction without the transport of materials, machinery and men, the uneasy collaboration, rivalry and entanglement between the NSKK and the Organisation Todt increased. On all fronts, both organizations worked together, but the number of NSKK Transportstandarte Todt—under the new minister of armament Albert Speer—was increased. Gradually the NSKK lost its dominance on transport matters, and Hühnlein's health and power declined.

The most important wartime NSKK-OT division was the NSKK Transportgruppe Todt, created in July 1942. Headed by Major General Wilhelm "Willi" Nagel and numbering some 70,000 men in October 1942, the Transportgruppe Todt expanded considerably and took over all OT transport duties. The NSKK-OT transport group also included a large *Transportflotte* (a fleet of barges and inland boats for river transport). From 1942, the NSKK attached a staff to each OT Einsatzgruppe (OT corps) to coordinate the collaboration.

Adolf Hühnlein died from cancer on June 18, 1942, and Hitler was present at his grandiose national funeral at Munich. Hühnlein was succeeded by NSKK-Obergruppenführer Erwin Kraus. Erwin Kraus (1894–1966), an engineer by training, had served as an infantry officer and later as an airman during the First World War. After the war he served in several Free Corps and joined Hitler's NSDAP in 1923. He became one of Hühnlein's assistants as Führer NSKK Gruppenstaffel Südwest (the region of Stuttgart) from 1930 to 1933, *Inspekteur für technische Ausbildung und Geräte des NSKK* (inspector for NSKK equipment) in 1935, and member of the Reichstag in 1936. He was appointed NSKK-Korpsführer on June 21, 1942, and remained in this function until the end of the war. Kraus could not prevent encroachments and was not able to sustain Speer's growing influence and power. Gradually he lost control of a part of the NSKK. In 1944 Kraus was appointed general inspector for the motorization of the Volkssturm, a post in which—because of Germany's chaotic situation and lack of fuel and vehicles—he had little to do. Right after the war Erwin Kraus was condemned by a denazification court to a three-and-a-half-year prison sentence as a prominent Nazi leader and fined 1,000 Marks. He was released in 1948 but had to act as a witness in 1953, this time for his involvement in the death of an NSKK man. When Kraus was trying to escape to Tyrol in late April 1945, an NSKK man named Lukat tried to steal one of his jumpers and Kraus had the man condemned to death and executed as a looter. Kraus was not directly involved in the execution; two other NSKK men were. One had already died and the other was never found, so the whole affair ended with a nonsuit. Erwin Kraus died in Munich on August 11, 1966.

As the Allies intensified the bombardments on German towns, from 1943 onwards, the Nazi Party authorities felt that a gesture would be appreciated by the people. As a result, the NSKK was more and more engaged to support the various existing rescue teams on the home front. Another special branch was hastily created, known as the NSKK Katastrophendienst (emergency service), which performed various roles including police, protection, heavy rescue, ambulance, firefighting, evacuation and debris-clearance duties.

By early 1944, the major NSKK units included the following.

- NSKK Transportgruppe Luftwaffe (including two brigades divided into six regiments);
- Motorobergruppe Alpenland (Alps) in Austria;
- Motorobergruppe Mitte (middle): Berlin, Franconia, Lower Rhine;
- Motorobergruppe Nord (north): Hamburg, Lower Saxony, Baltic Sea, Schleswig-Holstein;
- Motorobergruppe Nordost (northeast): Danzig, East Prussia, Wartheland;
- Motorobergruppe Ost (east): Leipzig, Lower and Upper Silesia;
- Motorobergruppe Süd (south): Bavaria, Hochland;
- Motorobergruppe Südwest (southwest): Rhine-Moselle, Swabia;
- Motorobergruppe Südost (southeast): Upper and Lower Danube, Sudetenland;
- Motorobergruppe West (west): Hessen, Thuringia, Westphalia.

In addition there were many NSKK transport units attached to the Organisation Todt in Russia, Italy and France.

Foreign Volunteers

From mid-1941 onwards, casualties in the Wehrmacht had become extremely high, particularly on the Russian Front, and more and more German nationals were drafted into the armed forces. To make up for the shortage of manpower, the NSKK had to rely more than ever upon foreign enlistment to fill its ranks. This was illegal, as the NSKK was a sub-branch of the NSDAP, whose membership was strictly "Aryan" and German, at least in theory. But as the war went on, and drivers and mechanics were badly needed, European foreigners were encouraged to enlist on short-term contracts as NSKK *Freiwilligen* (volunteers). Three occupied countries were particularly responsive: France, the Netherlands and Belgium. About 3,000 Flemish, 2,000 Walloons (mainly coming from the Belgium pro–Nazi parties AGRA and Rex), 10,000 Dutch (most of them from the pro–Nazi Party NSB) and 2,000 Frenchmen (from various pro–Nazi parties) volunteered and were recruited.

In Belgium the ultra-right party Vlaamsch Nationaal Verbond (VNV, Flemish National League), headed by the pro–Nazi leader Gustave de Clerq, had a paramilitary organization called the Dietsche Militie (Germanic militia) including four branches. One of these was the Dietsche Militie Motor Brigade (DMMB, transport brigade), which in 1943 was incorporated into the NSKK to form the NSKK-Regiment Flandern.

In French-speaking Wallonia the most important pro–Nazi Party was the nationalist, ultra-conservative Catholic, and anticommunist Rex movement, created in 1935 by the ambitious politician and journalist Léon Degrelle (1906–1994). The Rex party also had its own uniformed, paramilitary formations including a Brigade Volante (BV, transport brigade). This was incorporated into the Nazi transport organization to form a special foreign unit called NSKK-Rex.

In the Netherlands the Nationaal-Socialistische Beweging (NSB, National Socialist League) had an SA-like, paramilitary militia known as Weerafdeling (WA, defense detachment). For the purpose of the league's mobility, an organization was created in 1935 known as Motor Weerafdeling or Motor-WA, in fact a copy of the NSKK. Headed by H.J.A. Eman, the Motor-WA numbered about 400 members who became an addition to the NSKK when the kingdom of the Netherlands was defeated and occupied after May 1940.

NSKK-like formations were also created in other European occupied countries, in Denmark and Norway for example, but also in Eastern Europe, the Balkans and the Baltic lands.

There were indeed fundamentalist Christian, anti-democratic, anti–Semitic, and fascist ultraright parties whose members shared Nazi values, wished the establishment of the German order, and were eager to participate in the struggle against their hated enemies. Many volunteers were convinced that even wearing a German uniform they were serving their country. Many of these ideological "patriots" did not expect to be regarded and punished as traitors after the war. These men claimed to be saviors of the Western Christian civilization but were politically immature, as they were motivated by passion more than by reason. They were duped, or even worse, they fooled themselves. However, the bulk of foreign volunteers who joined the German army, the NSKK and the Waffen SS did so for no political reasons at all, and without any idea of what the Hitlerite spirit was and what Nazism included. Some were just boisterous young men, rebels rejecting the bourgeois order of their parents, careless adventurers, rootless mercenaries, deserters, ex–French-Foreign-Legion members, ex-servicemen or demobilized professional soldiers who enjoyed a life of adventure, soldiering and fighting, men who felt more at home in a uniform, living in mess and barracks, and who could never settle down into the monotonous routine of civilian life with a job, a home, a wife and children. These professional mercenaries and adventurers recognized the sheer military virtuosity and glamor of the German army and were keen to join such a magnificent fighting machine. They were seduced by the pride of belonging to what they thought was a prestigious elite. There were also romantically minded young men who saw membership in the NSKK as a heroic adventure in which they would have the opportunity to show off their courage, intrepidity, manliness, and boldness. For some young extremists the Nationalsozialistisch Kraftfahrkorps served as a stepping stone to join the prestigious Waffen SS. For example, a number of French NSKK volunteers were later allowed to be candidates for the SS armed forces. The few selected were regrouped to form the SS-Sturmbrigade 7 "Frankreich" (later to become a part of the 33rd Waffen-Grenadier Division der SS "Charlemagne").

Other applicants were just easily influenced persons misled by propaganda, attracted by banners, bands and parades; men who fancied themselves strutting around in slick German army or SS uniforms. Others were weak souls escaping problems at home, a pregnant girlfriend or an unhappy marriage, for example. Others were dragged onto the German side by misguided friends or by a popular officer. Many foreign volunteers were malcontents, disoriented, hungry, or unemployed, unable to support their families; or social misfits attracted by decent food, good pay, premiums and bonuses. In a period of uncertainty, despair, misery, unemployment and profound scarcity, to be a soldier—in whatever army—could mean individual survival. A few "volunteers" joined the NSKK because they were sought after by the Sicherheits Dienst (SD, the dreaded security service of the SS). Joining the NSKK could mean avoiding prison or a concentration camp.

For the purpose of training foreign volunteers, several centers were created in Germany but also in the occupied European countries: Vilvoorde and Diest in Belgium, as well as Zeist, The Hague, Heibloem, and Almelo in the Netherlands as already mentioned.

The volunteer system proved, however, insufficient to meet the German demand, and drastic measures were taken such as blackmail, rounding up and forced enlistment. *Volksdeutsche* (persons of "German blood" living abroad), western people (French Alsacians, Walloons) and northern "Germanic" Europeans (Dutch, Danes, Flemish) were reinforced by numerous units composed of a mosaic of people from central and Eastern Europe (Estonians, Latvians, Lithuanians, Ukrainians, Bulgarians, Croats, Serbs, Slovaks, etc.). There existed a Lithuanian NSKK unit formed towards the end of the Second World War, and there were also about 1,000 young Lithuanian boys and girls drafted into the service of the Luftwaffe as FlaK, signal, transport and searchlight helpers in the last months of the war. Photographic evidence also showed the existence of Norwegians in the Reichsarbeitdienst (RAD, National Labor Service)—a German auxiliary service not widely known for accepting foreign volunteers. Russian prisoners' camps were combed to recruit Hilfswillinge (HiWi, foreign auxiliaries) who chose to "volunteer" in order to escape the famine, bad treatment and certain death that awaited them in the overcrowded prisoner-of-war camps.

The use of foreigners was not always a good solution, as the lack of mastery of the German language led to misunderstandings, irritation and poor service. This was the case at the NSKK *Motorschule* in Tübingen in

Volunteer of the Belgian VNV/NSKK-Regiment Flandern. The depicted volunteer wears the German uniform with greatcoat and the typical steel helmet bearing the NSKK insignia on the left side. His Belgian nationality is indicated by a badge on the upper left sleeve displaying the Flemish coat of arms—a standing lion.

October 1943, when misunderstood orders gave rise to a mutiny. As for the rounding up of foreigners, of course, it created low morale and poor military value, which could lead to insubordination, desertion and even sabotage and rebellion, and consequently harsh German repression. The German attitude towards foreign volunteers was indeed very contradictory. On one hand they tried to attract and to unite all foreign pro–Nazi forces; on the other hand they rejected a lot of volunteers, and those selected were regarded as second-class auxiliaries, contemptible inferiors, despised and roughly handled, unfairly and unequally considered. Even the warmest pro–Nazis were often treated without any tact or respect for their different language, culture, mentality, custom or military traditions. This apparent contradiction was justified by the fact that the Nazis totally believed in themselves. They were madly proud, obsessively racist and sickly xenophobic; they were convinced that they did not need exterior help to achieve their conquests, and they did not wish to share their victories with foreigners. But the main reason was Hitler's lack of confidence in foreigners.

If they really had wanted them, the Germans could have had many more foreign troops, and these could have played a significant and decisive military role.

If foreign mercenaries were accepted in the NSKK (and other units of the German army including the Waffen SS), they formed second-class units, which did not become members of the "real German order" in the strict sense because they did not correspond to the extravagant Nazi racist and elitist claims. Foreign volunteers were called *Freiwillige* (volunteers) to distance them from the genuine and "pure" Germans. For many foreign volunteers, the result was disappointment and disillusionment. Those who had swallowed German propaganda rapidly discovered that things in the German army and in NSDAP organizations such as the NSKK or the Organisation Todt were not as rosy as they had been painted. By the end of the war when everything was lost, many foreign volunteers knew they would have to pay some price. Many eventually refused to take responsibility, deserted and tried to disappear in the chaos of Germany in the spring of 1945. Others were fully aware that they were rejected by their own family, considered abject traitors, and hated by their national community. Having lost all hope, they fought until the bitter end with the suicidal fatalism and the desperate bravado of those who have nothing left to lose.

Transportkorps Speer

As we have seen, the Motor Transportstandarte Speer (Transport Regiment Speer) had

NSKK Obersturmmann NSKK-Motorgruppe Luftwaffe. This saluting private first class wears the grayish-blue air force uniform with a short blouse. His rank is indicated by two silver bars worn on the forage cap and on the right collar patch. The left collar patch carries the emblem of the NSKK. The small blue, white and red shield with a central battle-axe (Pétain's Vichy Francisque) worn on the upper left sleeve indicates a French volunteer.

been formed in 1937 around a cadre from the NSKK school at Döberitz to assist Hitler's architect, Albert Speer, in his capacity of inspector general of the rebuilding of Berlin.

As previously said, in May 1938 Fritz Todt was given the task of completing the West

Wall (Siegfried Line), which had been started by the Heer almost two years earlier. For this task the Organisation Todt (OT) was officially formed and the NSKK supplied transport for the construction. These men were formed into the regiment-sized NSKK Transportstandarte Todt in September 1939, and were expanded to brigade strength into the NSKK Transportbrigade Todt in 1940.

Following the invasion of the USSR, Motor Transportstandarte Speer was expanded into NSKK Transportbrigade Speer and was attached to the Luftwaffe, where it was used in the construction of airfields.

As previously discussed, following the mysterious death of Fritz Todt in a plane crash on February 8, 1942, Albert Speer was appointed leader of the OT as well as minister for armaments and munitions. When NSKK-Korpsführer Adolf Hühnlein died and was succeeded by Erwin Kraus in 1942, it was agreed by Speer and Krauss that NSKK Transportbrigade Speer and NSKK Transportbrigade would merge into the NSKK Transportgruppe Todt with the exception of the non–Germanic volunteers, who would serve in a new formation known as Legion Speer (which soon had recruitment offices all over Europe), both to be commanded by NSKK-Gruppenführer Wilhelm Nagel. As of September 1943 the organization of the Legion Speer corresponded with the Einsatzgruppen of the Organisation Todt and comprised the following units:

- Legion Speer Italien (Italy) headquartered at Rome;
- Legion Speer Norwegen (Norway) headquartered at Oslo;
- Legion Speer Ost (east) headquartered at Kiev;
- Legion Speer Reich (home) headquartered at Berlin;
- Legion Speer Südost (southeast) headquartered at Belgrade;
- Legion Speer West (west) headquartered at Paris.

The NSKK Transportgruppe Todt primarily worked with building projects, while the branches of the Legion Speer worked primarily with military transports. The NSKK Transportgruppe Todt was again redesignated in October 1942: it became NSKK Transportgruppe Speer.

The NSKK Transportgruppe Speer was reorganized again in 1944 when it merged with Legion Speer and was made into an organization independent of the NSKK named Transportkorps Speer (TKS). At the head of the TKS, Speer appointed one of his deputies, Wilhelm Nagel. One reason for this reorganization was the confusion between the various auxiliary transport organizations and pressure from Martin Bormann to remove all non-Germanics from the ranks of the overtly Nazi Party organization NSKK. Another reason was that, after five years of war and because of the destruction caused by the massive and continuous Allied air attacks, the German transportation system had reached a predicament. The NSKK could no longer assume responsibility for meeting the most urgent transportation needs. Since victory largely depended on mobility and supply, the minister of armaments, Albert Speer—in an effort to reorganize an effective war economy—was actively plotting to free his transport units from Nazi Party NSKK control and influence, a strategy NSK-Korpsführer Erwin Kraus was powerless to avoid, given the power and authority enjoyed by Albert Speer.

The new Transportkorps Speer was created in June 1944 by the absorption of various units from the NSKK and the Organisation Todt. The headquarters were established at Kreuzbruch. The Transportkorps Speer soon included 47,727 men, including 17,000 Germans, 20,000 foreign volunteers and 800 Russian HiWis ("volunteering helpers"), with a fleet of about 35,000 cars, vans and trucks. Speer's efforts were, however, in vain. At the end of 1944, the transportation system found itself in a catastrophic situation. After the abortive Ardennes counter-offensive (the Battle of the Bulge) in the winter of 1944–1945, which vainly consumed the last German organized strength, the road transportation

German barge. This inland boat was built by the Scalenbau KG and Dyckerhoff and Widmann KG Companies from Ostswine, a region of Swinemünde in the period 1943–44, for the Transport Fleet Speer. As metal had become scarce, some boats had their hulls made of cheap concrete with a thickness of 80 mm. The ship had a length of 40.50 m, a width of 7.00 m, and was powered by two diesel engines. About 50 units were built.

system—and railway network, as well—had totally collapsed. There were no longer any trains, boats, cars, trucks, fuel or personnel available for provisioning the armies, for withdrawing the wounded and for carrying out the evacuation of hundreds of thousands of panicking refugees who fled westwards as the Soviets invaded the eastern part of Germany.

The Transportkorps Speer also included the Transportflotte Speer (TFS, waterway fleet). This had been created as early as 1937 by Albert Speer—then in his function of architect redesigning German cities to transport building material along the Spree, Havel and Elbe rivers to Berlin. In 1941, the fleet had about 10,000 personnel (mainly Norwegian volunteers) and 280 barges—originally intended for the abortive Operation Sealion, the invasion of Great Britain. The headquarters of the fleet were established originally in Berlin and then moved to Groningen (north Netherlands). The fleet was headed by Großkapitän (major general) Seyd. The Allied bombing of roads and railways increased the importance of transport by waterway, and by July 1944, the Transportflotte Speer had 2,000 inland ships with a tonnage of 500,000 serving a network of 31 coastal and inland harbors in Finland, Norway, Denmark, the Netherlands, Belgium, France, Romania and the Soviet Union.

Militarization of the NSKK

Originally the members of the NSKK were officially noncombatant civilians and thus not armed. But as the war went on, the communication lines in the occupied territories were often unsafe due to ambushes and sabotages—particularly in Russia and the Balkans. Transport columns were then accompanied by armed escorts, while drivers and mechanics were issued small arms such as pistols, submachine guns and grenades to defend themselves. As early as January 1939, for the purpose of self-defense, NSKK-Wehrstaffeln (defensive armed detachments) had been created. These units—totaling some 200,000 men by 1943—were also employed as a police force for security duties (e.g., guarding of vital plants and installations, arresting of vagrants, deserters and escapees from prisoner-of-war camps) and as anti-guerrilla fighting formations. By the end of the war, due to manpower shortages, NSKK members—both Germans and foreign volunteers—were drafted, trained and armed to form new fighting units. The 106th Panzer Brigade Feldherrnhalle, for example, was raised in autumn 1944 with customs officers, policemen, and Nationalsozialistisch Kraftfahrkorps drivers. The armored unit saw action in November 1944 in the Ardennes and the Rhineland. It fought until April 1945 when survivors surrendered to the U.S. Army.

By the closing phase of World War II many NSKK men were incorporated into hastily formed and improvised Kampfgruppen (combat groups), into the Waffen SS and into the Volkssturm, for pointless, desperate and bloody rear-guard combats. With the forming of the Volkssturm in October 1944, the Drivers' Corps became responsible for its automotive training.

It should be added that by that time, fanatical Nazi NSKK men were guilty of a number of war crimes. For example, in August 1944 during the liberation of Paris, NSKK members captured 13 French underground armed resisters from Choisy-le-Roi (a suburb near Paris). The prisoners were held as hostages and taken by the retreating Nazi column. At a place called Gué-à-Tresmes (near Meaux, département of Seine-et-Marne), the NSKK men, who did not need them any longer for their security, shot them.

At the beginning of May 1945, Germany surrendered. The various transport organizations were disbanded and the personnel of the Transportkorps Speer and NSKK were treated under the Geneva Convention as prisoners of war. Those captured by the Russians spent several years of harsh detention in work camps, where many of them died. Survivors were released only in the early 1950s.

RANKS

Once the NSKK had become a separate Nazi *Gliederung*, rank insignia were intro-

NSKK *Rottenführer* with overcoat.

duced. The members of the Nationalsozialistisches Kraftfahrkorps were given Nazi hierarchy ranks, which were displayed on black collar patches. Ranks, on the whole, were similar to those of the SA and SS, as listed below with their equivalents.

Unterführer
(Non-Commissioned Officers)

NSKK *Sturmmann*: private
NSKK *Obersturmmann*: private 1st class

NSKK

NSKK *Rottenführer*: private 1st class
NSKK *Scharführer*: corporal
NSKK *Oberscharführer*: sergeant
NSKK *Truppführer*: sergeant major

Führer *(Subaltern Officers)*

NSKK *Obertruppführer*: warrant officer
NSKK *Haupttruppführer*: warrant officer
NSKK *Sturmführer*: 2nd lieutenant
NSKK *Obersturmführer*: lieutenant
NSKK *Hauptsturmführer*: captain
NSKK *Staffelführer*: major
NSKK *Oberstaffelführer*: lieutenant colonel
NSKK *Standartenführer*: colonel

Höhere Führer *(General Officers)*

NSKK *Oberführer*: brigadier
NSKK *Brigadeführer*: brigadier general
NSKK *Gruppenführer*: major general
NSKK *Obergruppenführer*: lieutenant general
NSKK *Korpsführer*: chief of NSKK

Ranks were displayed on the left collar patch of the tunic (the right collar—from Oberstaffelführer downwards—displayed a patch with Sturm and regiment numbers). Although in many cases, the NSKK ranks were continued in the Transportkorps Speer, new ranks were created by the end of 1944, including the following:

Unterführer *(Non-Commissioned Officers)*

Kraftfahrer: driver or private
Oberkraftfahrer: private 1st class
Unterfahrmeister: corporal
Fahrmeister: sergeant
Oberfahrmeister: sergeant major
Führer (Subaltern Officers)
Stabfahrmeister: warrant officer
Feldkornett: 2nd lieutenant
Oberfeldkornett: lieutenant
Stabkapitän: captain
Oberstabkapitän: major
Oberfeldkapitän: lieutenant colonel
Oberstkapitän: colonel

Höhere Führer *(General Officers)*

Brigadecommandant: brigadier general
Gruppenkommandant: major general
Korpskommandant: lieutenant general

INSIGNIA

The emblem of the NSKK was a variant of the standard *Hoheitszeichen*, comprising an eagle with spread wings holding a swastika in its claws and—above the eagle—a scroll bearing the initials NSKK. The emblem was displayed on headgear and on the right collar patch of the tunic, and repeated on the belt buckles of officers and enlisted men.

The flag of the NSKK was a variant of the Nazi flag. It included a red rectangle with a white disc in the middle containing the brown-colored eagle, swastika and NSKK scroll.

Reflecting an overt Nazi organization, a current issue was the Nazi red brassard with a black swastika in a white disc worn on the upper left sleeve. As in the Organisation Todt and the Labor Service, the armband was quickly removed before being taken prisoner, as overt Nazi affiliation could result in direct death on or off the battlefield, particularly when being captured by revengeful Balkan partisans or trigger-happy Soviet troops.

Driver's award (*Kraftfahrbewahrungsabzeichen*).

Insignia

NSKK Dagger. The NSKK dagger was the same as that of the SA and SS. The wooden red-brown grip was decorated with a small metal (sometimes silver) swastika and eagle, and the blade bore the etched Gothic lettered motto *"Alles für Deutschland* [Everything for Germany]." An elegant 16th century "Holbein" Swiss-style, the *Dolch* (dagger) was carried in a steel scabbard (with silver- or nickel-plated fittings) suspended by a chain and attached to the waist belt. Daggers were awarded to qualified NSKK men who were members for years, to those who had achieved a set of standards, and those who passed tests of knowledge of Nazi arcana. The dagger was offered or granted, but although it had to be purchased by the holder, it was not considered personal property. So when a holder was expelled or had to leave the NSKK for any reason, he had to hand back the dagger. Production of the dagger ceased in 1942.

NSKK flag and medal. *Top:* NSKK camp and garrison flag. *Bottom:* Wartime female driver's badge. The alloy badge had enamel detailing with a red background, brown border and swastika in a white disc and *Kriegskraftfahrerin* (female driver) in a scroll.

The NSKK was assigned a dagger. This was of the SA style with a brown grip and black metal scabbard with the slogan "Alles für Deutschland [Everything for Germany]" inscribed on the blade. Generally these daggers were of the best quality. Each individual had to purchase his own when his uniform was issued.

The NSKK corps had its own badges, piping and insignia indicating ranks, regions and specialization, as well as various medals rewarding the achievements of the men. The Nazis were quick to realize that driving was the skill of the future, and they sponsored and promoted it to enhance the image of a new and modern nation on wheels. NSKK motoring plaques were issued in the 1930s. They recorded achievements, races and rallies undertaken by the drivers of the corps.

During the war there was a medal known

NSKK

NSKK Emblem.

NSKK unit collar patch (worn on the right side).

NSKK cloth badge. The badge was worn on the upper right sleeve.

as the *Kraftfahrbewahrungsabzeichen* (motor transport driver's award), which could be awarded to drivers who had distinguished themselves while driving in difficult conditions in certain eastern, northern and African theaters of war for a given number of operational days. The medal was issued in three

NSKK traffic control service gorget. The metal half-moon-shaped *Ringkragen* (gorget) was suspended by a chain around the neck. It was worn on duty by the members of the NSKK Verkehrserziehungsdienst (Education Traffic Service). The unit number, the NSKK swastika-and-eagle emblem and the lettering were treated with a luminous paint that shone in the dark. The gorget was worn by selected members of uniformed organizations to denote special service or duty. Two distinct styles of gorget existed, the heart-shaped and crescent-shaped, both descended from similar regalia used by the Imperial German Army. The obverse of each shield bore an appropriate badge and/or inscription, while the reverse was covered in cloth or stiff card and featured a protruding central prong. This prong was hooked through a convenient buttonhole in the tunic during wear, thereby holding the gorget plate firmly in position. The first official Nazi gorgets were produced in the late 1920s for SA standard bearers. It took the form of a heart-shaped, nickel-plated shield, sporting a gilded brass sunburst on which was superimposed a disc enclosing an eagle holding a Sonnenrad swastika—"Sun-Wheel" swastika—inscribed in a circle. The neck chain was made from tight-fitting nickel-plated wire links, and the backing cloth was of dark-colored wool. The gorget was used only when the wearer was actually engaged in the specific function or carrying his regimental flag. Individually designed gorgets were subsequently created and manufactured for standard bearers of the SS, NSKK, NSFK, RAD, HJ, Political Leadership, RLB, TeNo, Polizei, Reichsbahn, DRK, army, Luftwaffe and ex-servicemen's associations. Each bore insignia relevant to its own organization.

grades: gold, silver and bronze. The award displayed a driving wheel surrounded by oak leaves. It could be forfeited for neglect of a vehicle, exceeding the speed limit or causing

Insignia

NSKK cloth badge, worn on headgear.

NSKK Traffic Education Service Badge. The NSKK *Verkehrserziehungsdienst Abzeichen* (Traffic Education Service Badge), awarded after six months of service, was worn on the upper right sleeve of the service tunic or greatcoat. The shield-shaped aluminum badge was 72 mm in length and displayed the 1938 NSKK swastika-and-eagle pattern with the letters NSKK on a scroll arching above it. Below, in raised script, was the word *Verkehrserziehungsdienst*. The badge had three holes for sewing it to the sleeve.

NSKK *Hoheitszeichen* variant, worn on headgear.

Badge worn by the French NSKK volunteers. The cloth badge was worn on the upper right arm. It represented the French tricolor (blue, white and red) with a central black labrys (double-edged battle axe), the emblem of Marshal Pétain's Vichy government.

NSKK driver badge. The "NSKK *Raute*," the diamond-shaped black cloth specialty badge, was worn by NSKK drivers on the lower left arm.

NSKK

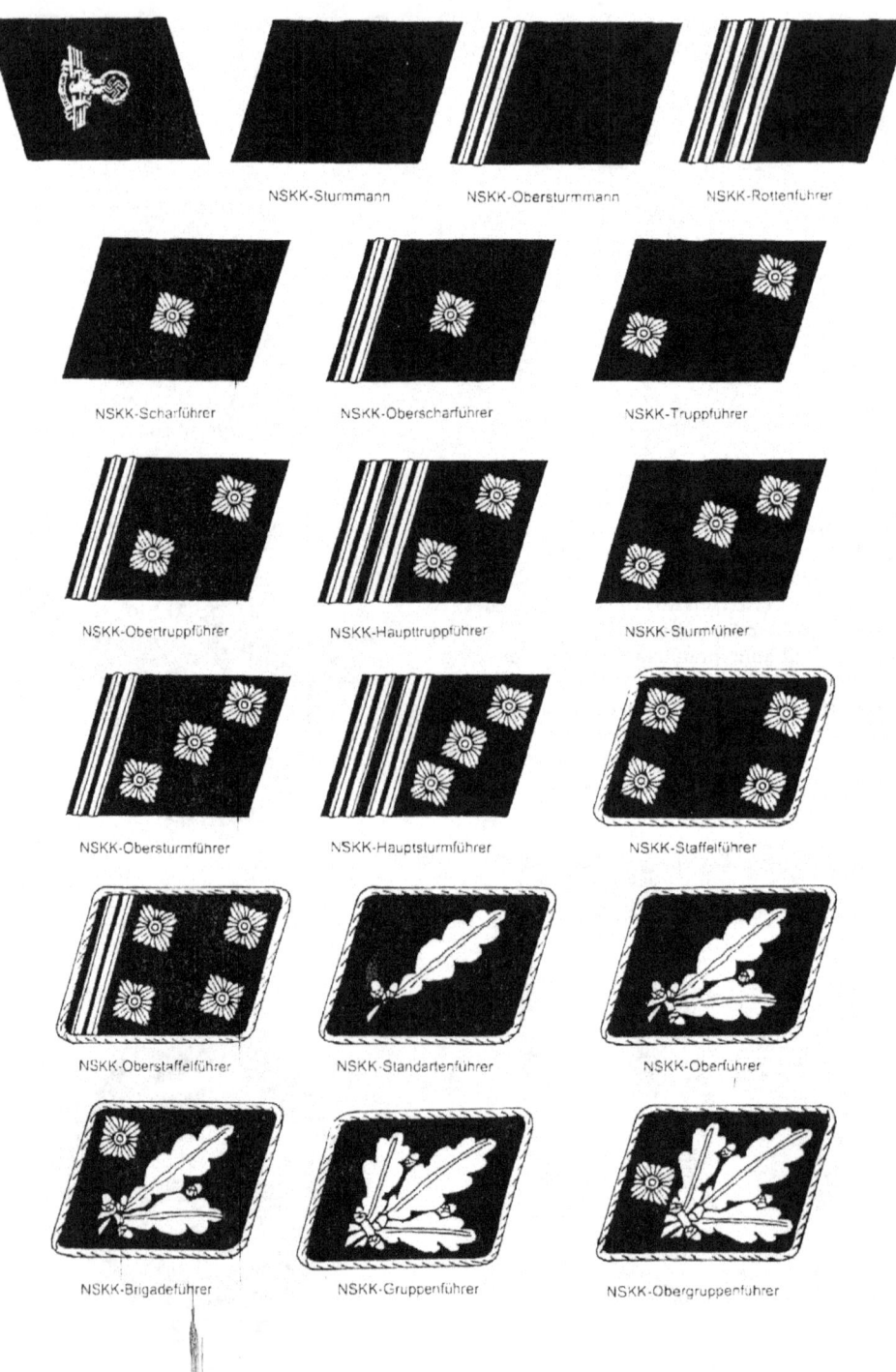

NSKK collar patches. The right collar patch (top left) showed the emblem of the corps or the numerals of *Sturm* and regiment. The left patch indicated the ranks, which were quite similar to those of the SA and SS.

Uniforms

Collar patch of the Transportkorps Speer.

Sports medal (*Sportabzeichen*). Sports played a central role in the Third Reich, and the emphasis was on virile outdoor activities, sports, competition and physical training. Members of all branches of the Nazi Party—including the NSKK—had to satisfy certain minimum requirement in the sphere of athletics, which were rewarded with medals and insignia.

NSKK Sturm pennant. The NSKK battalion pennant included a red triangular field with a black swastika in a white disk. In the upper left corner was a unit identification lozenge displaying in white Arabic numerals the number of the *Motorsturm* (battalion, here 2) above the number of the *Motorstandarte* (regiment, here 15). In the lower left corner there was an enlarged version of the NSKK driver's arm badge.

NSKK armband worn by auxiliaries tasked with traffic control. The armband was orange with black letters.

an accident under the influence of alcohol. There also existed a medal for the few NSKK wartime female drivers (*Kriegskraftfahrerin*).

The Drivers' Corps had a marching song called the "NSKK Marsch," composed by Adolf Hühnlein himself.

Uniforms

The members of the Nationalsozialistisch Kraftfahrkorps wore various sorts of uniforms. Initially the NSKK wore a khaki tunic and black riding breeches with a khaki shirt and black tie. The connection with the SA motorized corps was emphasized by the SA-style kepi, which had a black top and khaki sides.

With the onset of war, the NSKK rationalized its uniform, and then men wore a khaki tunic with a brown collar, a color that was repeated in the cap band. The officer's off-duty uniform was rather similar to that of the NSDAP with peaked cap, olive brown tunic, waist belt, riding breeches and leather boots.

On duty, members of the NSKK wore various fatigue overalls and the standard *Drillichanzug* (fatigue uniform). This uniform—

NSKK

NSKK private first class. This private first class (*Obersturmmann*) wears a peaked field cap and olive brown uniform.

Crash helmet.

NSKK black side cap. Note that the rank of *Oberscharführer* (corporal) is indicated both on collar patch and side cap.

composed of tunic and trousers—was made of strong unbleached denim material.

As the war went on some NSKK men considered themselves increasingly to be soldiers of the Wehrmacht, as they more often wore uniforms and insignia that made them virtually indistinguishable from their comrades in the armed forces. Members of the NSKK Motorgruppe Luftwaffe wore the air force light blue-grey uniform composed of a short jacket, trousers and boots, but they had black overseas caps with the NSKK eagle on the left, and the sleeve displayed the NSKK diamond. On the cuff was the title with the number of the NSKK Transport Regiment.

Uniforms

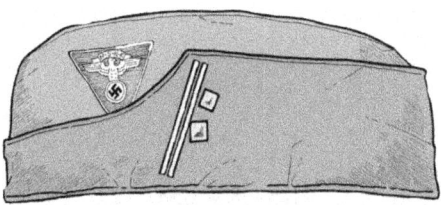

NSKK Mütze. The NSKK black side cap displays the rank of *Obertruppführer* (sergeant major).

M35 helmet. The standard German army steel helmet type 1935, when worn by NSKK members, displayed the NSKK decal (scroll, eagle and swastika) on the left side. On the right side the helmet had a German tricolor.

NSKK policeman. The depicted *Obersturmmann* (private 1st class) of the NSKK Wehrstaffeln on duty wears the standard army M1935 steel helmet and a gorget (a half-moon shaped metal plate held by chains) bearing the emblem of the corps. Policemen were generally armed with light weapons, e.g., a PKK police pistol.

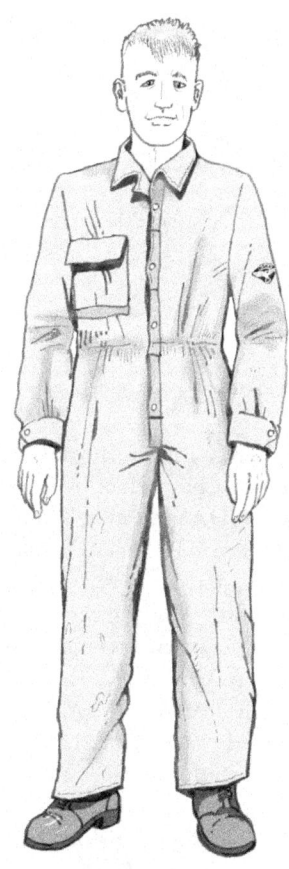

Work overall.

NSKK

Left: NSKK *Sturmmann* (with Luftwaffe uniform); *right:* NSKK *Sturmführer*.

NSKK *Sturmführer* (2nd lieutenant). The service uniform included a peaked cap, a four-pocket, olive brown tunic, a red brassard with swastika, black breeches and leather riding boots.

The NSKK was the only overtly Nazi organization to be part of the Deutsches Afrika Korps (DAK, headed by the famous field marshal Erwin Rommel). The 4th Motor Transport Regiment served and operated vehicles in North Africa in the period 1941–1943. NSKK members serving in the DAK wore the tan tropical Afrika Korps uniform. Officially this uniform comprised an olive-green, light field tunic with khaki shirt, drill shorts, knee-length stockings, canvas-topped lace-up boots and a brimmed, tropical cork helmet. But like their British and Commonwealth adversaries, the Germans adopted a fairly relaxed attitude towards military uniforms in the field. NSKK members wore all kind of German-made clothing but also civilian, captured British and Commonwealth dress and equipment. They might also drive captured Allied vehicles.

Sailors of the NSKK waterway fleet and Transportflotte Speer wore a dark blue uniform based on that of the military seamen.

The *Sonderbekleidung* of the Deutschen Panzertruppen (Special German Panzer black uniform) was often worn by NSKK men who trained the army tank drivers. The black

Uniforms

Left: NSKK *Truppführer* (Sergeant), 1939; *center:* NSKK *Truppführer*, Transport Korps Speer; *right:* Captain. This captain of Transport Korps Speer wears a dark blue uniform with peaked cap, a double-breasted tunic with black collar and matching trousers.

Panzer *Feldjacke* was a short, hip-length, double-breasted, tight-fitting jacket, without external pockets or other external features that would snag. The Panzer *Feldhose* (trousers) were the same for all ranks. They were black, full length and rather baggy. They were fastened around the ankle and usually tucked into the universal *Marschstiefel* (marching jackboots), giving a deep "pulled-down" effect. The jacket collar patches were the most eye-catching feature since they displayed a white or silver metal *Totenkopf* (death's head). The combination of black uniform and death's head was dramatic and fearsome.

Headgear worn by the members of the NSKK varied considerably. In the early years a SA-style kepi with chinstrap was worn, displaying the NSKK scroll, eagle and swastika at the front. Before the war, the typical Motor-SA-styled padded *Sturzhelm* (crash helmet) was worn while driving an open-topped car or a motorbike, but also at parades, ceremonies and rallies. The crash helmet was originally used by pilots of the Imperial German Air Force during World War I. It was adopted by the Motor SA circa 1928 and later by the NSKK with the addition of a large metal swastika-and-eagle insignia displayed at the

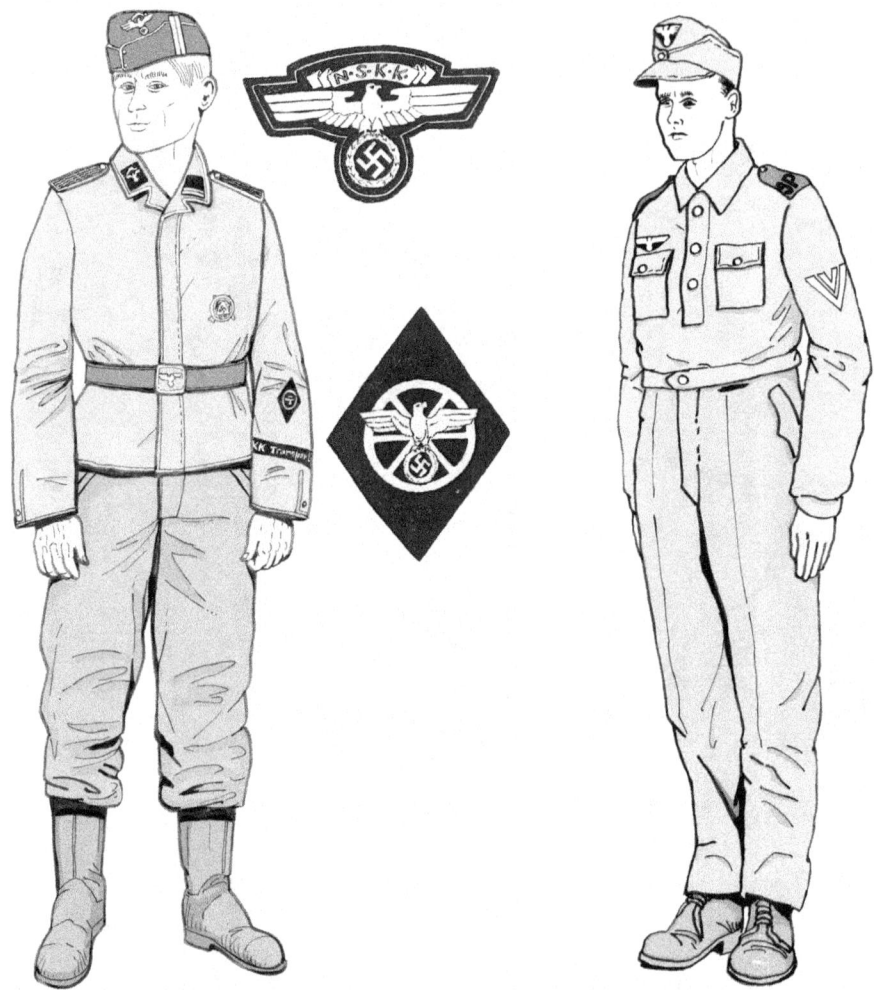

Left: NSKK corporal. The depicted *Obersturmmann* (corporal) of the NSKK Motorgruppe Luftwaffe wears the German air force's light blue-gray uniform composed of a short jacket and matching trousers; *right:* Driver first class. The depicted *Hauptkraftfahrer* (private-driver first class) of the Transportkorps Speer (in late 1944) wears a two-piece, olive brown motoring uniform composed of a soft peaked field cap, a short pullover denim blouse and trousers. His rank was indicated by chevron on the left arm.

front. Made of thick black leather, the crash helmet had reinforced ribs, a comb, a short leather visor, a back neck-guard, and earflaps connected to the chinstrap. The national motor corps acceptance stamp was in the liner. The crash helmet was gradually discarded in the late 1930s, and motorcyclists and drivers generally wore the standard Wehrmacht M1935 steel helmet. As troops employed in hazardous frontline duties, many NSKK units were issued combat helmets, most often standard Wehrmacht M1935 steel helmets with goggles protecting the eyes. The steel helmets were drawn from Heer (German ground army) or Luftwaffe surplus—generally with the addition of the NSKK decal (eagle/swastika/scroll) appearing on the left side of the helmet, and the German tricolor on the right side.

A distinctive, peakless black cloth side cap was introduced in 1936. It displayed the wearer's rank up to and including the rank of

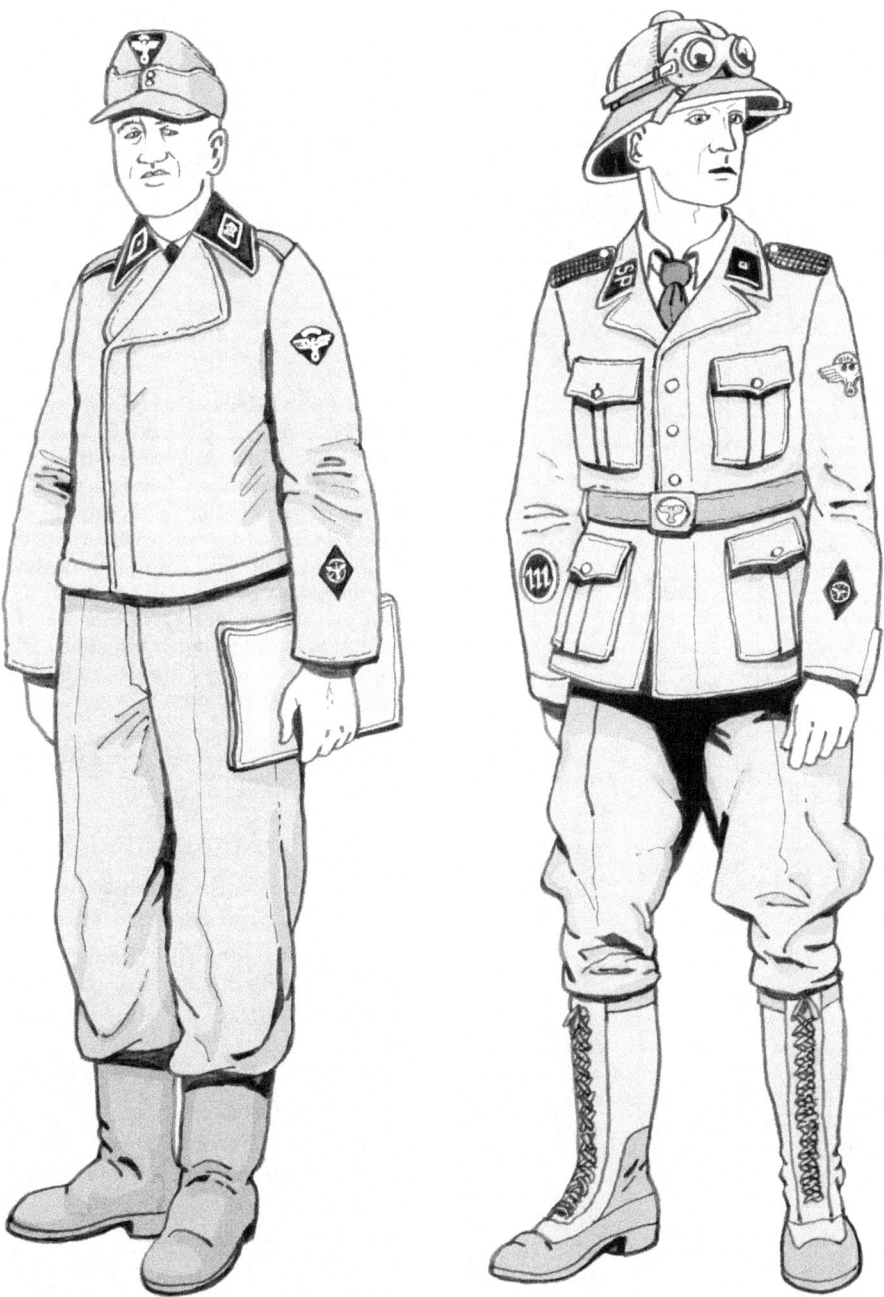

Left: Tank instructor. The NSKK instructor wears the black Panzer uniform of the armored forces with soft peaked cap and marching boots; *right:* Corporal (North Africa, 1941). The NSKK served on all World War II fronts including in North Africa. Newly arrived in North Africa, this NSKK *Oberscharführer* (Corporal) wears the freshly issued tropical suit of the Deutsches Afrika Korps (DAK) including an olive-green tunic, trousers, high lace-up boots, and tropical pith helmet. On the right sleeve he wears an oval specialty badge with the letter M of *Mekaniker* (mechanic). Note the use of shirt and tie, a practice rapidly discontinued due to the hot climate and the harsh conditions of desert warfare.

Tropical pith helmet. This helmet was worn by NSKK men serving in North Africa. It was made from compressed cork covered with segments of olive-green canvas cloth. It had a ventilation hole on top, leather binding on the edge of the rim, leather sweatband, leather chinstrap, and red cloth lining. The Afrika Korps pith helmet carried the red, white and black army shield on the right side and the NSKK eagle on the left. The tropical helmet was rather unpopular with the troops and was soon discarded in favor of the popular peaked field cap.

Winter suit. Winter suits existed in several versions, all donned over the regular uniform. A variant included a thick pullover jacket with three front pockets and attached hood, and a thick pair of matching trousers. Some winter suits were reversible, with one side camouflaged in green/brown patterns, and the other side completely white for use in the snow.

NSKK-Haupttruppführer by a system of white metal pips and SA/SS pattern silver braid patch. In the prewar period and during the early stages of World War II, NSKK tank driver instructors wore a black, padded *Schutzmütze* (protection beret) as part of the special black Panzer uniform. This consisted of a protective crash liner fitted with a beret cover with a short tail. The previously discussed *Feldmütze* (peakless forage cap or side cap) and the *Einheitsfeldmütze* (soft peaked cap) were also widely worn.

Aftermath

In 1945 the NSKK was disbanded and the Nuremberg Tribunal declared it a condemned organization (although not a criminal one). To conclude this discussion of the NSKK and German motorization, the following must be added.

It is generally believed that the Germans were in the forefront of mechanization, as shown by the renowned Panzer divisions. The fact was that they were a good deal less advanced in basic military mechanization than most other countries. The German army always suffered motor vehicle shortage. Although many civilian transport trucks and many enemy captured vehicles were pressed into German service, production and replacements could never match the losses, attrition and destruction of transport vehicles. So far behind were the Germans, as a matter of fact, that most of their field artillery went to war in 1939—and even later—behind horse teams.

Opel Blitz light truck with gas generator. Powered by coal and gas instead of diesel oil, this conversion of the Opel truck showed what efforts the Germans had to go to in the face of an ever-growing fuel shortage as World War II progressed. In the last year of the war, front lines were pushed back from the oil fields, and Allied air bombing took a heavier toll on their fuel reserves.

Logistics became increasingly complicated as the tonnage of supplies to be carried multiplied. An army's rapid advance was a supply officer's nightmare; as soldiers and tanks moved farther away from railheads, supplies dwindled.

If some divisions were well equipped, the average German *Versorgungskolonne* (motorized supply column) often looked like a parade of worn-out, broken down, pitifully inadequate vehicles. In certain extreme conditions (in northern Africa or on the Russian front, for example), instead of trucks carrying troops, it was the soldiers who were obliged to disembark and push the trucks through loose sand or thick, sticky mud. In the North African campaign, shortages of fuel and supplies as well as inadequate transport were one of the reasons for Rommel's failure. In Russia snow and ice, but also ambushes and sabotages by partisans, made road movement slow and hazardous. After mid–1944 and until the end of the war, all daylight movements were utterly dangerous as the sky was totally dominated by the Allied air forces. By then the Germans were under quasi-constant observation, bombing and strafing. Before they got anywhere near the front, they had already lost many vehicles, weapons, equipment and men in attacks from the air.

CHAPTER 4

DEUTSCHER VOLKSSTURM (GERMAN POPULAR HOME GUARD)

SITUATION IN THE WINTER OF 1944–1945

By the end of 1944 it was obvious that Germany was doomed to lose the war. On June 6, 1944, the Allies had landed in Normandy, France. The German forces in the West had been defeated and by August 25, Paris and large parts of France were liberated. By September 1944, the Germans had fallen back to their own border, and in a bold attempt to outflank them the Allies launched an airborne offensive in southern Holland. But the British and Polish parachutists were defeated at Arnhem, and the advance came to a halt. From December 1944 to January 1945, the Germans used their last reserves in a final and hopeless counter-offensive in the Belgian Ardennes, known as the Battle of the Bulge, which the Allies won but which had heavy losses on both sides. The scene was set for the final act, the invasion and conquest of Germany.

On the Eastern Front, the Russians had destroyed the German Army Group Center, opened new offensives in January 1945 and entered Warsaw. By the end of the month the Red Army was on the river Oder, less than 100 miles from Berlin. In February 1945, the Allied troops entered Germany in the West. On March 1945, they led their armies into the heart of the Reich. In the meantime the Russians captured Vienna—capital of Austria—and liberated Prague—capital of Czechoslovakia. By that time, German soldiers hardly knew what was happening, air cover was nonexistent, communications were breaking down, many units were left without orders, and the knowledge of ultimate defeat was spreading throughout all ranks. Only Hitler and a few Nazi diehards still refused to admit how desperate the situation had become, or to abandon hope of reversing the predicament by a dramatic stroke. The Allied advances went on until April 27, when Russian and American forces met at Torgau, central Germany. On May 2, Berlin was captured after bitter, pointless and hopeless fighting. Two days earlier Hitler, finally realizing that all was lost, had committed suicide, and six days later Nazi Germany surrendered.

CREATION OF THE VOLKSSTURM

Of the measures taken to mobilize the last manpower resources of the German nation, the most extreme was the creation of the Volkssturm or Deutscher Volkssturm (German Popular Army), a national militia designed to supplement the defenses of the homeland. However, calling upon a large part of the population and organizing citizens into a territorial militia in case of emergency was not a new thing in 1944. There are many cases recorded in history. For example, nonprofessional militias were raised during the American Revolutionary War (1775–1783), e.g., the Lexington Militia, commanded by John Parker. The Germans and Austrians had raised irregular forces in the period 1805–1807 against the French. The British created the Home Guard in mid–1940 when they found themselves under the threat of a Nazi invasion. The Soviet Union mobilized a temporary "People's Army" to support the regular Red Army in the summer of 1941. What was different about the Volkssturm was that it was set up not by the traditional German army, but by the Nazi Party on Adolf Hitler's order. The territorial militia was intended to serve a double purpose, as far as the Nazi Party was concerned: first, to strengthen the defense of the Reich; and, second, to keep a large part of the population so thoroughly under military control that any incipient revolt against Hitler's regime would have a hard time thriving. It was the intention to have a strong and hard core of Nazi fanatics dominating the Volkssturm at all levels.

The German word *Sturm* actually means tempest or hurricane, but also assault or attack, revealing that the Führer still placed Germany in an aggressive position, and that he intended to unleash a cyclone of furious violence upon his enemies. In fact, the Volkssturm consisted of defensive home units. The Volkssturm was created on September 25, 1944, by Hitler's decree. Symbolically the formation of the German people's "assault force" was publicly announced on October 18, 1944. This was the anniversary of the great victory over the French emperor Napoléon at Leipzig in 1813, the so-called Battle of the Nations, which was followed by the withdrawal of the French invaders and heralded the end of Napoléon's empire. With Germany a nation in arms, the Nazis wanted to put themselves in the historical tradition of Prussia. On the whole, the call for the Volkssturm did not arouse the same popular enthusiasm as in 1813.

When the Volkssturm was created in autumn 1944, the Allied progression on the Western front had been marked by several local defensive German victories, which prolonged the war into the spring of 1945. As already said, at Arnhem in south Netherlands, Montgomery's airborne Operation Market Garden had ended up as a failure. On the Western Front, Aachen (Aix-la-Chapelle) had been successfully defended. For 85 days the Germans troops had denied the Allies the use of the great Belgian port of Antwerp, which could not

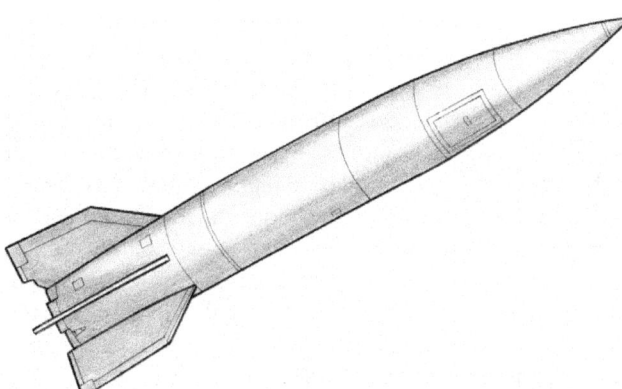

V2 Rocket. The V-2 was an unmanned, guided, ballistic missile. It was guided by an advanced gyroscopic system and propelled by a mixture of ethyl alcohol, water, and liquid oxygen fuel. The rocket was 46 ft. (14 m) in length, had a maximum speed of 3,355 mph (5,400 km/h), rose to an altitude of 52 to 60 miles (83 to 93 km) and had a range of 200 to 225 miles (321 to 362 km). It carried an explosive warhead weighing approximately one ton (738 kg) that was capable of destroying a whole city block. The V2 was first fired operationally in September 1944 against London and Antwerp (Belgium) with devastating effects.

be opened to traffic before the end of November 1944. These comparative successes gave fresh heart to the Wehrmacht and the German people, and they provided for Hitler and his minister of propaganda, Josef Göbbels, precious time that they turned to good account. These events appeared to justify Hitler's determination to maintain the struggle and Göbbels' boast that the Allies could be halted at the borders of Germany. The temporary German façade of recovery rallied the people for the supreme effort, which the Führer now demanded of them.

These short-term military successes also coincided with the publication of the postwar plan concerning the treatment of defeated Germany. This proposal for the future became known as the Morgenthau Plan because it was fathered by the American secretary of the treasury Henry J. Morgenthau, Jr. The essence of the scheme planned by Morgenthau was that postwar Germany should be dismembered and converted into an agricultural and pastoral country deprived of industry. The revelation of the Morgenthau Plan enabled Göbbels to produce "evidences" and warnings that the enemies of the Reich intended to pursue the extermination of the German people. Harping on the dire consequence of defeat, Göbbels instilled into the German public a profound dread of both the Russians and the Western Allies. The fact that Henry Morgenthau was a Jew enabled him to launch another anti–Semitic propaganda campaign arguing that the German people could not expect mercy, and that they would be faced with starvation and enslavement. Actually, President Roosevelt considered that Morgenthau's proposal was irrational and dangerous for the future of Europe. However, he could not publicly disown it for electoral reasons, as his Republican opponents would have accused him of lacking the determination to carry the war through to complete victory. Anyway, by coupling the supposed consequences of the Morgenthau Plan and the unconditional surrender demanded by the Allies, Göbbels could convince a part of the German people that their only hope of saving the nation and themselves lay in giving unconditional obedience to the Führer and determined resistance to their enemies. Moreover, since the failed attack on Hitler's life on July 20, 1944, it was realized by many soldiers and a part of the nation that any internal revolution would only precipitate the collapse of Germany and would cause a repetition of the chaos of 1918. It was probably this fear of chaos, the dread of anarchy and civil war, the desperate straits to which the bulk of the German urban population had been reduced by Allied air bombing, the absence of hope for mercy and a decent future, the destruction and dislocation of the very essentials of life, that created an ultimate community of interest between Hitler, the Nazi Party, the Wehrmacht and a part of the German people. Throughout the autumn of 1944, although the Allied bombing was heavier than ever before, the German people worked with unbroken vigor to repair the damages and maintain the economy of total war. A common slogan displayed in the ruins of the German cities by that time was, "Our walls may collapse but not our morale." Thus paradoxically, as winter and the invading armies closed in upon them, some of the German people and their armed forces—instead of rising in revolt against the Nazi regime—rallied to uphold Hitler's rule, the very man whose megalomania had led them to defeat and ruin.

The idea of a popular army originated in plans made by General Adolf Heusinger, chief of the general staff of the army, to raise a territorial militia in East Prussia. The plan was first put in action in summer 1944 by Gauleiter Erich Koch, who disregarded both the Wehrmacht and the SS, whom he treated with equal contempt. Without informing the responsible Army Group under Colonel General Rheinhardt, Koch had defensive positions constructed using invalids, retirees and teenagers. Koch also took charge of the search for deserters and stragglers, and raised all able men to form a small citizen army called Ostpreussen Volkssturm (East Prussia Home Guard). He requisitioned the armaments factories in East Prussia and refused any expert military advice for his force. Dilettante and megalomaniac though he was, Gauleiter Koch had had an inspiring idea. His force fought with some success in Goldap and Gumbinen. With the military situation worsening and the fighting getting perilously close to German soil, Hitler and his henchmen still viewed the war through their illogical and sick Nazi ideology. For them the war was a clash of races in which there was not option for peace negotiations or surrender, but only victory or total destruction of Germany. Therefore the war was to be continued until the bitter end. In this context it was decided to develop a civilian army on national scale on the Koch model but under the aegis of the Nazi Party. Hitler still believed that additional fanaticized troops could prevent the Allies from a rapid advance. The Volkssturm was to unleash such a storm of fury and inflict such casualties that Allied morale would crumble and the coalition would collapse. If only the whole German people would fight hard and long enough, Hitler and company could win time in order to engage the "miracle weapons." It was hoped that the flying bomb V1, the long-range ballistic rocket V2 and the new type–XXI submarine could reverse the outcome of the war and force the Allies to beg for a truce. The decision to create the Volkssturm was supported by Josef Göbbels (minister of propaganda and newly appointed Reich plenipotentiary for total war) who saw a possible propaganda exploitation and an increase of his personal power.

The slogan "*Unsere Mauern brachen, aber unsere Herzen nicht* [Our walls broke, but not our hearts] was commonly daubed or printed on official posters and improvised signs in bombed sites in German towns. Despite large-scale death, destruction and suffering, civilian morale in Germany did not collapse as the controversial "Bomber Harris" (Air Marshal Sir Arthur Harris, heading the RAF Bomber Command) had hoped.

COMMAND

Because of internal rivalry within the Nazi Party top leadership, the authority over the Volkssturm was mixed. Indeed the more the Third Reich shrank under the Allies' hammer blows, the more strident became the struggle for personal power at the top of the collapsing Nazi state. Finally it was agreed that the Volkssturm would be equipped, armed and commanded by Reichsführer Heinrich Himmler's SS, as commander in chief of the home forces. But as a direct consequence of the July bomb plot against Hitler, the Volkssturm was not placed under the Wehrmacht control. It was recruited, organized, and politically led by the NSDAP under the more "reliable" leadership of Reichsleiter Martin Bormann, who acted on Hitler's behalf.

Now that the war had moved onto German territory, the defeated and unreliable Wehrmacht was discredited. Now leadership was the prerogative of the SS and NSDAP. More and more Nazi leaders argued that the military situation had gone wrong because not enough scope had been given to the NSDAP. If the Nazi Party had had its way, it would have provided military leaders and generals imbued with Nazi spirit. Many thought that it was a pity that SA chief of staff Ernst Röhm's effort in 1934 to form a Nazi popular armed force had been thwarted by the Wehrmacht. Now many NSDAP leaders thought that it was high time for the party to take control over the military, which in their eyes had proved not only incompetent but also treacherous. The Volkssturm was actually intended to be Bormann's private army and escaped both the army and Himmler's control. It marked, in fact, the start of the decline of Himmler and the rise of Martin Bormann, head of the party chancellery, managing director of the Nazi Party, Hitler's *éminence grise*, and jealous doorkeeper to the dictator's office. Bormann was assisted by several Stabführer (chiefs of staff). The chief of the SA (Sturm Abteilung, or Storm Troops), Wilhelm Schepmann, was designated inspector of weapons training; the chief of the NSKK (Nazi Motor Corps) Erwin Kraus was appointed inspector of technical training; NSDAP Oberbefehlsleiter Helmut Friedrichs was responsible for organization and political affairs; and SS-Gruppenführer Gottlob Berger represented the SS. A staff of Wehrmacht officers, commanded by Oberst (colonel) Hans Kissel, was also responsible for equipment, weapons and training. Helmut Friedrichs and Gottlob Berger achieved a comparatively good working relationship, but Bormann and Himmler frequently clashed for control of the Popular Army, a conflicting situation exacerbated by the confused and overlapping chain of command.

The Volkssturm was indeed badly organized and ill commanded. It occupied a kind of netherworld among the military. Although its members had the status of Wehrmachtsgefolge and were expected to support and fight alongside the German army in time of emergency, they were not considered part of the army. At the top level there was resentment between NSDAP and SS. At lower levels, there was a lack of competent military leaders and an absence of any clearly defined division of authority between the SS and the Nazi Party, between the military and civilian agencies. At all levels, this vagueness created trouble and confusion for soldiers and civilian leadership alike. There were no clear operational plans, no one knew from whom orders were to be taken, and no one was eager to clarify the chain of command of the force.

The Volkssturm was definitely a bottom-of-the-barrel organization. Although it succeeded in mustering millions of men for local defense inside the Reich, a conservative estimate indicated that a large part of this force included men who were not totally physically fit for military service.

Organization

All available men (excluding Jews, Gypsies, criminals, foreigners and German natives who were already in the armed forces and paramilitary formations) whose jobs were not deemed absolutely necessary were drafted for the defense of the fatherland. The conscription was organized in four *Aufgeboten* (levies) of men born from 1884 to 1928 (thus from 16 to 60 years of age in 1944) to make a planned strength of 6 million.

The first levy included 1.2 million men forming 1,850 battalions (of which 400 were deployed in border zones). It was composed of all physically fit 20–60-year-old men without essential war work exemption, including all available Nazi Party members and officials, Allgemeine SS (the senior, nonpermanent members of the SS), SA ("Brownshirts" or assault troops), NSKK (drivers and mechanics), members of the NSFK (Nazi Air Corps) and other conscripts. They were assigned for frontline duty, would be quartered in barracks, and were liable for service anywhere within their Gau (region).

The second levy, totaling 2.8 million guards forming 4,860 *Abteilungen* (1,050 battalions in frontier district), concerned all 20–60-year-olds with essential war exemptions. They were usually organized in factory battalions, quartered at home and liable for duty within their own district.

The third levy totaled about 600,000 teenagers, aged 16–19 plus some 15-year-old volunteers (mostly Hitler Youth), forming about 1,040 battalions for local defense.

The fourth levy—composed of men of limited physical ability—counted 1.4 million 20–60-year-olds unfit for active military service. They formed 2,430 battalions for guard and surveillance duty in prisons, concentration camps, and prisoner-of-war camps.

The Volkssturm was prohibited from operating outside Germany, but four battalions were constituted from Germans living abroad. Battalions 400 and 402 were recruited in Denmark, and battalions 605 and 610 in the protectorate of Bohemia-Moravia (former Czech provinces). The improvised Volkssturm was unofficially reinforced by volunteering members of local traditional rifle associations known as *Standschützen* that existed in northern and southern Tyrol and in Vorarlberg, all Alpine provinces of the pre-1918 Austrian Empire. According to ancient traditional prerogatives, the *Standschützen* were called up for the defense of their home country in case of war, and had the status of a territorial militia. In the First World War, for example, in 1915 after Italy declared war on Austria by attacking Tyrol, the *Standschützen* were mobilized to defend their mountain frontiers since nearly all the regular Austrian forces were engaged on the East Front fighting the Russians. The *Standschützen* were regarded and organized as rifle clubs or associations during peacetime and did not have any specific military training. In remembrance of the old traditions, the Volkssturm riflemen units of Tyrol and Vorarlberg received special identification badges worn on the left upper sleeve. The edelweiss insignia of the type worn by mountain troops was often worn on the left side of the mountain cap.

The Volkssturm also included young girls of the Hitler Youth Movement as well as women and young women from the NS-Frauenschaft (Nazi Women's League), who provided rear-echelon support such as logistics and medical care.

In one capacity or another, many of the Volkssturm personnel, male and female, had already contributed their services to the German war effort when the call to arms was issued. It must be remembered that dozens of Nazi semi-military services, associations, and political organizations had regimented practically every walk of German life since the seizure of power by the Nazis in January 1933. Because of these organizations, and owing to a very efficient and ruthless police system managed by the SS, the Nazi authorities had a very fair knowledge of the military and service possibilities of every male in Germany. Much had been done to exploit German manpower on a part-time basis wherever full-time service could not be performed. Thus service in the Volkssturm became merely an added duty for many men who already had part-time jobs and activities in other defense organizations or who worked in war industries. As the Nazis envisioned it, a man who performed ARP (air-raid precautions) tasks during an air attack, who had a route to guard as a member of the Streifendienst (patrol service), or who was a skilled laborer in an armaments factory would obviously take his post in a Volkssturm squad and would readily fight as an infantryman when his home area was attacked by Allied forces. As much as possible abilities, physical fitness, and the war work of the recruits were taken into account. Limited-service personnel were given local or static defense missions. Invalids and cripples were employed for administrative tasks and headquarters work. Although youths of 16 were included in the Volkssturm, the lower age brackets in general were likely not to be represented very generously, in view of the fact that the German armed forces increasingly drafted boys younger than 18.

Despite the fact that the Volkssturm was inducting by age classes, an appeal for "volunteers" was conducted in the usual Nazi manner. Working through the factory cells of the DAF (German Labor Front) organization and other groups directly supervised by the party, Nazi leaders could induce the entire personnel of certain factories and businesses to "volunteer" *en bloc*. The result was that recruits poured in as fast as the training facilities could handle them, and faster than if they all had been drafted formally.

All members of the Volkssturm had to swear an oath—taken in public on village and town squares—to protect their fatherland.

Children, elderly people and women were employed to dig trenches and anti-tank ditches, to erect barbed wire, obstacles, roadblocks, blockades and barriers. In many cases they were also issued weapons to participate actively in the hopeless defense of their villages and towns.

As said above, the Volkssturm recruits were the responsibility of the local Nazi Party officials, and so each of Germany's 42 *Gaue* (regions) constituted a Volkssturmabschnitt (Home Guard District).

The standard basic unit of the Volkssturm was the *Abteilung* (battalion). A *Gau* was composed on average of 20 Kreise (counties), which provided about 12 *Abteilungen* (battalions). Each battalion was allocated a number within its district; e.g., Abt. 25/97 meant 97th Battalion in District 25, East Prussia. In theory, each battalion included a staff commanding three or four *Kompanien* (companies). Each company was divided into three or four *Züge* (platoons) containing three or four 10-men *Gruppen* (squads).

The first levy of the Volkssturm—the most suitable for active warfare—also included several Sondereinheiten (Special Units). There was—at least on paper—a medical service at battalion level with medical officers, orderlies and nurses. In frontier districts there were Panzerwarndiensten (Tank Warning Squads), and each company was supposed to have one or more Panzernahbekämpfungstrupp (Anti-tank Close Combat Squads) composed of volunteers armed with anti-tank weapons. In East Prussia there was the Nachtjagdstaffel 1 (night-fighter squadron) manned by men of the NSFK (Nazi Flyers Corps) equipped with light aircraft. There were only a few genuine *Kampf Abteilungen* (combat battalions). These included several machine-guns units, a few artillery battalions armed with obsolete guns, and companies specialized in engineering and demolition. But due to local NSDAP local officials' lack of experience and preparedness the Volkssturm soon appeared to be a waste of time and efforts, not to speak of human lives.

Uniforms

Uniforms and equipment were regulated by Order No. 318/44 specifying that "every kind of uniform and weatherproof sports, outdoor and working clothing" was permitted, with emphasis on durable shoes, warm gear, greatcoats and outdoor headgear. The NSDAP *Gauleiter* was required to provide all dispensable stocks of uniforms of the Party, but obviously and inevitably the Volkssturm was armed and equipped with scraps, discarded surplus and leftovers. Draftees were not issued regular uniforms. They were ordered to provide their own clothing and to kit themselves out with appropriate equipment. As can be imagined, people used a great variety of available

Uniforms

Left: Bataillonsführer. Senior officers of the Volkssturm were usually NSDAP officials. The depicted *Bataillonsführer* (major) wears a uniform of the Nazi Party with the Volkssturm armband. He is armed with a MP40 submachine gun; *right:* Civilian drafted into the Volkssturm, 1945. The man is armed with a Panzerfaust.

uniforms, including army, party and paramilitary equipment, and even First World War vintage gear. However, many of the men went to war in their civilian clothing or with a mixture of military and civilian items, the emphasis being of course on casual wear, overcoats, warm clothing and robust outdoor shoes. Old SA, DAF, Organisation Todt or NSDAP uniforms were rather unpopular because Volkssturm men did not relish being mistaken for Nazi Party members if captured. Efforts were made to provide army issue when possible. The militiamen favored military items of some sort—e.g., Luftwaffe shirts, tunic, trousers and greatcoats even in non-matching combinations, as well as Heer-Wehrmacht uniforms—the latter often outmoded or even no longer serviceable uniforms. Being captured in civilian clothing could be extremely risky, as the men could be arrested and shot on the spot as illegal partisans. Italian, Czech, French and other captured uniforms were sometimes redyed military field-gray. Civil uniforms such as those of streetcar crews, zookeepers, postmen, railwaymen, and mailmen were also sought after and worn. Shirts, underwear

Left: Policeman drafted into the Volkssturm. The depicted *Hauptwachtmeister* (NCO) wears the field-grey police tunic, which had a more greenish hue than that used by the army, often referred to as "police green." The four-pocketed tunic had a contrasting, mid-brown collar and cuffs and traditional orange Gendarmerie piping on the front collar and cuffs. On the left arm he wears the Volkssturm armband and the police-style eagle–swastika–oak-leaf emblem embroidered in orange thread. He wears a salvaged Luftwaffe steel helmet and is armed with a pistol and a Panzerfaust; *right:* NCO *Schutzpolizei* man drafted into the Volkssturm.

and socks were whatever the men provided for themselves. Volkssturm battalions thus presented a ragtag appearance, in dress as well as armament, and their shabby, untidy, mixed and motley image inspired little confidence. The lack of complete official uniforms caused a great deal of disgruntlement throughout the new militia. Many members felt that they were assuming the duties of soldiers with none of the privileges. Incidentally, there was no remuneration for service in the Volkssturm, except when a member was taking part in actual combat.

The only standard, identifiable item was an *Armelbinde* (armband). The Nazi authorities asserted that this piece of cloth officially made Volkssturm men members of the Wehrmachtsgefolge (Armed Forces Auxiliaries). The armband was worn on the upper left arm when performing duties as a member of the Volkssturm, ensuring a precarious combatant status. The Hague Regulations required indeed that legal combatants would be identified from a distance

Uniforms

Left: Civilians drafted into the Volkssturm. Due to large-scale lack of supplies, many Volkssturm draftees served in their own civilian clothing; *right:* HJ boy in the Volkssturm. The depicted Hitler Youth private wears the dark blue HJ winter uniform with M1933 black ski-cap with HJ diamond cap badge, and M1938 dark blue trousers. Insignia included HJ and Volkssturm armbands on the left arm. On the right upper sleeve he wears two silver *Panzervernichtungsabzeichen* (tank destruction badge, instituted in March 1942) for his single-handed destruction of two Soviet tanks. He is armed with the latest Sturmgewehr StG 44 (assault rifle model 1944) with its attendant ammunition magazine pouches fixed on the waist belt.

by uniform or armband. The official version of the armband was supposed to measure 7 cm in width. It had white Latin capital lettering on a black background with a national emblem often—but not always—adjacent to the lettering. The lower and upper edges were in red, thus completing the national colors. The armband had to carry the wording Deutscher Volkssturm Wehrmacht between two *Reichsadler* (emblem featuring an eagle with outstretched wings and a swastika). In practice, because of shortage of everything and since armbands were produced locally, the word *Wehrmacht* was sometimes omitted, and there was considerable design variation: e.g., plain white or other light colors with the wording hastily inscribed by hand or printed in black on various materials including cotton, silk, rayon or even strips of linen tablecloth.

Medical service was regulated by Order No. 393/44 of the Party Chancellery, dated November 9, 1944. Each member of the medical service had to wear the army-style red cross armband on the left upper sleeve.

Equipment was restricted to the most necessary items. At a minimum, the possession of a rucksack or backpack, blanket, field bag, mess kit, canteen, cup, knife, fork and spoon was considered essential.

Each man was issued an identification

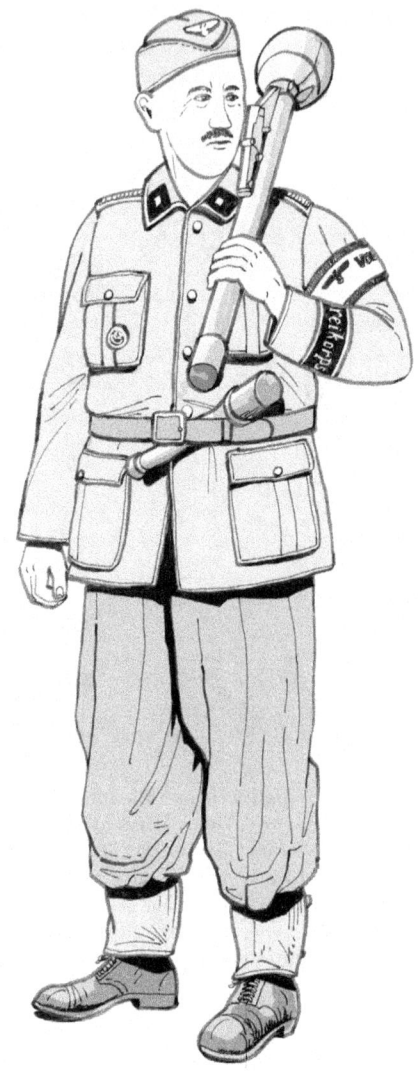

Above: Squad leader, Freikorps Sauerland, 1944; *below:* Volkssturm armband.

disk (made of zinc or aluminum) perforated in its center in order to be separable into two equal halves. If the bearer was killed, one half remained with the body for identification, and the second half provided a record of casualties. Each part of the ID carried the initials DV (Deutscher Volkssturm) and the numbers of battalion and company. The militiamen were also issued a 16-page Volkssturm paybook containing photo and information of the bearer, service and health record, and equipment and weapons issued.

By Order No. 358/44 of the Party Chancellery, dated October 30, 1944, all Volkssturm battalions were issued flags. As these were supplied by the Party, they were of the basic NSDAP style, i.e., a black swastika on a white central disc on a red field. In addition all Volkssturm battalion colors had to bear a black patch on the upper inner corner, displaying the number of the respective *Gau* (region) and the number of the battalion (e.g., 14/115), with letters measuring 6 cm high, done in machine embroidery.

When possible, members of the Volkssturm tank-warning service were issued a gorget bearing the inscription *Panzerwarndienst* stenciled in luminous paint on a metal breastplate similar to that of the Feldgendarmerie (Military Police).

Just like the rest of the uniform, headgear included a wide range of military and civilian items, untidy and incongruously varied in character. Because of the shortages of war, an enormous variety of headdress was worn by the Volkssturm. Anything was possible regarding what sort of uniform and headgear was worn, including visored caps, forage caps, peakless hats, berets, mountains caps, and brimmed hats, worn with or without insignia or cockade. Helmets, when available, also displayed a wide variety including Wehrmacht steel helmets from the M35 to M42 series; vintage World War I helmets like the M1916 and M1918; and helmets from the civilian and civil organizations ranging from the Luftschutz "gladiator style" to fireman and police helmets. In some cases, captured enemy helmets were also issued, the most common being the French crested "Adrian" style and the Soviet M1936 and M1940. Many helmets did not bear any insignia except those previously used by another organization, such as the Luftschutz, fire/police, and Wehrmacht. Some Volkssturm formations had their unit designations painted directly onto their helmets.

Ranks

There was no indication of rank on the shoulder straps. Rank, introduced by Order No. 318/44, was indicated as much as possible by collar patches using a black background and small, square stars identical to those in use by the SS, SA, NSKK, NSFK and other Nazi-affiliated organizations. The collar insignia had the form of a black rhomboid measuring 5 × 6 cm, bearing one to four aluminum-colored pips according to the rank appointment, and sewn onto both corners of the collar of the tunic and greatcoat. For want of collar patches (or collar tabs), the pips were sometimes affixed directly onto the collar in the same pattern as prescribed for the collar patch. The approximate ranks, their equivalents and the known insignia of ranks were as follows, from highest to lowest:

Reichsleiter: Nazi Party Leader
Stabsführer: General
Gauleiter: Lieutenant General
Gaustabsführer: Major General
Kreisleiter: Colonel
Kreisstabsführer: Lieutenant Colonel
Bataillonsführer: Battalion Leader (four pips positioned in each corner)
Kompaniefführer: Company Leader (three diagonally placed pips)
Zugführer: Platoon Leader (two pips diagonally near the forward lower and rear upper corners pips)

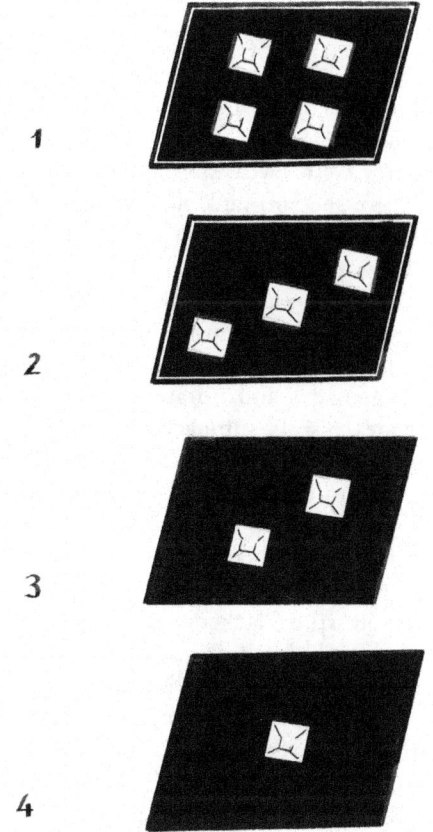

Volkssturm ranks: (1) Bataillonsführer (Battalion Leader); (2) Kompagnieführer (Company Leader); (3) Zugführer (Section Leader); (4) Gruppenführer (Squad leader)

Gruppenführer: Corporal (one centered pip)
Volkssturmmann: Private (no pip)

Medical personnel ranks were established in accordance with Order No. 393/44 dated November 9, 1944 as follows:

Bataillonsarzt (Battalion Medical Officer) including three pips and a caduceus of white metal to the rear of the patches
Sanitätsdienstgrad (Medical Sergeant) with one pip

Weapons

The civilian recruits of non-conscription age constituting the German Volkssturm were poorly trained. Some had World War I experience; others none at all. Training sessions—held on Sundays and during evenings—consisted of little more than drills, marching, and propaganda. Veterans and invalids of the army hastily instructed the men in 48-hour training programs in infantry tactics with special emphasis on defensive and anti-tank close combat. The rifle was the basic weapon and—in theory, at least—members of the Volkssturm were expected to master other weapons. These included the Panzerfaust (anti-tank rocket launcher), the Panzerschreck (bazooka), egg hand grenades and potato-masher hand grenades, pistols, submachine guns, mortars, and machine guns, as well as various sorts of anti-personnel and anti-tank mines and booby traps. In practice, weapons, ammunitions and equipment consisted of whatever could be found in army stores. The Volkssturm lacked communications, vehicles, field kitchens and bakery equipment. It was also drastically short of heavy equipment, fuel and transport, support artillery, armored vehicles and tanks. Even small arms were scarce. There were not enough of them to equip the first and second levies. The third and fourth levies were not issued arms at all, and had to manage with their own personal hunting or sporting rifles when available. The issued weapons—including rifles, pistols and machine guns—came from every country that Germany had defeated and occupied. Besides German-made weapons, there were Italian, Russian, French, Belgian, Dutch, Norwegian, Czech and even British captured guns. There were no fewer than 15 different types of rifles and 10 sorts of machine guns. Finding ammunitions and spare parts for this hodgepodge of arms was hopeless. So desperate were the confusion and shortages that the average ammunition supply of each Volkssturm combatant was less than five rounds per rifle. Food rations were meager, people simply had to make do with what they had, and shortages generated widespread frustration and disgruntlement. Given the lack of means, extensive combat was thus beyond most units' capability. As can be imagined, having to beg, borrow or scavenge for basic sustenance did not enhance fighting spirit and confidence. Civilian clothing, eclectic uniforms, outdated and foreign weapons, improvised and incompetent leadership, and general lack of everything obviously tended to produce low morale.

Worthy of mention is a German submachine gun created in late 1944 in the Primitiv-Waffen-Programm (basic weapon program), an attempt to develop and produce a large number of cheap but effective weapons for the Volkssturm. Designed by a certain engineer Karl Barnitzke of the Gustloffwerke Suhl Company, the gas-delayed blowback Volkssturmgewehr FG 45 was derived from the Mauser 98K. In order to simplify production, the cheap submachine gun was constituted of cheap and poor-quality parts, had a rough finish, and fired the 7.92 mm short cartridge, which had been adopted for the MP 43 assault gun. Ammunitions were contained in the same MP 43 30-round magazine fitted in the bottom of the gun. It was intended for easy manufacturing by non-specialist personnel, in improvised factories, and made from nonessential materials. The Volkssturm submachine gun had a weight of 4.6 kg and an overall length of 885 mm. It was a very basic weapon with no attention to durability, and it was prone to jam if not properly maintained; but it provided plenty of firepower in a relatively compact package. When production started, the war had nearly come to its end. About 10,000 Volkssturm submachine guns were probably made, but the number that reached frontline troops is not known.

With the same idea in mind, several other cheap weapons were designed. The Volkssturmpistole—produced by firms such as Mauser, Gustloff and Walther—was a very cheap pistol, easily assembled and firing 9-mm ammunition. Here again only a few were produced and few ever reached the troops at the front.

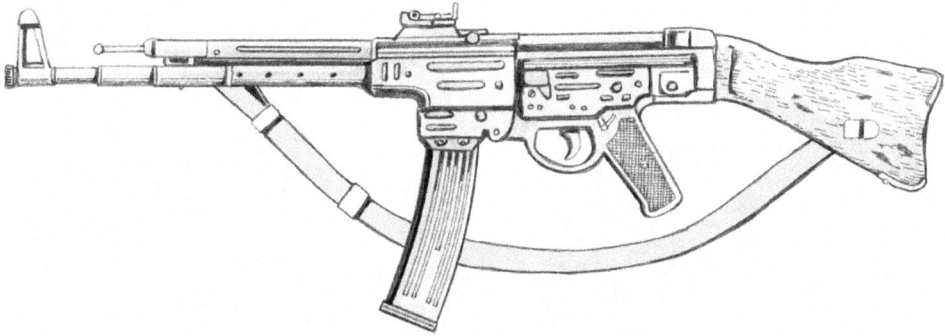

Sturmgewehr, 1944. Also called Maschinepistole 43 (MP 43), this weapon was designed and manufactured by the Erfurter Maschinefabrik Haenel und Suhl (Erma). The MK43, issued in July 1943, was an all-metal weapon (with a wooden butt). It weighed 5.1 kg and the detachable magazine contained 30 rounds. In 1944 the MK 43 was slightly improved and renamed Sturmgewehr (StG 44) or MPi 44; it proved an excellent assault weapon. Intended to replace the obsolete Mauser 98K rifles, about 300,000 MK 43/MPi 44s were issued in the last two years of the war. Most of the production was allocated to the elite Waffen SS. The new rifles came too late to replace other service weapons, and they could not make any impact on the outcome of the war.

The 7.92-mm Volkssturm Gewehr 1 (VG1) was a small carbine made in the last days of World War II. It had a crudely made bolt and stock, and used the magazine of the semi-automatic Model 43 rifle. There was a variant known as Volkssturm Karbine 98 (VK98). The 7.92-mm VK98 used the Model 98 action combined with miscellaneous barrels from old German and foreign Mauser rifles. The stock was very crude and of unfinished, unseasoned wood.

The Machinenpistole 3008 (MP 3008), produced by the ship and aircraft building Company Blohm and Voss, was a cheap copy of the British Sten submachine gun but with a vertical magazine and a pistol grip.

In the last years of the war, the Germans developed small and low-weight anti-tank weapons. The Panzerschreck (literally, tank terror), officially designated 8.8-cm Raketenpanzerbüchse 43 (RPzB 43), often nicknamed *Ofenrohr* (stove pipe), was a copy of the U.S. bazooka. It was operated by two men (a shooter and a loader) and often was fitted with a shield protecting the gunner. It had a simple, smoothbore barrel that electrically fired a 3-kg shaped-charge or HEAT (High Explosive Anti-Tank) warhead placed on a rocket. The projectile could penetrate 10 cm of armor at a range of about 200 m.

The Panzerfaust—issued in late 1943—provided the individual infantryman with the ability to engage tanks at very close range. It was a simple, cheap and effective one-round weapon consisting of a simple tube containing the propelling charge. It weighed about 6 kg (131 lb.) and fired a fin-stabilized 3.5-lb. hollow-charge bomb, which could penetrate 203 mm of armor. After striking its target, the shaped charge in the warhead directed the force of the explosion inwards, punching a concentrated

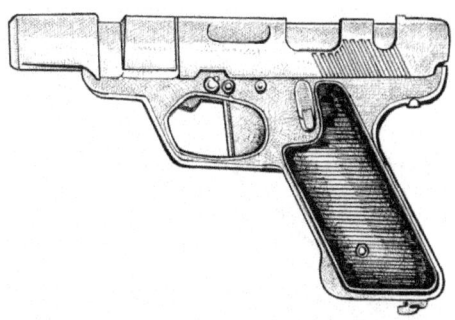

Volkspistole prototype Mauser.

Deutscher Volkssturm

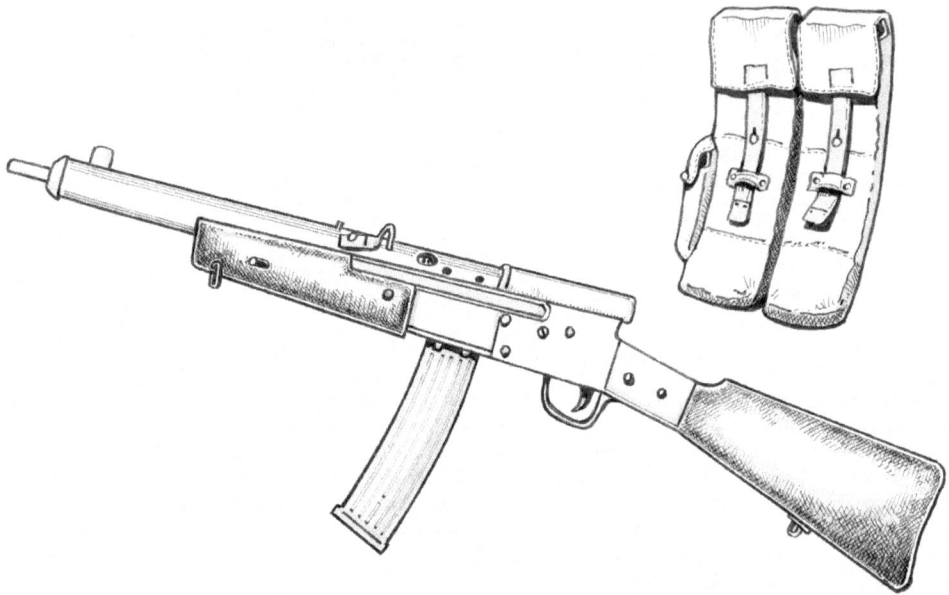

Volkssturm Gewehr 7.92 mm. The 30-round magazines were carried in pouches fixed on the waist belt.

jet of molten metal and gas through the armor plating of the tank. Before, during and after firing the Panzerfaust operator was always in a very dangerous situation. The launching tube carried the words "*Achtung! Feuerstrahl!* (Beware of Jet Flame)" to warn the unwary user of the highly dangerous jet of flame that extended rearwards from the tube when fired. Indeed the Panzerfaust (and the Panzerschreck as well) emitted a back-blast of about 10 m with a dangerous jet of fire and smoke that could inflict seri-

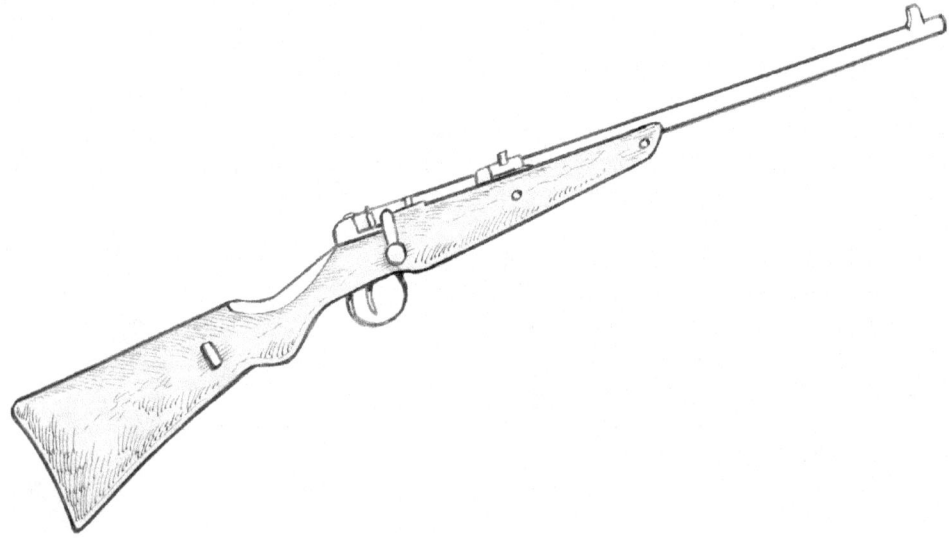

Volkssturm carbine VK98.

Weapons

Panzerschreck. The German anti-tank rocket launcher RPzB 43 had an overall length of 1.4 m, a weight (empty) of 9.5 kg, and a range of 150–200 m.

Panzerfaust.

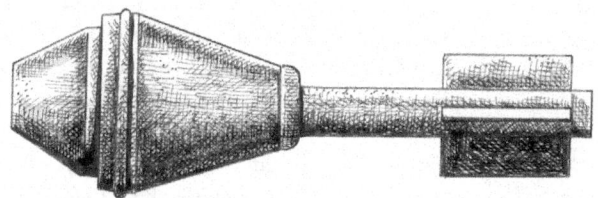

ous injury on anyone in its path. The back-blast flame made it potentially lethal to the operator if he used the weapon from an enclosed space. Moreover, the Panzerfaust's limited range required firers with nerves of steel who had to hide until targets were close and who had to run away quickly after firing. The back-blast flame instantly disclosed the user's position and inevitably invited enemy fire, as parties of infantrymen accompanied armored vehicles. The Panzerfaust existed in several improved versions with ranges of 60 and 100 m.

Another anti-tank weapon was a kind of grenade, known as Panzerwurfmine L. It was a hollow-charge warhead fitted with a finned tail for stabilization and guidance. Weighing 1.35 kg (2.98 lb.), the grenade was relatively small, light, and handy, but it was an uneasy and dangerous weapon, requiring much skill and a lot of courage for use in an effective manner. The user gripped the handle of the grenade, and when ready swung his arm forward and released the handle. As soon as the grenade was in flight four canvas fins unfolded from the handle, and the drogue effect of these fins maintained the warhead in its correct forward position for

Panzerfaust projectile. The Panzerfaust projectile was a shaped charge or HEAT (High Explosive Anti-Tank) warhead, which was stabilized in flight by several folding fins at the rear. By shaping the explosives in an inverted cone, the explosive effect could be channeled into a very small spot on the target. This superheated jet of fire and molten copper then burned and drilled through the armor. While this produced only a small hole in the armor, the fire and copper tended to ignite anything inside the vehicle. Military vehicles were/are stuffed with flammables (people count as flammables) or explosives, so any penetration of the armor by the Panzerfaust projectile had devastating consequences.

maximum effect as it struck. The grenade's range largely depended on the physical strength of the thrower (the range was at maximum 30 m or 32.7 yards), but its hollow charge was very potent. It could knock out even the heaviest Allied tanks. These grenades were therefore not in general use but mainly issued to very specialized close-in tank-destroyer squads.

THE VOLKSSTURM AT WAR

The Volkssturm's mission was manyfold. The men were tasked with guarding key positions, bridges, industrial sites, power plants, public buildings and other essential installations. They played a surveillance role in concentration camps and prisons and—in case the occasion arose—were ordered to crush a feared uprising by the estimated 10 million foreign (slave) workers and prisoners of war who populated Germany against their will. The Volkssturm recruits were to eliminate agents and sabotage groups. In addition, they were to hunt deserters, escapees and shot-down Allied airmen, and manned quiet sectors of the front. They should surround and contain seaborne and airborne landings in their districts. Rapidly, as the front lines collapsed everywhere in early 1945, the Volkssturm recruits were deployed as common infantrymen in combat zones to plug gaps in the front after enemy breakthroughs.

Under almost constant air attack, without any proper weapons and equipment, and lacking food and shelter, most Volkssturm men were used more as a labor force than as a fighting army; they had to build defenses, establish roadblocks, dig trenches and anti-tank ditches, help clear damage, guard stranded trains against pillaging, evacuate usable goods from destroyed buildings, and fight fires. Göbbels' propaganda asserted that the Volkssturm was "unshaken, resolute to fight, and certain of victory." But, of course, the reality was quite different. Intended to mirror King Frederick William III's Prussian Landsehr from 1813 against the French Emperor Napoleon I, the Volkssturm on the whole did not generate a wave of enthusiasm, as discipline was harsh. Orders mandated punishment for desertion, loss of weapons, defeatism, and dereliction of duty. Military and SS police patrols operated behind the front, arresting anyone suspect of leaving his post without orders. Nazi officials and flying SS courts-martial could mete out the death penalty (by hanging or firing squad) for deserters, stragglers, saboteurs, and defeatists.

Although most units had few weapons, little ammunition, no uniforms and poorly trained old men, a few Volkssturm units stood out by being better organized and equipped. The Freikorps Sauerland, for example, was a large Volkssturm unit, and probably one of the most cohesive formations of its type, with its own insignia and attempts at a uniformed look. Freikorps Sauerland was established by order of the NSDAP *Gauleiter* of *Gau* Westphalen-Süd (South Westphalia) and was raised during the autumn of 1944. The name was taken from the nationalist free corps active during the unrest right after World War I. Only volunteers were accepted, still giving the unit a field strength of several battalions, and as Volkssturm units, it was considered "elite." Members of Volkssturm Sauerland were issued field grey or brown uniforms from the Organisation Todt or RAD (National Labor Service) and fitted with standard Volkssturm rank insignia. Special insignia were established for the unit, consisting of a white cuff title bearing the inscription "Freikorps Sauerland," a sleeve patch and a helmet decal. Helmets were usually from the Luftschutz (Air Protection Service) or of the M42 type. Weapons were generally older German and foreign (Czech, Italian, French, etc.) rifles, plus the ubiquitous Panzerfaust and hand grenades.

Not all planned Volkssturm battalions were formed, so disorganized was the administration, so great the lack of means, and so widespread the confusion and chaos in the last months of the war. But at least 700 battalions saw combat action. Grossly outmatched and overwhelmed by Allied firepower, their fate was sealed from the start. An honorable surrender was about the best that Volkssturm troops could hope to achieve. In the west, battalions Essen and Westmark were formed and tried to oppose the western Allies. Battalions drafted from the border districts in the east (e.g., Danzig, East Prussia, Brandenburg, Lower and Upper Silesia, Pomerania, and Wartheland—all facing Russian armies) also fought. Obviously, Volkssturm units fighting the Russians had other motivations than those in the west. Given these variations it is misleading to imagine a typical Volkssturm militiaman. In public all people would express national-socialist fervor and confidence that the war still could be won, but in private a definite sense of doubt and trepidation prevailed, now that the fighting was so close. Kids and grandfathers found themselves facing imminent enemy attacks, and soon they were in the front line, in the middle of the battlefield. Lines of defenses with minefields, anti-tank ditches, trenches, artillery and machine-gun positions protected by earthworks were established. These makeshift fortifications were often erected with the forced contribution of foreign laborers, camp inmates and prisoners. Girls manned anti-aircraft guns, grandfathers fired with their hunting rifles, and youths shot with Panzerfausts on barricades.

All in all, the Volkssturm were an ill-prepared, poorly armed, heterogeneous body composed of old civilian men—some of poor health—with little warlikeness and low pugnacity, and boys with a high morale and great motivation—at least those who belonged to the fanatic Hitler Youth. German soldiers nicknamed Volkssturm men "troops casseroles" because they were composed of "old meat and young vegetables." In Berlin the men of the Volkssturm were called Bismarck Jugend (Bismarck Youth) because of their old age—a reference to Chancellor Otto von Bismarck (1815–1898). Far too young or too old, little trained, with insufficient weapons and ammunition, and lacking coherent command and motivation, the Volkssturm recruits were unable to stop or even slow down the systematic onslaught of the Allied armies. Hitler deceived himself into believing that a drafted civilian force, led by militarily inexperienced Nazi leaders, could save his regime. The improvised militia had very little impact on the outcome of the war, but it pointlessly increased casualties on both sides. Volkssturm guardsmen faced Allied armies that were determined to win the war regardless of the lives that it might cost.

As the Allies—and more particularly the Russians—drove deeper in Germany, many draftees ignored the call-up, and many Volkssturm units deserted or surrendered. There were at times so many of them that the Allied High Command declared them "Disarmed Enemy Personnel" (DEP) in order to avoid processing through the regular prisoner-of-war camps. Many leaders deliberately disbanded their troops and sent them back home, as there was really nothing else they could do.

Some units fought fanatically, though, because they believed Göbbels' propaganda that the Russians would kill them all and their families anyway. Sometimes fanaticism bordering on madness was driven by fear and despair. Others units fought hopeless rear-guard combats in improvised *Festungen* (fortresses) because they were obliged to do so by the SS. Indeed, marauding gangs of SS men and Nazi policemen, roving the country in search of deserters, took justice into their own hands. They halted anyone and checked identities. As already said, any man suspected of leaving his unit was summarily shot or was hung from the nearest tree or streetlight post as an example to others. The determination of certain militia-

Badge of Volkssturm Sauerland.

men of the Volkssturm to fight until the end was strengthened by the knowledge that any premature surrender would be treated as desertion. When the names of deserters were known and ascertained, these were made known to the civilian population at home, and their next of kin were looked upon as enemies of the German people. Inexorably caught between the devil and the deep blue sea, many people perished on and off the front lines.

Aftermath

The total of the Volkssturm casualties was never precisely known. About 175,000 recruits were listed as missing in action after the war. In addition, the Russians acted against the hated Germans with a particular savagery. Many Volkssturm men caught with arms were summarily executed as illegal guerrillas by trigger-happy Soviet troops. The Russians were vengeance-minded; they were determined to repay the German population with the same atrocities the German soldiers had inflicted on the Russian people. As they looted and raped on large scale, many people—especially women—committed suicide. Another result of the terrifying fear of the Soviet troops' advance was a massive evacuation of some three million German civilians from the eastern provinces. Heading westwards along congested, snow-swept roads harassed by Polish guerrilla fighters, the general evacuation was escorted by remnants of Volkssturm recruits and other formations of the collapsing German army. Many died from exposure, hunger, exhaustion and combat.

In March 1945, Hitler had issued the Nerobefehl ("Nero Order," named after the infamous Roman emperor, AD 54–68). This decree commanded a scorched-earth policy that would completely destroy Germany's industrial infrastructure, all electrical plants, all coal mines, all water and sewage plants, bridges, factories and rolling stock. The orders fortunately were not totally obeyed or universally carried out due to the opposition of several leaders, among them Albert Speer, but much destruction was deliberately effected. By that time Germany was in total chaos.

The Volkssturm and the Nerobefehl showed Hitler's determination to fight to the last man. It was an ultimate crime, a final expression of complete despair, the *Götterdämmerung* (twilight of the gods), the total collapse of the Third Reich, which sent to death the entire German people. If Hitler was to be defeated, he would fight for every house, and nothing would be left. In Hitler's mind a great people must die heroically; that was a historic necessity. So the ordinary men, women and children of Germany had to die for failing to win his war, and they could expect no sympathy from their Führer. As Hitler saw it, it was they who had let him down by failing to overcome. Hitler had once declared: "If the German people are incapable of winning the war, then they can rot!" He remained true to his megalomaniacal original program: *Weltmacht oder Niedergang* (world power or ruin). In his sick and ruthless *Weltanschauung* (view of the world), he considered that if Germany lost the war, that would mean that the nation had not stood the test of strength, and in that case the whole German people deserved no better than to be totally destroyed.

Service in the Volkssturm did not generate the camaraderie that was relived, renewed and celebrated after the war in German veterans' associations. The Volkssturm had had too brief an existence to forge military traditions; it had extremely poor fighting records and members of relatively advanced age. Created by the Nazis in a moment of chaos, it was ultimately an army that most militiamen who had served in it simply wanted to forget.

Chapter 5

Other Military Affiliated Units

As a conclusion to this work about the four official Wehrmachtgefolge, it might be interesting to have a look at other Nazi-affiliated organizations.

As we have seen, the topic of German World War II auxiliary forces is a complex one. There were numerous, sometimes overlapping, organizations that were auxiliaries to the regular armed forces. In fact, the whole Nazi system was—from the start—a preparation to war. And consequently, not only the four official Wehrmachtsgefolge and the overtly Nazi fronts and leagues but also every state, private or civilian association, agency, formation, club, organization, group or movement was auxiliary to the armed forces and serving a more or less important support role—directly or indirectly. Virtually all segments of German society were enlisted into highly structured organizations of common interest. The leaders of Nazi Germany created a large number of different organizations for the purpose of helping them stay in power. Although membership in the Nazi Party was never mandatory or universal, nearly everyone belonged to some leagues, fronts or formations that were connected to the NSDAP. Nobody could exist during Hitler's regime in Nazi Germany without recognizing that politics and control had permeated almost every aspect of everyday life. The Nazi leadership rearmed and strengthened the national military, but at the same time set up an extensive state security and police apparatus under the control of the SS and created their own personal party army, the Waffen SS. Through the staffing of most government positions with Nazi Party members, by 1935 the German national government and the Nazi Party had become virtually one and the same. This process started after the seizure of power in 1933 and was practically completed by 1938 through the policy of *Gleichschaltung*—a series of measures, decrees, and laws for the coordination and unification of the Reich resulting in a highly authoritarian, one-party state. By then local and regional state governments had lost all legislative power. All official state organizations were coordinated and Nazified; all senior and junior civil servants were selected along racial lines and got instructions and directives from superiors. These orders included, notably, mentally and practically preparing the population for war; fostering membership in the German *Volksgemeinschaft* (community); controlling political opinions, behavior, discipline, and willingness to collaborate with Nazi authorities; designating "enemies of the German people," notably the Democrats, Socialists, and Communists, and the Jewish community; and collaborating with the police for the repression of these enemies.

Because of their anti–Semitism and racism, the Nazis could not manage or did not want to bring scientists, military generals and businessmen together in a coordinated war effort, and they suffered greatly because of it. Between 1933 and 1939 many great names in German art and science fled the country or were dismissed or imprisoned. There is no doubt now that a Nazi regime without racism and anti–Semitism would have produced long-distance rockets with nuclear warheads and probably would have won World War II. Instead of husbanding their scientists and businessmen, the Nazi German authorities conscripted them into the army, along with manual workers and clerks. German scientists enjoyed a higher status than their British counterparts, but they lacked a central coordinating body that would have allowed them to bring science from laboratory to battlefield at great speed. Between 1939 and 1945, the Nazi regime did little or nothing to revise the role of science in the war. In 1940 the German General Staff and Hitler clung to the tactics of *Blitzkrieg* (short and decisive battle). So there were no long-term war plans, and it was decreed that no research or development should be pursued unless it promised substantial military results within four months.

Members of Nazi-affiliated organizations wore uniforms and insignia. The Nazis used eye-catching symbols, uniforms and regalia in variety and volume as trappings of power. The inevitable Nazi eagle-and-swastika emblem was displayed everywhere: carved in stone on buildings; printed on posters, official papers and forms, certificates and diplomas, and postage stamps; but also worn in various designs and materials on tunics, badges, brooches, pins, belt buckles, daggers, decorations, vehicles and soon to remind the public of the omnipresence of the Party. Nazi regalia presented a somewhat junky character. They were made of relative cheap materials such as plastic, nonprecious metals, porcelain, and leather. On the whole badges and insignia were quite cheap and sold for a few *pfennigs*, but they helped spread a strong symbolism and pride throughout the people. In a society in which a lot of people wore a uniform with insignia and medals, and in which everyone had to work for what the Nazis regarded as the "common good," the man or woman in civilian dress was often suspected as a slacker.

Detailed plans existed for the rapid mobilization of all the Nazi organizations in case of the actual invasion of, or immediate military threat to, any part of Germany proper. Elaborate administrative preparations had been made for their operational control and chain of command in case of emergency. This arrangement for the emergency defense of German soil was in sharp contrast to the established prerogatives of the army, whose members were officially the only bearers of arms, and which had to share its authority and defensive role with its principal rivals: the SS and the NSDAP.

Many overtly Nazi fronts, organizations, leagues and associations existed with the aim of favoring or enforcing strict obedience to Nazi authority at the expense of personal freedom. To name, list or discuss all would be prohibitive, and only some of them will be briefly surveyed here below as a conclusion to this book.

STURM ABTEILUNG (SA)

The Sturm Abteilung of the NSDAP (SA, assault detachments of the Nazi Party) were created in August 1920. They were strongly armed squads intended to protect Nazi meetings, to provoke disturbance, to break up other parties' meetings, and to beat up political opponents as part of a deliberate campaign of intimidation. After 1925 the name *Braunhemden* (Brownshirts) was also given because of the color of their uniforms. Under the leadership of Hitler's close political associate Ernst Röhm (1887–1934), the militia grew to become a huge, ruthless and radical paramilitary force. Although it mutinied on several occasions

Other Military Affiliated Units

Left: SA *Scharführer*, 1933. The typical SA uniform included a brown kepi; a two-pocketed brown shirt (actually a sort of short blouse with a shirt underneath); a brown tie; a swastika armband; a cross-belt (across the shoulder) and a waist belt with various forms of buckles; brown or black breeches; and black riding leather boots. Top left: emblem of the SA; *right:* SA *Gruppenführer*, 1933. Senior SA officers carried a dagger bearing the motto *"Unserer Führer—Unser Glaube* [Our Leader—Our Faith]" or the slogan *"Alles für Deutschland* [Everything for Germany]." SA men who had joined before December 31, 1931, personally received from Ernst Röhm daggers inscribed *"In herzlicher Freundschaft* [In heart felt friendship]." After Röhm's elimination in June 1934, those daggers were either withdrawn or had their inscription erased.

in the early 1930s, the SA was one of the instruments that brought Hitler to power in Germany in January 1933. After the seizure of power, the SA grew tremendously because of opening widely to all people who wanted to join—including the unemployed but also thugs and social outcasts. For a while members had the status of Hilfspolizei (Auxiliary Police). Ruthlessly they hunted, arrested and interrogated all suspects and supposed or real "enemies" of the newly established Nazi regime. These enemies included Communists, Socialists, trade-union leaders, Jews, Democrats, Catholics, Protestants, Conservatives, pacifists, foreigners, Gypsies, Jehovah's Witnesses, Freemasons, homosexuals, modern artists and even common citizens and dissident Nazis who knew too much or who preached a diverging gospel. This was the first step of *Gleichschaltung*, the uniformization, total nazification and subordination of the German people to the now all-powerful NSDAP. Once the Nazi dictatorship had been established, the usefulness of the SA was limited to Germany's new leadership. By early 1934, it became clear that the turbulent SA thugs were a terror for the German population, a disturbance for civil and public order, a cumbersome ally and an embarrassment for the NSDAP, and also a superfluous financial burden. The ambitious Ernst Röhm—who had always demanded the primacy of the SA soldier above the NSDAP politician—called in harsh words for a "Second Revolution." In fact, Röhm wanted to replace the traditional national army with his SA men, with himself as commander in chief. But he had become an object of disgust to the bourgeois order, a threat to Hitler's own power, and a challenge to the *Reichswehr*. In the struggle for power, Röhm and the SA leadership became increasingly isolated by their more conservative rivals: Hitler and the Nazi Party, the fast-growing SS, the army generals and the German public at large. After a period of brooding and hesitation, Hitler solved the crisis by ordering a bloody purge (known as the Night of the Long Knives) at the end of June 1934, during which Ernst Röhm, a part of the SA top leadership, and several "annoying" personalities not involved with the SA were executed without trial. The purge of the SA was carried out by Himmler's SS, and in its wake the SS gained considerable power. After the Night of Long Knives, the SA was not disbanded, and in Röhm's place Hitler appointed the loyal and colorless SA *Obergruppenführer* Viktor Lutze (1890–1943). The day of the radical political bullies had ended with the death of Ernst Röhm and the purging of the radical elements. The SA corps was disarmed, completely reorganized, totally deprived of political power, relegated to a backseat role, assigned mundane tasks, and turned into a veterans' association in charge of the pre-military training units of the SA Reserve and the boys of the

After the purge of June 1934, the SA lost all power. Here a member of the SA Reserve is collecting in the street for the Winterhilfswerk (WHW), the official Winter Relief Organization.

Hitler Jugend (Hitler Youth). When World War II broke out, the strength of the SA was greatly depleted, as many of its younger and fitter members were drafted into the Wehrmacht. After the death of Viktor Lutze in 1943, the SA staff chief was *Obergruppenführer* Wilhelm Schepmann (1894–1970). By then the German SA was composed in majority of aged or partially disabled men or those deemed unfit for regular military service. Some served in the

German army reserve as guards for prisoners of war, and in civil defense units such as firemen, auxiliary policemen, and air raid precaution wardens.

WAFFEN SS

The Waffen SS were combat formations of the Schutz-Staffeln of the NSDAP (SS, protection squads of the Nazi Party). Tactically they were related to the Wehrmacht, but they were directly placed under the command of Himmler and Hitler. They represented a small but important armed force serving Germany's war efforts on all fronts.

Originating from a tiny group of highly selected and loyal bodyguards intended to protect Adolf Hitler, and originally a part of the SA, the SS became a huge organization within the Nazi Party, a private army within the Wehrmacht and a state within the state. Headed by SS *Reichsführer* Heinrich Himmler (1900–1945), the SS had numerous tasks: maintenance of the Nazi order; control of the German population; internal and foreign intelligence; and elimination of enemies of the Reich in the concentration camps, just to name a few. Another of Himmler's ambitions was to become a military commander. Indeed, once an army cadet but too young to take part in World War I (he was born in 1900), Himmler had always secretly longed to be at the head of a fighting formation. With Hitler's backing, Himmler developed his own permanent SS armed force, which was organized after 1935. The military SS were highly selected, militarily trained and organized. They wore uniforms and lived in barracks. Called originally Verfügungstruppen (SS-VT, Reserve or Task Troops), the corps grew to a large army during World War II, with only a small part being an elite force. The idea of the Waffen SS had a part of its military origins in the World War I Stroßtruppen (Assault Troops). These were small infantry units, trained to attack independently, in which the typical rigid Pruss-

Early SS man c. 1925. The Schutz Staffeln (SS, Protection Squads), like no other institution in the Third Reich, represented the arrogance of Nazi ideology and the criminal nature of Hitler's regime. The origin of the SS was a small squad created in 1923 as a personal group of bodyguards to Hitler called Stoßtrupp Adolf Hitler. In early 1925, the unit was reshaped and took the name Schutzkommando, then Sturmstaffeln, and finally in November 1925 Schutz-Staffeln (SS in short), under which it became infamous.

ian discipline was transformed into a closer comradeship between officers and men based on mutual trust. Politically, during the immediate post–World War I years, the Freikorps (free corps) were also fundamental to the future development of the Waffen SS. These were units of demobilized servicemen who remained loyal to the authoritarian creed of the imperial army. Nationalist, rightist, fanatic and revanchist, the free corps expected continuing military privileges and a voice in national affairs. Both Stoßtruppen and Freikorps put the emphasis on warrior qualities, high motivation and esprit de corps. It was those qualities and that spirit that were intended to reappear in a new form and along strict Nazi racial lines within the Waffen SS. Himmler was determined that the SS military branch should become the nucleus of a postwar German national police and army service. In April 1936, the SS-Verfügungstruppe and the SS-Totenkopfverbände (Death's Heads, concentration camp guards) were declared organizations in service of the State, and officially financed by the budget of the Ministry of the Interior. In October 1936 an inspectorate was set up and placed under direction of retired lieutenant general Paul

Left: SS Sturmmann Totenkopf unit. SS-Totenkopfverbände (SS-TV, Death's Head units) were composed of professional, armed, uniformed SS men living in barracks. They had rudimentary military training and were intended to form *Bereitschaftstruppen* (special political mobile troops) stationed at key points across the Reich to protect by arms the Nazi regime from an internal revolt. As no such threat appeared, the anti-insurrection SS-TV force was assigned to run prisons and concentration camps set up by Hermann Göring in 1933 to house and "re-educate" all political opponents. In early 1940 a number of Death's Head formations were drafted to form a Waffen SS unit called the 3rd SS Panzerdivision Totenkopf; *far left:* the death's head (*Totenkopf*), which was one the SS symbols, worn at the front of headgear; *right:* Waffen SS *Unterscharführer*. The depicted Waffen SS sergeant wears the standard German army uniform. Distinctive insignia are the collar patches (SS badge on right, and rank on left); the Nazi eagle-and-swastika worn on the upper left arm (instead of on the right breast pocket, as by the army); the waist belt with buckle carrying the SS motto "My Honor Is Loyalty"; the cuff-title sewn on the lower left sleeve, indicating unit.

Hausser (1880–1972), who became a key figure in the development and growth of SS troops. Increasing international tension and German involvement in Franco's civil war in Spain gave impetus to the preparation of the SS-VT. From the start, the SS-VT, with their vague, illegal status, were intended to be the Führer's personal, flexible and reliable instrument for special political tasks. This applied to the camp guards, SS-Totenkopfverbände, too. Both SS armed corps were expressions of Himmler's paranoia and Hitler's obsessive fear of internal plots supposedly led by Jews, communists, monarchists, Free Masons, Catholics and reactionary Prussian officers.

The Heer (German regular ground army) rejected, for obvious reasons, the idea of an SS army outside its control. Thus, the prewar years were dominated by a perpetual struggle between the army and the SS on the strength, organization and function of the SS-VT. One of the army's points of opposition towards the SS-VT was based on its potential drain on the manpower pool. Between 1935 and 1938, the cunning and hypocritical Hitler could not afford to alienate the army. Owing to various compromises, the army was successful in limiting the growth of the armed SS. Only a small share of German conscripts and officers were allocated to it. Until the eve of the war, its overall strength, including the *Totenkopf* concentration camp guards, did not exceed 23,000 men.

In 1938, owing to lies, manipulation and forged documents creating scandals, Hitler purged the army's high command by dismissing generals Blomberg, von Fritsch and several others. The dictator abolished the Ministry of Defense, created the Oberkommando der Wehrmacht (OKW, High Command of Armed Forces) and maneuvered himself to the position of Führer und Oberster Befehlhaber der Wehrmacht (leader and supreme commander of the defense forces). Hitler assumed personal military command and managed to impose the SS-VT. When World War II started, Himmler wanted his small, private army to take part in the combat. The SS Verfügungstruppen were reinforced with regiments of Totenkopfverbände and drafted members of the Ordnungpolizei (uniformed police). In July 1940, Himmler's forces were renamed Waffen SS (literally, armed SS). Owing to potentialities and the action of the Allgemeine SS (the nonpermanent branch of the organization), by exploiting the law to suit himself, and by ruthlessly confiscating Jewish property, Himmler could swell his army, recruit Germanic foreigners, and find funds to equip his private armed forces. Although the regular Heer watched the SS with dislike and distrust, and although the generals tried to obstruct him, the Reichsführer Himmler managed to constitute a formidable elite force. The Waffen SS, organized by General Inspector Paul Hausser, was divided into units similar in strength to those of the Heer (German ground army). However, Himmler and Hausser made successful use of popular historical memories by giving each SS unit an identifiable title alluding to an important episode or prestigious hero of Germany's past. Reflecting Himmler's Ger-

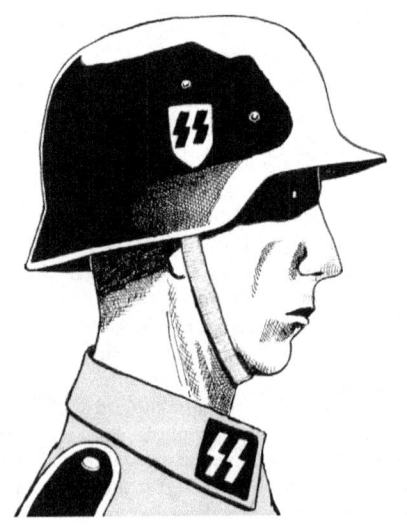

Waffen SS helmet.

manic paganism and mystical urges, every unit was identifiable by a badge on a shield carrying a strong meaning: runes, medieval heraldry and national symbols. A newly formed SS division was "christened" by ceremonials in some style. The SS's device was "*Meine Ehre heißt Treue* (My Honor Is Loyalty)." The SS army was militarily commanded by Hitler himself and administered by Himmler, who carried the official title of Reichführer der SS und Chef der Deutschen Polizei. During the campaigns of 1939–1940, the Waffen SS proved that it could fight as well as the German army, though many still harbored grave suspicions and resentment concerning the political nature of Himmler's troops. Officers enlisted in the Waffen SS for 25 years, NCOs served for 12 years and privates for 4. The Waffen SS authorities were very choosy about membership—at least originally. The emphasis was on physical aptitude, fitness, warlikeness, military skills, toughness, endurability and pugnacity, but also on race. The Waffen SS was intended to reflect the "master race." In the beginning, the Reichsführer insisted that the candidates were to be racially pure—that is, of good German stock—and able to prove their Germanic roots with "untainted" descent (non–Jewish, non–Slavic) back to 1800 (officers back to 1750). This nonsense about race was relaxed during the war when the Waffen SS needed more fighting men. Most of the elitist demands were abandoned when World War II begun. After 1940, in order to increase the number of combatants, the Waffen SS opened its ranks to *Volksdeutsche*. These "racial" Germans from northern European Germanic lands (Scandinavia, Holland, Flanders) were considered to be people of "similar blood." Where power was at stake, even a perfectionist like Himmler could abandon racial quality for quantity. After 1942, the Waffen SS was open to "impure" volunteers from Western and Eastern Europe (France, Wallony and others). During the winter of 1943–1944,

Waffen SS camouflage smock. As far as uniform was concerned, Waffen SS soldiers were prototypes of modern infantrymen, wearing an effective camouflage smock. Called a *Tarnjacke*, it combined various colors such as brown, green, red, pink, yellow, grey and black printed in various irregular patterns. Camouflaged uniforms were rather expensive and a few were issued to the army, but most of them were allocated with priority to elite troops such paratroopers and Waffen SS. The special Waffen SS combat smock had elasticated cuffs, was tunic length, collarless and had a lace-up neck. It was worn over the standard tunic and had slits to give access to the tunic pockets. The *Tarnjacke* existed in several variants, some reversible with a mottled pattern on one side for autumn wear, and a different pattern featuring mainly green and brown on the other side for spring and summer wear. The depicted Waffen SS private is armed with a pistol in a leather holster and an MG 34 machine gun. Note the use of *Gamasche* (gaiters) made of canvas; these were worn more and more frequently by German troops in place of marching boots after 1943 when leather became scarce.

the Waffen SS underwent its most profound mutation. It became a pan–European, international army. Some physical demands were lowered and all racial selection criteria were abandoned for the sake of growth. In order to compensate for the dramatic casualties suffered in the German-Soviet war, through 1945, the recruitment (and rounding up) was progressively opened to other racial groups. Even Russian mercenaries, Baltic nationals, Slave *Untermenschen* ("subhumans") from Central Europe and Muslims from the Balkans were welcome.

In 1943, the first SS *Panzerdivisionen* (armored divisions) were created and rapidly proved hard nuts to crack for the Allies. The Waffen SS was virtually a private army with its own staff (SS-Führungs Hauptamt), and by the end of the war the corps counted some 38 divisions (infantry, mountain, cavalry and armored), which were organized separately from the regular Heer and had their own badges of ranks, flags, insignia and emblems.

The main emblems of the SS were the double-lightning S rune (worn on collar patch) and the *Totenkopf* (death's head), worn on headgear. Weapons, equipment, vehicles, armored cars, tanks and uniforms were similar to those of the regular German army, but the most distinctive item of uniform worn

Untersturmführer (first lieutenant), 7th Division Prinz Eugen. The 7th Freiwilligen Gebirgsdivision Prinz Eugen (Mountain Division of Volunteers) was raised in late 1941. Its designation referred to Franz Eugen, prince of Savoy-Carignan (1663–1736), who successfully led the Austrian army against the Turks and against the French king Louis XIV. Its insignia (top right) displayed the Proto-Germanic rune of Odal (letter O, and symbol of inherited state). The Leontopodium Alpinum, better known as Edelweiss—a rare white flower found high in the Alps Mountains (middle right)—was the symbolic insignia designating a mountain unit. The 7th Waffen SS division was composed of *Volksdeutsche* ("racial" German minorities living beyond the borders of the Reich), mainly voluntarily recruited, some were rounded up in Transylvania, Hungary and pro–Nazi Croatia. Commanded by SS Obergruppenführer Arthur Phlebs between January 1942 and May 1943 and later by SS Obersturmbannführer Otto Kumm, the counterinsurgency mountain unit was especially trained to combat Tito's partisans in Yugoslavia, Bosnia and Montenegro. The division is infamous for its cruelty and the massive atrocities committed against civilians in Montenegro.

by the Waffen SS was the *Tarnjacke* (camouflage smock) with matching camouflage helmet cover. By the later stage of the war, a part of the regular army came to admire Himmler's warriors. The top fighting Waffen SS soldiers gained a reputation for fanatical bravery, dependability and steadfastness in the worst conditions. They were sometimes the only troops who could be relied upon to fight on while those around them retreated. In the last two years of World War II, Himmler's private army offered a component that the generals of the regular national Heer simply could not refuse. The Waffen SS had seven armored divisions: the 1st SS Panzerdivision Leibstandarte Adolf Hitler, the 2nd SS Panzerdivision Das Reich, the 3rd SS Panzerdivision Totenkopf, the 5th SS Panzerdivision Wiking, the 9th SS Panzerdivision Hohenstaufen, the 10th SS Panzerdivision Frundsberg and the 12th SS Panzerdivision Hitler Jugend. These were actually the elite units, which constituted a fearsome fighting machine, known as "Hitler's fire brigade," rushing from menaced fronts to collapsing points all across Europe and Russia to restore apparently impossible situations and to hold back the overwhelming weight of numbers on the Allied side.

After the attempt on Hitler's life on July 20, 1944, Himmler's power was paradoxically strengthened; in fact, the SS Reichsfürer had failed to fulfill his task, this being from the start Hitler's protection and security. Nonetheless, the German army was obliged to accept him as commander-in-chief, and all armed forces came under direct control of the SS. Despite Himmler's total lack of military experience, he was then given command of the army group Vistula. While head of NSDAP Martin Bormann constituted the Volkssturm (people's home guard), the Reichsführer SS hastily created the Volksgrenadierdivisionen (people's grenadier divisions). New Waffen SS divisions—both German and foreign—were raised by harsh methods and large-scale conscription, but most Waffen SS units created in 1944 and 1945 were far under regular strength, poorly armed, badly trained and mediocrely led. In the end, Heinrich Himmler was such a bad military commander that Hitler dismissed him on March 13, 1945.

During the last months of the war, even the best Waffen SS divisions were no longer the mighty formations of the previous years. Combat attrition had cost them many of their best troops and weapons. The quality of the replacements they received could not hope to match that of those they had lost. In strict military terms the value of the foreign Waffen SS divisions was generally poor because of degeneration due to atrocious civil wars and unproductive combats for local issues. Many Waffen SS divisions raised with foreigners in 1944–1945 were failures and generally despised by the original German Waffen SS formations. Only a suicidal spirit kept a few Waffen SS units as effective and tough fighting machines until the very last weeks of the war. In many occasions, they succeeded in stemming the Allies and inflicted enormous casualties. Enthusiasm and bravery counted for little against the well-equipped and highly professional Allied forces. Finally the frequency and the intensity of the Allied large-scale offensives on all fronts gave the exhausted and decimated Waffen SS men no chance. They were driven back inexorably, and ultimately, they were outnumbered and defeated. In the end fanaticism proved unable to prevent the final defeat of Hitler's regime.

One cannot leave the subject of Waffen SS without noting, however briefly, the record of atrocities committed by Himmler's private army. The Waffen SS built up a reputation of hard fighting soldiers, but they were not Soldaten wie anderen (ordinary combatants), or—as has been sometimes suggested—merely a fourth regular service of the Wehrmacht. The heavy SS military training and the indoctrination in

Nazi ideology produced a new type of warrior rarely equaled in the history of warfare. The Waffen SS were brainwashed to feel superior, always to obey, to kill and to die without ever asking a question. The indoctrination implanted new norms of behavior into the SS that robbed them of their powers of moral judgment and replaced them with coldheartedness, cruelty, impatience and an excessive, narrow group egoism. They were—on the whole—ultra-Nazi, fanatical mercenaries and ruthless adventurers who committed numerous atrocities and war crimes, both on and off the battlefield. The numbers of razed villages, massacred civilians, exterminated Jews, prisoners of war shot in cold blood, and other crimes were unspeakable. The Waffen SS were the standard-bearers of Nazism and, not without reason and evidence, the "elite corps" of the Third Reich was declared a criminal organization by the tribunal of Nuremberg in 1946.

After the war Paul Hausser became a member of the HIAG Hilfsgemeinschaft auf Gegenseitigkeit der Angehörigen der ehemaligen Waffen-SS (Mutual Help Association of Former Waffen-SS Members)—an organization founded in 1951, which sought to rehabilitate the reputation and legal status of former Waffen-SS members.

HITLER YOUTH (HJ)

The Hitler Jugend (HJ, Hitler Youth) was originally the junior branch of the SA. The first NSDAP-related organization of German youth was the Jugendbund der NSDAP (League of the Youth of the National Socialist Party), which was announced on March 8, 1922. Gustav Adolf Lenk (born in October 1903 in Munich) was promoted leader of the Jugendbund at age 19. In the beginning the Hitler Youth was to be disguised much as the SA had been—as an organization of sport and physical fitness clubs so that the still-prevailing Versailles conditions limiting the size of the German army could be given a

HJ winter uniform. The Hitler Youth winter uniform was dark blue and included a single-button cap or a peakless forage cap; a warm two-pocket pullover field blouse; and thick, baggy trousers. The waist belt buckle bears the motto "*Blut und Ehre* [Blood and Honor]," and on the left arm are displayed the triangular black region badge and the white and red HJ armband. The rank of *Scharführer* (corporal) is indicated by two square silver stars on the black shoulder strap.

reverential nod. The youth organization—actually a breeding ground for young Nazi activists—was divided into the Jungmannschaften (boys 14–16 years old) and the Jungsturm Adolf Hitler (16–18 years old). It fell under the command of the chief of the SA and was headed by Lieutenant Johann Ulrich Klintzsch, and the 300 youth

Left to right: The insignia of the Junior Hitler Youth (10–14 years) was the rune letter S in a black oval cloth badge, worn on the upper left arm with the black triangular region badge; Pimpf Deutsches Jungvolk (Junior Hitler Youth), who wore a uniform composed of a peakless forage cap, a brown shirt with a black neckerchief, leather waist and shoulder belts, black corduroy shorts, white or gray stockings, and heavy marching shoes; The Hitler Youth knife (with its leather sheath) with the motto "*Blut und Ehre* [Blood and Honor]" on the blade; BdM girl wearing a sport suit, consisting of a white singlet with the HJ diamond-shaped emblem on the breast, black shorts and light shoes.

members wore uniforms similar to those of the SA. In April 1926, the very descriptive name Hitler Jugend (HJ, Hitler Youth) appeared for the first time, revealing the personality cult devoted to Adolf Hitler. On July 3–4, 1926, at the Reichparteitag (Nazi Party Day) held in Weimar, the Hitler Youth was formally established with Kurt Gruber as Reichsführer of the HJ (leader of the Hitler Youth). Gruber was replaced by Baldur von Schirach (1907–1974) in October 1931. The Hitler Youth was reorganized by von Schirach and then included four main sections. For the boys aged 10 to 14 there was the Deutscher Jungvolk (DJ, German Youth), and for boys 14–18 the Hitler Youth proper (HJ). The girls were divided into the Jungmädelbund (JMB, League of Young Girls) ages 10 to 14, and the Bund deutscher Mädel (BdM, German Girls League), ages 14 to 18. In May 1932, the four branches of the Hitler Youth were made totally independent from the SA administration. Under the dynamic direction of Baldur von Schirach the HJ became a powerful organization of the NSDAP. After 1933, it developed into one of the firmest structures of the Nazi state with two

Other Military Affiliated Units

Girl of the HJ-BdM. The uniform included a black cap or beret; a white shirt with a black tie or black neckerchief; a short, brown, four-pocketed tunic; and a black or dark blue skirt. The black triangular badge indicating the region and the red and white diamond-shaped Hitler Youth insignia were worn on the upper left sleeve.

main aims: the boys had to prepare for war and the girls had to be future mothers. In 1943 a special Waffen SS division was formed with HJ boys aged 16 to 17, the 12th Panzerdivision Hitlerjugend, which saw action during the Battle of Normandy in July 1944.

Nazi Flyers Corps (NSFK)

According to the stipulations of the Treaty of Versailles in 1919, Germany had no right to possess an air force, but in the 1920s a highly centralized civilian aviation organization appeared in the framework of the commercial airline company Lufthansa. At the same time, flying, gliding and ballooning were popular activities developed and performed in private clubs and in the Deutsche Luftsportverband (DLV, German Air Sport League). The DLV was created by the Nazis in March 1933. Its chairman was Hermann Göring and its vice-chairman was the SA chief Ernst Röhm. Its purpose was to channel and develop air-mindedness in Germany, and also to rally World War I veteran pilots and aces for propaganda aims. Heroes such as Bruno Lörzer and Ernst Udet joined and played a significant role in the creation of the Luftwaffe in 1935.

The organization soon grew in size and purpose as the Nazis incorporated all existing civilian aviation clubs. The DLV continued to exist after the Luftwaffe was officially founded in 1935 but to a much smaller degree. Many DLV members transferred to the regular military air force, and as many of these prior members were also staunch Nazi Party members, this gave the new Luftwaffe a strong Nazi ideological base, in contrast to the other branches of the German army, which mostly comprised "Old Guard" officers from the German traditional aristocracy and conservative bourgeoisie.

In April 1937 the DLV was dissolved and replaced with a new organization named the Nationalsozialistisch Fliegerkorps

Emblem of the DLV.

Nazi Flyers Corps (NSFK)

(NSFK, Nazi Flyers Corps). Although considered an independent Nazi Party organization (like the NSKK and the RAD), the NSFK was a state-registered association subordinate to the *Reichsluftfahrtministerium* (RLM, Reich Minister for Air Travel) established in April 1933 and headed by Reichsmarschall (Commander-in-Chief) Hermann Göring (1893–1946), before the renunciation of the Treaty of Versailles and the unveiling of the Luftwaffe. The RLM was a ministry tasked with the development and production of aircraft. It had a test site at Rechlin, a municipality in Mecklenburg, Western Pomerania, Germany. The town's airport had a long history and was the Luftwaffe's main testing ground for new aircraft designs during the period of the Third Reich.

That the NSFK was made subordinate to the RLM was ordered by Hermann Göring, who wanted all services and organizations connected with the air force to be under his leadership. As a result the NSFK was not commanded by a high-ranking Nazi official but by a senior Luftwaffe officer who carried the title of NSF-Korpsführer, and who was directly responsible to Hermann Göring: General der Flieger Friedrich Christiansen (1879–1972), until June 1943, when he was appointed Wehrmachtsbefehlshaber in den Niederlanden (Supreme Commander of the Wehrmacht/Governor in the Netherlands). Then Christiansen was replaced with the veteran and retired Luftwaffe Generaloberst Alfred Keller (1882–1974), who remained NSF-Korpsführer until the German surrender in May 1945. Göring's control over all aspects of aviation in Germany became absolute.

It is interesting to note that the Nazi Party did

Emblem of the Nationalsozialistisches Fliegerkorps (NSFK).

not know precisely what to do with the NSFK top leadership within the hierarchy of the NSDAP. They always listed the NSFK *Korpsführer* under the *Reichsleiters* but above the *Hauptbefehlsleiters*. It was only near the end of the war that the NSFK Korpsführer Keller was invited to the *Reichsleiter/Gauleiter* meetings at the Führer Headquarters. Previously, Christiansen had been excluded from such wartime assemblies.

The NSFK was mainly a voluntary organization with a small core of paid personnel. Voluntary members were not allowed to have any other Nazi Party affiliations. The

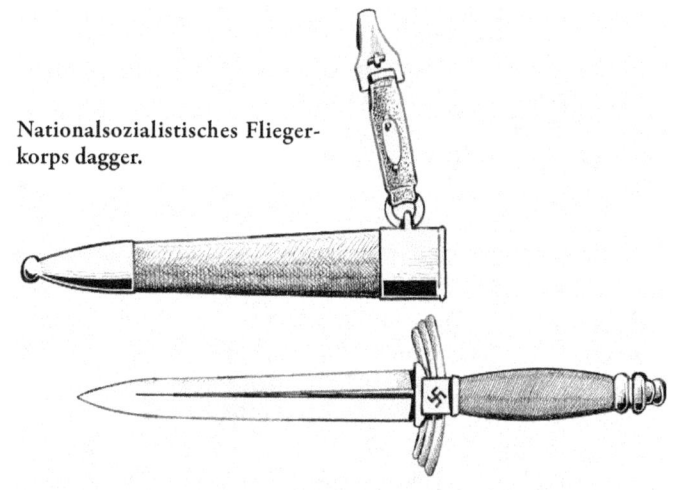

Nationalsozialistisches Fliegerkorps dagger.

NSFK was partly financed by voluntary contributions from private individuals, from the RLM and from the Luftwaffe.

Like the DLV before it, the NSFK's main purpose was to promote interest and development of air sports, notably gliding and ballooning. The NSFK was used as a means to channel energy, to exploit youth enthusiasm in aeronautics with a view of training future combat pilots and technical support personnel, and to keep the reservists of the aviation troops in training.

Closely related to both the Luftwaffe and the Nazi Party NSDAP, the organization of the NSFK, like that of the SA, SS and NSKK, was based on military units comprising *Rotten* and *Scharen* (squads), *Sturmen* (companies), *Sturmbannen* (battalions), *Standarten* (regiments) and *Gruppen* (divisions).

As with all Nazi organizations, the NSFK was a male-dominated association, but females were not discouraged from participating in events and were also allowed membership and access to flight training. Female members of the DLV and the NSFK were far more rare than their male counterparts, but they did exist in small numbers. Unfortunately, little is known about the women's participation and female crew in the NSFK.

Members, of course, wore uniforms, had distinctive insignia and used a system of ranks similar to those of the SA, SS, and NSKK. As with most Nazi paramilitary groups, rank patches were worn on a single collar opposite a badge of unit membership. The exception was for the ranks *Standartenführer* and above, which displayed rank insignia on both collars. As of 1934, the NSFK ranks were as follows: NSFK *Mann* (private); NSFK *Sturmmann* (private 1st class); NSFK *Rottenführer* (corporal); NSFK *Scharführer* (corporal); NSFK *Oberscharführer* (sergeant); NSFK *Truppführer* (staff sergeant); NSFK *Obertruppführer* (master sergeant); NSFK *Sturmführer* (second lieutenant); NSFK *Obersturmführer* (first lieutenant); NSFK

NSFK *Sturmbannführer* (battalion leader).

Hauptsturmführer (captain); NSFK *Sturmbannführer* (major); NSFK *Obersturmbannführer* (lieutenant colonel); NSFK *Standartenführer* (colonel); NSFK *Oberführer* (colonel); NSFK *Brigadeführer* (brigadier general); NSFK *Gruppenführer* (major general); NSFK *Obergruppenführer* (lieutenant general); and NSF *Korpsführer* (leader of the corps).

The emblem of the corps was Icarus, the winged man of Greek mythology, with stretched-out wings and a swastika—a strik-

Nazi Flyers Corps (NSFK)

Glider-pilot badge. Instituted in January 1942, it was intended to distinguish advanced qualification beyond existing NSFK awards. The silvered pin badge (45 mm in diameter) with enamel seagulls was worn on the lower left breast of uniforms.

Ballooning badge. The embroidered cloth DLV-NSFK ballooning badge (70 × 56 mm) was worn on the left pocket of the tunic.

ing image for an organization intended to foster air-mindedness. The emblem in metal form was displayed at the front of headgear, and in cloth form it was originally worn on the right upper sleeve of the tunic and later displayed above the right breast pocket of the tunic and on the traditional brown shirt. The winged Icarus symbol served as the basis for many NSFK forms, flags, medals, badges and emblems.

The NSFK uniform included a kind of SA-styled blue-grey kepi, and a yellow or silver piped blue-grey *Dienstmütze* (beret); a SA-styled brown or Luftwaffe grey service dress with tunic and matching trousers; and a pale blue shirt with a black tie. The collar of the tunic had badges displaying unit details and ranks. The facing color, used only as piping and underlay, was

Right: NSFK balloon.

Other Military Affiliated Units

NSFK SG-38 instruction glider. The SG-38 was designed in 1938 to be a training glider for basic flight training by the Nationalsozialistisches Fliegerkorps (NSFK). It was an absolutely minimalist aircraft, consisting of a high, strut-braced wing connected to a conventional empennage by an open-truss framework. It was made of wood with the wings, tail surfaces and inverted "V" kingpost all finished in doped aircraft-fabric covering. For take-off and landing the glider was fitted with a skid mounted on shock-absorbing springs. The pilot sat on a simple seat in the open air, without cockpit or windshield. The usual launch method was by bungee cord from a sloped hill. The high-wing aircraft was easy to fly, light, and cheap, and also very easy to maintain and repair.

bright yellow. For working and outdoor activities, members also wore a variety of greatcoats, overalls, boilers, flight suits and fatigue outfits.

The NSFK knife was officially adopted in April 1937 for wear by all personal of the NSFK. Old stocks of the earlier DLV knife were reissued to the NSFK with the addition of the NSFK scabbard inspection-stampings. So with this it is possible to find them with both markings. The knife continued to be produced until 1944, a total over 150,000 then being in circulation.

The NSFK was particularly charged with training the Hitler Jugend (HJ, Hitler Youth) before and during the Second World War to provide voluntary recruits for the Luftwaffe. For this purpose the Hitler Youth had a special branch known as the Flieger HJ, closely collaborating with the NSFK for the training of future combat pilots for fighters and bombers, as well as ground personnel for technical and administrative duties. At the age of 14, members of Hitler Youth could begin their training toward earning their glider pilot's rating.

As with the NSKK organization, sporting events of all kinds were popular and thus encouraged and organized by the NSFK.

Before the outbreak of World War II events organized by the NSFK involved model-building with flying competitions of the completed projects, and aeronautical classes followed by building and flying actual glider aircraft. The NSFK was divided into three sections—powered flight, gliders and ballooning—but glider flying was the mainstay activity of the NSFK. The corps owned 16 gliding aviation schools and 3 larger State Soaring Schools, the most famous being the Wasserkuppe in the Rhön Mountains where the Fliegerdenkmal had been erected as a memorial to Germany's World War I fallen airmen.

The NSFK also operated a ski school at

Zell-am-See in the region of Salzburg, Austria. The gliders used by the NSFK included several types, notably the Schneider/DFS Grunau Baby II glider, introduced in 1932; the DFS Kranich II, a two-seat advanced training glider introduced in 1935; the DFS model Schulgleiter SG38, the standard basic gliding trainer introduced in 1938; and the DFS Olympia Meise, a high-performance, single-seat sailplane introduced in 1939. The initials DFS mean Deutsche Forschungsanstalt für Segelflug (German Institute for Glider Flight), which was founded in 1933. The institute's purpose was to centralize and coordinate all technical research on gliders in the new Nazi Reich. During the war the DFS produced military assault gliders and conducted research and experiments on jet and rocket propulsion.

NSFK gliders were often painted in a cream color. Markings and numbering were applied in black paint on the sides of the fuselage and on the lower surface of wings. Markings included a D (Deutschland, Germany) followed by a number representing the specific NSFK *Gruppe*, and the glider's assigned number within that *Gruppe* or sometimes its own number among all gliders in Germany. A typical registration marking would look like this, for example: D-2-13. The Nazi Germany national emblem (a red band with a white circle containing a black swastika) was applied on both sides of the tail rudder.

Occasionally, the NSFK Icarus emblem could also be found applied just ahead of the cockpit, on the port side or on the nose of the glider. On occasion, slightly different markings can be observed in period photos, but the above description relates the markings generally found on most NSFK gliders.

Although participation in the NSFK could eventually lead to a pilot license, the Luftwaffe did not recognize the NSFK certificate. A NSFK pilot would still need to complete flight training with the German air force to become a Luftwaffe pilot.

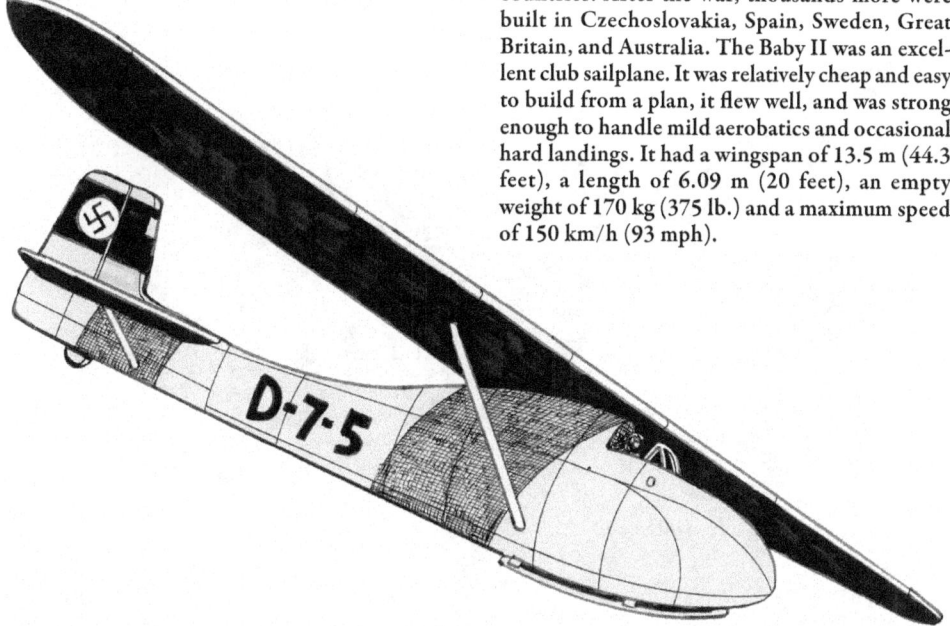

Grunau Baby II training glider. Introduced in 1933, the Grunau Baby was designed by Edmund Schneider. It became the most popular glider of all time. Thousands were constructed in Germany from 1933 to 1939, and during World War II, factory records indicated that 4,104 units rolled from workshops in Germany and the occupied countries. After the war, thousands more were built in Czechoslovakia, Spain, Sweden, Great Britain, and Australia. The Baby II was an excellent club sailplane. It was relatively cheap and easy to build from a plan, it flew well, and was strong enough to handle mild aerobatics and occasional hard landings. It had a wingspan of 13.5 m (44.3 feet), a length of 6.09 m (20 feet), an empty weight of 170 kg (375 lb.) and a maximum speed of 150 km/h (93 mph).

Other Military Affiliated Units

The Luftwaffe also had a number of glider-pilot schools located throughout the Reich. The attendees of these Luftwaffe glider centers were generally qualified pilots who volunteered to become assault gliders. During World War II the Luftwaffe tested numerous designs and used a variety of transport and combat gliders, including the DFS 230 Assault Glider; the DFS 331 Assault Glider; the Gotha Go 242 Transport glider; the Gotha Go 345 Assault Glider; the Gotha Ka 430 Transport/Assault Glider; the huge Junkers Ju 322 Assault Glider; and the Messerschmitt Me 321 Transport Glide, the largest production glider ever used by a military service.

The NSFK also played a role in the formation of newly created paratrooper units. Developed by Luftwaffe General Kurt Student (1890–1978), the German *Fallschirmjäger* (paratroopers) were a small, elite force that played a significant role during World War II. Using gliders and parachutes, the carefully selected and highly trained German airborne units achieved some remarkable successes in 1940, notably the capture of the reputedly impregnable Fort Eben Emael in Belgium and the seizure of bridges on the Rhine River and airfields near Rotterdam in the Netherlands. However, the casualties suffered at the landing in Crete in May 1941, though leading to the capture of the Greek island, were judged too costly by Hitler for him to permit a repetition. Paradoxically, as the likelihood of

NSFK Sponsoring member lapel badge. Issued to German citizens over the age of 18 who regularly contributed to the Flying Corps, the nickel pin had a wingspan of 24 mm and the circle a diameter of 21 mm. The "F" at the bottom stands for *Förderer* (sponsor).

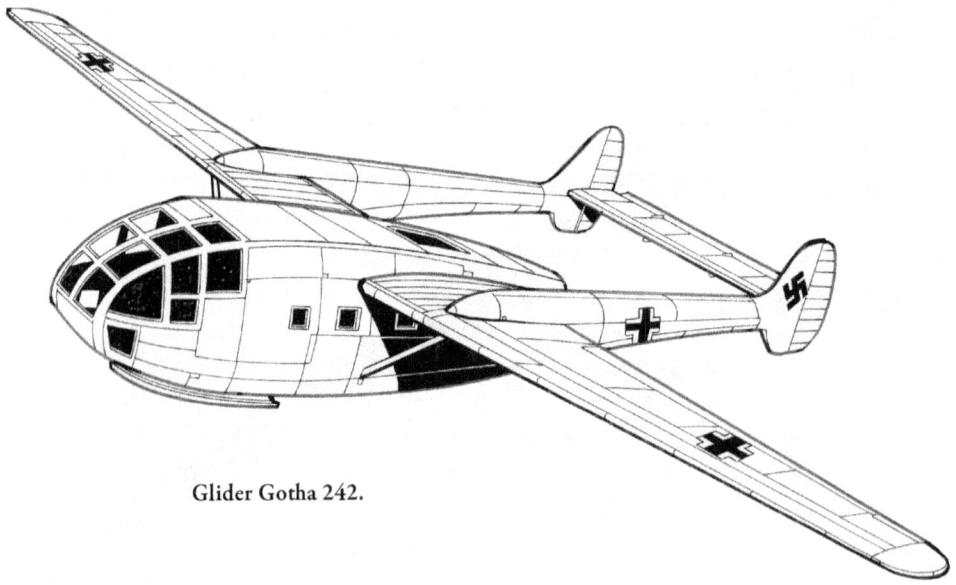

Glider Gotha 242.

Nazi Flyers Corps (NSFK)

Commemorative badge of NSFK Group 16 (Southwest), Great Flight Day, June 19, 1938, Mannheim. The nickel-plated badge had a diameter of 40 mm and displayed a stylized Bücker Bü 133 Jungmeister training airplane.

NSFK radio operator cloth badge.

Radio operator badge. The NSFK Bordfunker Abzeichen (radio operator triangle) was worn on the lower left sleeve. Introduced in 1941, it was machine woven on a grey-blue background. It was awarded to students who had demonstrated proficiency in radio communications, electronics and physics, and who had earned the gliding proficiency B certificate.

Germany Flight 1937. The NSFK Deutschlandflug Table Award 1937 was an aluminum, bronze-plated 97-mm × 85-mm badge. On the reverse there was a quote from Korpsführer Friedrich Christiansen reading: *"Mit unserem Führer im gleichen Schritt und Tritt fliegen wir für unser ewiges Deutschland* [Keeping pace with our leader we fly for our eternal Germany]."

another large-scale airborne operation receded, the parachute forces expanded, earning a reputation as formidable infantry fighters as they attracted a steady flow of young volunteers of the highest caliber from throughout the German air force, army and Hitler Youth. Until the end of the war, the highly regarded and respected German parachute forces grew to ten divisions, which were used as elite infantry assault troops.

During the war, the NSFK's task was to further air-mindedness among the public at large, but the emphasis was on the training of prospective pilots and specialized manpower for the German air force, producing a constant flow of skilled personnel and thereby functioning as a reserve pool for the German air force. By the end of the war members of the NSFK performed air defense duties such as reserve FlaK (anti-

Other Military Affiliated Units

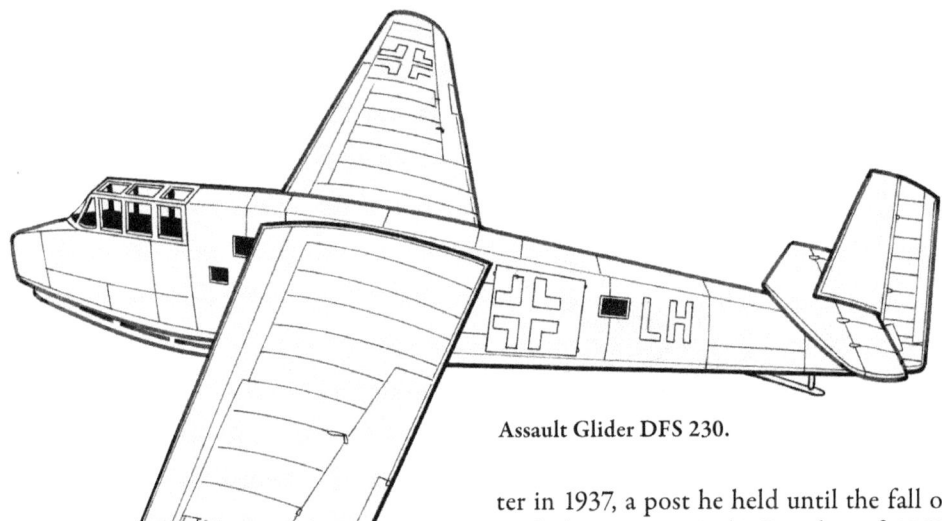

Assault Glider DFS 230.

aircraft artillery) service. By the end of 1944 and in the beginning of 1945, as in many other Nazi organizations, some NSKF members were drafted into the Volkssturm or into other last-ditch combat groups placed under command of the SS and NSDAP.

NATIONAL GERMAN RAILWAY COMPANY (DRG)

The Deutsche Reichsbahn Gesellschaft (DRG), also called Deutsche Reichsbahn (DR), was the National German Railway Company, the trains and equipment that it consisted of, and the men and women who made up the entire breadth of services that were required for it to operate.

Since 1926, the German State Railway Company was headed by engineer and railway expert Julius Dorpmüller (1869–1945). After the Nazis came to power, the highly regarded Dorpmüller became chairman of the Motorways Management Committee. He was appointed Reich Transport Minister in 1937, a post he held until the fall of Hitler's regime in 1945. By a law of 1939, the DR was made a public service, a nationally owned undertaking operating on a self-supporting financial basis with a considerable measure of administrative autonomy. In 1938 the railway system covered about 35,000 miles of track, of which 1,500 miles were electrically operated. The DR was a first-class railway system, well equipped with excellent locomotives and good rolling stock. After 1938 and during the war, owing to German conquests in Europe and Russia, the DR greatly expanded. It then operated about 500,000 miles of track and the num-

Deutsche Reichsbahn emblem.

ber of employed rose from 800,000 in 1937 to 1,400,000 in 1942. The DR was one of the most important facets of the German economy during the Second World War. The German economy during the period centered on rail transportation, and coal was the single most important item in this equation—at least 90 percent of all coal used in Germany was transported via rail. German industry, both military and civilian, could not survive without coal and the vital railways that carried it. Without rail, there was no coal, and without coal, the industrial might of Germany was doomed to failure. All other industrial necessities, as well as German passengers, goods, and freight, also required the German railways.

Deutsche Reichsbahn collar tab.

Deutsche Reichsbahn cap. The trim on the cap was bright red.

The DR played an important role during the war to transport supply, materials and troops from one front to another.

The DR was also a vital part of Hitler's program of racial extermination. The Reichsbahn and its personnel were not responsible but were highly instrumental in the deportation of opponents of the regime to the concentration camps, and the elimination of the European Jewish community to the extermination camps—the so-called Final Solution of the "Jewish Question." Transported in atrocious conditions, in overcrowded boxcars with practically no food, no water and no sanitary facilities for days, Jews and other enemies of the regime were charged the price of a one-way ticket to the gas chambers, while children under 10 or 12 years paid half price. The receipts taken in by the state-owned Deutsche Reichsbahn for mass deportations in the period between 1938 and 1945 reached a sum of $664,525,820.34. There is now no doubt that without the mass transportation of the railways, the scale of the Shoah would not have been possible. The most modern, accurate numbers on the scale of the Holocaust (c. six million) still rely partly on shipping records of the German Railway Company. It should be noted that in late 1944—at a time of general collapse on all fronts—the Nazi scheme of extermination of the European Jews went ahead, at considerable cost to the German war effort. Transports to extermination camps such as Auschwitz continued at a time when labor and rolling stock were badly needed for armaments and troop reinforcement, evacuation of casualties and refugees along a series of disintegrating fronts. At a time when the war was already lost, the continuation of the "Final Solution to the Jewish Question"—which Hitler had discussed more than 20 years before and decided to organize on an industrial scale at the Wannsee Conference of January 1942—clearly indicated that Hitler, being incapable of envisioning his own survival, was

Other Military Affiliated Units

Left: RBD Officer. The rank displayed on the collar patches indicated the pay-grade groups (here groups 8 and 7A). The black upper-sleeve badge showed the yellow Nazi eagle-and-swastika, and the lettering RBD (Reichsbahndirektion) and the railway district; *center:* Captain, Railway Police. The Bahnschutzpolizei included personnel responsible for railway security. Their duties varied from checking travel papers and ID to defending trains against partisan attacks. The depicted *Oberabteilungsführer* (captain) wears the light grey service uniform; *right:* Female auxiliary. The RDB auxiliary wears a dark blue forage cap, a dark blue tunic, and black trousers.

lured by the prospect of a universal annihilation that included his enemies, his victims, his own people and himself.

Civilian life was subjected to increasing militarization, and even organizations as innocent as the Reichspost (Postal Service) had members wearing uniforms. As might be expected, the Nazi government rationalized the administrative organization of the DR and introduced standardized uniform and insignia. The emblem of the DR was a winged wheel. The railway uniforms during the Nazi period of 1933 to 1945 were similar to those worn during the Weimar period (1919–1933) with the addition of typical Nazi badges and insignias bearing the eagle and swastika. The basic color was dark blue and included a Prussian-style tunic and cap, jacket, greatcoat and black trousers. The belt buckle had the winged wheel above a swastika surrounded by a wreath with the words *Deutsche Reichsbahn*. The eye-catching DR uniform survived the war with obvious modifications. The DR was a uniformed, non-military company, and its structure did not include a rank system based on military hierarchy. Instead the company was divided into four main worker classifications (indicated by collar patches and cap cords) and subdivided into 23 pay categories (indicated by shoulder straps). This was modified in February 1941 when a collar patch and shoulder straps system was introduced. Old and new "ranking" systems and insignia, however, were mixed until the end of the war owing to lack of

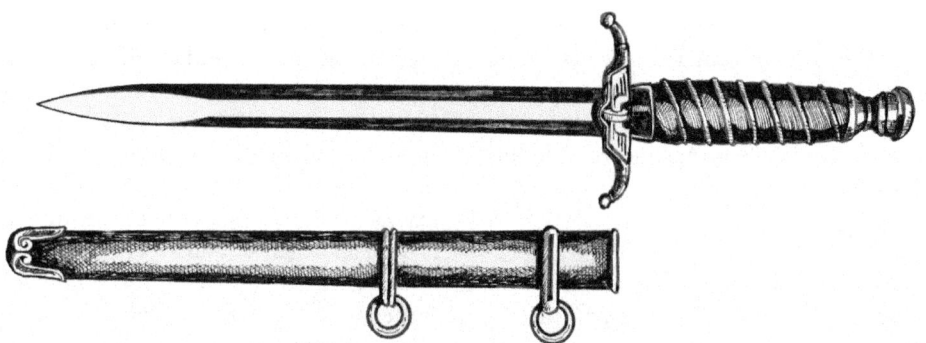

DBR dagger. Introduced in 1938, the Bahnschutz dagger was designed by the artist Paul Casberg and manufactured by the Carl Eickhorn Company from Solingen. It was 40 cm in length and its crossguard was decorated with the railway emblem—a winged wheel.

means for the total introduction and issue of uniform innovations. High-ranking officials had a dagger featuring the winged wheel on the guard. Laborers on the railroad wore an overall or a fatigue suit with a DR armband.

Some specialized personnel of the DR served and operated the huge cannons of the army's *Eisenbahnartillerie* (E-Art, heavy artillery mounted on railway).

The technical skills of the DR personnel were also employed in the operation of *Eisenbahn Panzerzüge* (Eis. Pz-Zug, armored trains). Some 80 armored trains were operated during World War II by the German forces, mainly on the Balkan and eastern fronts. Early in 1942 arose the concept of a polyvalent armored train in the form of the BP 42. This new type of train combined potent artillery and anti-aircraft guns with a strong infantry capability. The Deutsche Reichsbahn Gesellschaft saw armored trains as a way to preserve and advance a military presence. By keeping a strong military face on this state-owned railroad, the DR looked to increase both its state funding and its national prestige.

The DR also had lightly armed security formations. The Bahnschutzpolizei (BZP, Railway Protection) was formed in 1933 by the Eisenbahn Verwaltung (Railway Administration) in order to assure the safety and security of rolling stock and buildings of the company in its entire network. Personnel and officers investigated trespassing on rail property, assaults against passengers, sabotage targeting the railway, arson, pickpocketing, ticket fraud, robbery and theft of personal belongings, baggage or freight. As the war progressed, the Bahnschutzpolizei also checked travel papers and identity documents, and sometimes took arms for defense against partisan attacks in occupied territories. The Bahnschutzpolizei was organized into *Bezirke* (districts) and *Abteilungen* (detachments), each totaling about 150 men. These were divided into three *Züge* (squads or companies) and each *Zug* included four *Gruppen* (groups) composed of a dozen men.

The Bahnschutzpolizei ranks were as follows: BZP *Anwärter* (private); BZP *Mann* (private 1st class); BZP *Stellvertreter-Gruppenführer* (deputy corporal); BZP *Gruppenführer* (corporal); BZP *Obergruppenführer* (sergeant); BZP *Unterzugführer* (staff sergeant); BZP *Zugführer* (master sergeant); BZP *Oberzugführer* (second lieutenant); BZP *Abteilungsführer* (first lieutenant); BZP *Oberabteilungsführer* (captain); BZP *Abteilunfshauptführer* (major); BZP *Bezirkführer* (lieutenant colonel); BZP *Bezirkhauptführer* (colonel); *Stabsführer der BZP* (brigadier general); and *Chef der BZP* (chief of railway police). Members of the Bahnschutz were not policemen proper but

Other Military Affiliated Units

functionaries wearing a uniform. On occasion, they could be called upon to assist the regular police. By 1941 the uniform was changed and replaced by a light blue dress with a cuff title bearing the word Bahnschutzpolizei.

Ordnungspolizei (Orpo)

Nazi Germany was an authoritarian police state with many police and intelligence services repressing and spying on the population, such as the infamous Gestapo (Secret State Police) and the SS Sicherheitsdienst (Security Service of the SS). In April 1934 Heinrich Himmler (SS-Chief) was appointed chief of the German Police in the Ministry of Interior, and the lines between the national police and the Nazi private SS began to blur.

The Ordnungspolizei (Orpo, literally the "order police") was the organization of regular, domestic uniformed police composed

Left: Policeman of the Ordnungspolizei wearing a greatcoat; *right:* Policeman of the Ordnungspolizei. The depicted policeman of the Gendarmerie (rural police) wears the green uniform with the typical shako (conical, peaked hat). When worn on parade, a horsehair plume was inserted behind the cockade down to the left side of the shako.

Ordnungspolizei (Orpo)

Left: Fireman of Feuerschutzpolizei, c. 1939. This *Wachtmeister* of the Fire Protection Police (incorporated into the Orpo) wears a dark blue uniform with deep rose pink piping, and with police insignia (eagle and swastika in a laurel wreath) on the upper left sleeve. His head is protected with the standard German steel helmet. Members of these units were responsible for fighting fires as well as for keeping general order in conjunction with other police forces; *right:* Wasserschutzpolizei *Meister*, c. 1939. The Wasserschutzpolizei (Water Protection Police)—a branch of the Schutzpolizei—was responsible for monitoring the inland waterways and canals in both Germany and occupied territories. The depicted *Meister* (senior NCO) wears the dark blue walking-out dress composed of cap, naval-cut jacket (with police sleeve eagle) and straight trousers.

of Schutzpolizei (security police), Gemeinde Polizei (urban police) and Gendarmerie (rural police), each with many sub-branches. The Orpo—totaling some 250,000 policemen in 1939—also included various technical, administrative and auxiliary services such as rescue squads, police units on rivers, and air-defense units. Fire-protection police and fire brigades had been part of the Orpo since 1938. The Orpo was charged with ensuring interior order, and therefore it was militarily structured and organized with uniforms and ranks similar to those of the Wehrmacht. The Orpo passed into the control of the SS in 1936 and was headed by SS Oberstgruppenführer Kurt Dalüge (1897–1946). At the regional level the Orpo was controlled by inspectors called Inspekteur der Ordungspolizei (IdO) in each *Land* (province). In the annexed territories and later in the occupied European countries a senior officer was in charge, called the Befehlshaber der Ordnungspolizei (BdO, Commander of the Orpo). As the Orpo spread during the war to occupied countries, and it was militarized and indoctrinated. It became far more a military force than an organization of public servants. In addition to the routine police work that was carried on, some hundred battalions were raised (each about 550 men) and served in the ranks of the Wehrmacht as antipartisan units. Some members of the Orpo were drafted in 1940 to form the 4th Waffen SS Panzergrenadierdivision "Polizei 1." Some Orpo policemen—particularly those who were under disciplinary punishment—volunteered to constitute Einsatzgruppen (mass murder squads) in Russia in 1942–43. Other volunteers formed SS-Polizei regiments in 1943. In early 1945 Orpo policemen were drafted into the Volkssturm and to form the 35th Waffen SS grenadier division "Polizei nr.2."

The ranks of the Orpo were as follows: *Chef der Deutschen Polizei* (chief of the German police); *Generaloberst der Polizei* (colonel general of police); *General der Polizei* (general of police); *Generalleutnant der Polizei* (lieutenant general of police); *Generalmajor der Polizei* (major general of police); *Oberst* (colonel); *Oberstleutnant* (lieutenant colonel); *Major* (major); *Hauptmann* (captain); *Oberleutnant* (senior lieutenant); *Leutnant* (lieutenant); *Meister* (master); *Hauptwachtmeister* (head watch master); *Revieroberwachtmeister* (precinct senior watch master); *Oberwachtmeister* (senior watch master); *Wachtmeister* (watch master); *Rottmeister* (corporal); and *Unterwachtmeister* (policeman).

The Allies considered the Orpo a dangerous service, and right after the German capitulation in May 1945, the organization was purged of its Nazi members. It was,

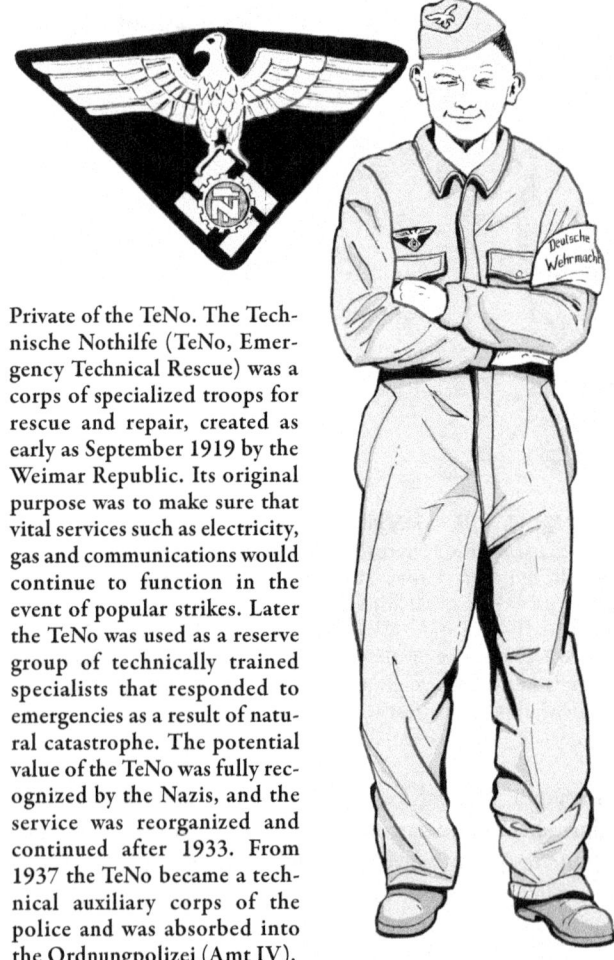

Private of the TeNo. The Technische Nothilfe (TeNo, Emergency Technical Rescue) was a corps of specialized troops for rescue and repair, created as early as September 1919 by the Weimar Republic. Its original purpose was to make sure that vital services such as electricity, gas and communications would continue to function in the event of popular strikes. Later the TeNo was used as a reserve group of technically trained specialists that responded to emergencies as a result of natural catastrophe. The potential value of the TeNo was fully recognized by the Nazis, and the service was reorganized and continued after 1933. From 1937 the TeNo became a technical auxiliary corps of the police and was absorbed into the Ordnungpolizei (Amt IV).

Emblem of the TeNo. The emblem was composed of the letter T (evoking the shape of a hammer) with superimposed N, both placed within a cogwheel superimposed on a swastika.

however, rapidly reactivated to maintain order. In the postwar period the Ordnungpolizei became the Volkspolizei (Vopo) in communist Eastern Germany (DDR) and—under its original name Schutzpolizei (Schupo)—in the western Federal Republic of Germany (BRD).

GERMAN POSTAL SERVICE

The Deutsche Reichspost (German Postal Service) was established as a state monopoly after the unification of 1871. Its official name was Kaiserliche Post und Telegraphenverwaltung (Imperial Administration of Post and Telegraph). Between 1924 and 1934 it was operated as a state-owned enterprise. During the period 1934–1945, it was an autonomous administration that combined all postal, telegraph and telephone services in Germany's 38 postal zones. The Reichspostministerium (Ministry of Post) located at Berlin was divided into seven departments, and was responsible for coordinating all administration; for example, deciding the principles for the use of the services, determining employees' pay scale and charges, and introducing of new services. The Reichspost operated a fleet of motor vehicles (with its own repair and

BdM girl employed as postal auxiliary. The BdM girl wears the female Hitler Youth uniform consisting of side cap with diamond-shaped HJ organization badge, white blouse with black necktie and leather slipknot, brown four-pocket suede tunic with a "Reichspost" armband, dark blue Melton cloth skirt, white socks and black shoes. She carries mail in a large, black leather satchel. *Top left:* Diamond-shaped emblem of the Hitler Jugend (Hitler Youth).

Postal service armband. The armband, worn on the left arm by those serving in the postal service as auxiliaries, was dark blue with yellow lettering.

Other Military Affiliated Units

Cloth badge of the Reichspost.

maintenance services), principally for the conveyance of mail but also for the transportation of passengers in remote rural regions deprived of railways. It also had several mail airplanes and mailships for international post.

During the war, the shortage of manpower forced many of the state organizations to make increasing use of boys, women and girls. For example, members of the Bund deutscher Mädel (BdM, League of German Girls, the female branch of the Hitler Youth) were encouraged to volunteer for a wide range of jobs in an effort to keep essential services running, including driving buses, trams and underground railways, as well as sorting and delivering mail.

The Reichspost employees were fully qualified civil servants and wore a uniform

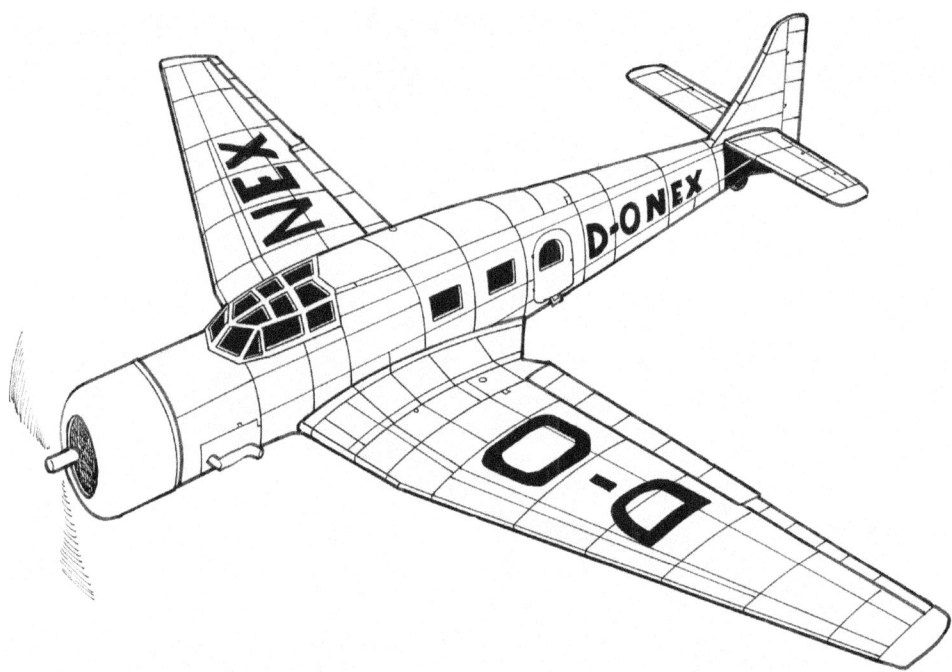

Junkers Ju 160. The Junkers Ju 160 made its first flight in 1934. It was a cantilever, single-engine, high-performance commercial monoplane put into service in 1937 on the express routes for airmail and Deutsche Lufthansa. It carried a crew of two and had accommodations for six passengers. The Ju 160 had a retractable undercarriage and was of all-metal construction with smooth sheet-metal covering. It was fitted with a 650-hp BMW Hornet engine. Fully loaded, the plane weighed 7,710 lb. It had a cruising speed of 186 mph and a range of 1,000 km. During World War II the civilian postal planes were militarized and transferred to the German Luftwaffe.

when on duty. The official dress included a dark blue jacket with orange piping and black trousers. A series of 20 different collar patches indicated ranks. The Deutsche Reichspost employed many women who after 1940 were issued with a uniform of their own. This consisted of a dark blue, orange-piped beret, a blouse, a blue jacket with armband carrying the words "Deutsche Reichspost," matching skirt or slacks, and black shoes.

The *Postschutz* (Postal Protection Service) was created in March 1933. Its task was the protection and security of all post offices, facilities, and establishments. Prior to 1942 the Postschutz was placed under the control of the National Ministry of Post and Telegraph, and headed by the postmaster general and NSKK *Obergruppenführer* Dr. Ohnesorge. After March 1942, the Postschutz was incorporated into the Allgemeine SS (the general pool of SS men composed of full-time, part-time, active, retired and honorary members) and then named SS-Postschutz. By 1942 the Postschutz had a total of 4,500 men in service and was made up of older men or men who were not fit enough for frontline service. While under SS control the Postschutz worked in close cooperation with the SS Funkschutz (SS Broadcast Protection), who policed official radio stations, raided illicit broadcasting stations, and detected illegal listening to foreign broadcasting stations. Members of the Postschutz wore field grey uniforms, and after the reorganization of 1942 SS-style rank collar patches were introduced.

Conclusion

The total strength of the German army auxiliary forces was about 3,800,000 in 1944, and this figure illustrates the core of Hitler's National Socialism. War was the natural extension of the violent Nazi system. War was ideological and happened to be Hitler's main and ultimate goal. War was the centerpiece of the reconstruction of Nazi German society after 1933. Ideological war was fought in order to create and maintain a regime and a society in which the Germans could share the conquest, domination and annihilation of others. It was supposed to reach its climax with the anticipated domination of the Germans—part of a new "master race" in a racist empire—over other "inferior races."

The numerous auxiliary forces, Nazi Party agencies, associations, fronts, and organizations were by nature not regular armed forces but auxiliaries to them. In fact, the only true auxiliary forces were the Wehrmachtsgefolge, or armed forces auxiliaries, which were those formations or organizations that were not a part of the armed forces, but which served such an important support role that they were militarized and given protection under the Geneva Convention. As we have seen, the official armed forces auxiliaries consisted of the Organisation Todt, Reicharbeitsdienst, NSKK, and the Deutscher Volkssturm. Although some of the armed forces auxiliaries were militarized, it was specifically decreed that they were not to achieve armed forces status equal to the Heer, Luftwaffe or Kriegsmarine. The Wehrmachtsgefolge, however, provided all manners of support to the German armed forces in the form of added transportation, construction help, garrison and security work, combat engineering, railway repair, anti-aircraft defense, air-raid protection and early warning services, and in the end, even frontline combat duty. The other forms of auxiliary formations, although not specifically known as Wehrmachtsgefolge, such as the Hitler Jugend (Hitler Youth), Kraft durch Freude (an entertainment association), Deutsche Reichsbahn (Railway Company), and Deutsches Rotes Kreuz (German Red Cross), also provided invaluable support to the Wehrmacht. Many of the auxiliary organizations—directly or indirectly connected to the German armed forces—were thrown into the last-ditch attempt at preventing total defeat as World War II came to a close, many members being used in direct combat roles as the fronts collapsed. Those described in this book are by no means all such organizations that existed during World War II, but they are those that most directly supported the Wehrmacht or the war in general during and prior to World War II.

By Law No. 5 (Denazification Decree) issued by the American military govern-

Conclusion

ment on May 31, 1945, the Nazi Party, with all its institutions, formations, associations, fronts, and armed forces auxiliaries, was disbanded and declared illegal. As already pointed out, members of the Wehrmachtsgefolge had never shown any inclination to organize themselves, and veterans' auxiliary associations never became a feature of post–World War II Germany. Another point showing how little appeal the Wehrmachtsgefolge have today is that World War II re-enactors mostly ignore them in spite of the fact that Volkssturm re-enacting, for example, would be considerably cheaper and easier than any other World War II German army units.

The process of *Entnazifizierung* (denazification) was intended to eradicate Nazism. It was a very complicated task for the Allies. All persons involved in Nazism—including members of the Wehrmacht auxiliary forces—were removed from public positions, and by 1946 the process became more systematic. The Allied Control Council had defined five categories of persons associated with Hitler's regime.

- Category 1 was applied to major offenders and high-ranking Nazi officers, who were sentenced to death or life imprisonment.
- Category 2 concerned activists, militarists or profiteers, who were to be sentenced to a maximum of ten years' imprisonment.
- Category 3 included lesser offenders deserving leniency, who were to be placed on probation or given two or three years' imprisonment.
- Category 4 concerned followers who were nominal supporters of the Nazi regime, who were to be placed under police surveillance and in some cases obliged to pay a fine.
- Category 5 included exonerated individuals who themselves had suffered from Nazi oppression and who were to be released.

The process of denazification, however, was a complex task, which proceeded slowly and with difficulty in an increasingly tense international background, which soon led to the so-called Cold War, pitting the United States in the West and the U.S.S.R. in the East against each other. All surviving Nazis were interrogated about their past, and officers holding the rank of major (or SA or SS *Sturmbannführer*) or higher were arrested for inquiry. Many sought to disassociate and distance themselves from the guilt for the excesses, atrocities and genocide of National Socialism. Many minimized their role in Hitler's regime, and some of those deserving punishment were able to escape.

The document that formally concluded the Second World War in Europe was signed at Reims (Champagne, France) on May 7, 1945. From 1939 to 1945, death and

Surrender: the fate of all German forces in 1945.

destruction had reached a worldwide scale. World War II took the lives of more people than any other war in history, upwards of 37 million, both civilian and military. This includes almost 6 million Jews murdered in the hideous Nazi death camps, 20 million Russians and more than 4 million Poles who died as a result of war and persecution. The war resulted in large-scale movements of population, and changed completely the international status of nations regarded as great powers. In spite of victory, Great Britain and France lost their dominance. From 1945 onwards, world affairs were dominated for many years by two superpowers, the United States and the Soviet Union, the latter taking steps to ensure that the countries of Eastern Europe embraced communism. Japan and Germany lost their status in defeat. After the fall of Hitler's regime, statesmen concerned with the peace treaties were fully alive to the danger of repeating the errors of World War I's 1919 Versailles peace treaty. The charter of the United Nations was signed in June 1945 but the Allies were faced with problems of immense complexity. Right after the war, Germany and Austria were divided into American, British, French, and Soviet occupation zones. Germany was split between the two global blocks in the East and West during the Cold War, and reunited in 1990.

Appendix

World War II Chronology

1918
Nov. 11—World War I ends with German defeat.

1919
April 28—League of Nations founded.
June 28—Signing of the Treaty of Versailles.

1921
July 29—Adolf Hitler becomes leader of National Socialist or "Nazi" Party.

1923
Nov. 8/9—The Beer Hall Putsch.

1925
July 18—Hitler's book *Mein Kampf* published.

1926
Sept. 8—Germany admitted to League of Nations.

1929
Oct. 29—Stock market on Wall Street crashes.

1930
Sept. 14—Germans elect Nazis, making them the 2nd largest political party in Germany.

1932
Nov. 8—Roosevelt elected president of the United States.

1933
Jan. 30—Adolf Hitler becomes chancellor of Germany.
Feb. 27—The Reichstag burns.
March 12—First concentration camp opened at Oranienburg outside Berlin.
March 23—Enabling Act gives Hitler dictatorial power.
April 1—Nazi boycott of Jewish-owned shops.
May 10—Nazis burn books in Germany.
June—Nazis open Dachau concentration camp.
July 14—Nazi Party declared only party in Germany.
Oct. 14—Germany quits the League of Nations.

1934
June 30—The "Night of the Long Knives."
July 25—Nazis murder Austrian chancellor Dollfuss.
Aug. 2—German president Hindenburg dies.
Aug. 19—Adolf Hitler becomes führer of Germany.

1935
March 16—Hitler violates the Treaty of Versailles by introducing military conscription.
Sept. 15—German Jews stripped of rights by Nuremberg Race Laws.

1936
Feb. 10—The German Gestapo is placed above the law.
March 7—German troops occupy the Rhineland.
May 9—Mussolini's Italian forces take Ethiopia.
July 18—Civil war erupts in Spain.
Aug. 1—Olympic Games begin in Berlin.
Oct. 1—Franco declared head of Spanish state.

1937
June 11—Soviet leader Stalin begins a purge of Red Army generals.

Appendix

Nov. 5—Hitler reveals war plans during Hossbach Conference.

1938

March 12/13—Germany announces *Anschluss* (union) with Austria.

Aug. 12—German military mobilizes.

Sept. 30—British prime minister Chamberlain appeases Hitler at Munich.

Oct. 15—German troops occupy the Sudetenland; Czech government resigns.

Nov. 9/10—Kristallnacht—The Night of Broken Glass.

1939

Jan. 30—Hitler threatens Jews during Reichstag speech.

March 15/16—Nazis take Czechoslovakia.

March 28—Spanish Civil War ends.

May 22—Nazis sign "Pact of Steel" with Italy.

Aug. 23—Nazis and Soviets sign pact.

Aug. 25—Britain and Poland sign a mutual assistance treaty.

Aug. 31—British fleet mobilizes; civilian evacuations begin from London.

Sept. 1—Nazis invade Poland.

Sept. 3—Britain, France, Australia and New Zealand declare war on Germany.

Sept. 4—British Royal Air Force attacks the German navy.

Sept. 5—United States proclaims neutrality; German troops cross the Vistula River in Poland.

Sept. 10—Canada declares war on Germany; Battle of the Atlantic begins.

Sept. 17—Soviets invade Poland.

Sept. 27—Warsaw surrenders to Nazis; Reinhard Heydrich becomes the leader of new Reich Main Security Office (RSHA).

Sept. 29—Nazis and Soviets divide up Poland.

Oct.—Nazis begin euthanasia on sick and disabled persons in Germany.

Nov. 8—Assassination attempt on Hitler fails.

Nov. 30—Soviets attack Finland.

Dec. 14—Soviet Union expelled from the League of Nations.

1940

Jan. 8—Rationing begins in Britain.

March 12—Finland signs a peace treaty with Soviets.

March 16—Germans bomb Scapa Flow naval base near Scotland.

April 9—Nazis invade Denmark and Norway.

May 10—Nazis invade France, Belgium, Luxembourg and the Netherlands; Winston Churchill becomes British prime minister.

May 15—Holland surrenders to the Nazis.

May 26—Evacuation of Allied troops from Dunkirk begins.

May 28—Belgium surrenders to the Nazis.

June 3—Germans bomb Paris; Dunkirk evacuation ends.

June 10—Norway surrenders to the Nazis; Italy declares war on Britain and France.

June 14—Germans enter Paris.

June 16—Marshal Pétain becomes French prime minister.

June 18—Hitler and Mussolini meet in Munich; Soviets begin occupation of the Baltic States.

June 22—France signs an armistice with the Nazis.

June 23—Hitler tours Paris.

June 28—Britain recognizes Gen. Charles de Gaulle as the Free French leader.

July 1—German U-boats attack merchant ships in the Atlantic.

July 5—French Vichy government breaks off relations with Britain.

July 10—Battle of Britain begins.

July 23—Soviets take Lithuania, Latvia and Estonia.

Aug. 3–19—Italians occupy British Somaliland in East Africa.

Aug. 13—German bombing offensive against airfields and factories in England.

Aug. 15—Air battles and daylight raids over Britain.

Aug. 17—Hitler declares a blockade of the British Isles.

Aug. 23/24—First German air raids on central London.

Aug. 25/26—First British air raid on Berlin.

Sept. 3—Hitler plans Operation Sealion (the invasion of Britain).

Sept. 7—German blitz against England begins.

Sept. 13—Italians invade Egypt.

Sept. 15—Massive German air raids on London, Southampton, Bristol, Cardiff, Liverpool and Manchester.

Sept. 16—United States military conscription bill passed.

Sept. 27—Tripartite (Axis) Pact signed by Germany, Italy and Japan.

Oct. 7—German troops enter Romania.
Oct. 12—Germans postpone Operation Sealion until spring of 1941.
Oct. 28—Italy invades Greece.
Nov. 5—Roosevelt re-elected as U.S. president.
Nov. 10/11—A torpedo bomber raid cripples the Italian fleet at Taranto, Italy.
Nov. 14/15—Germans bomb Coventry, England.
Nov. 20—Hungary joins the Axis Powers.
Nov. 22—Greeks defeat the Italian 9th Army.
Nov. 23—Romania joins the Axis Powers.
Dec. 9/10—British begin a western desert offensive in North Africa against the Italians.
Dec. 29/30—Massive German air raid on London.

1941

Jan. 22—Tobruk in North Africa falls to the British and Australians.
Feb. 11—British forces advance into Italian Somaliland in East Africa.
Feb. 12—German general Erwin Rommel arrives in Tripoli, North Africa.
Feb. 14—First units of German "Afrika Korps" arrive in North Africa.
March 7—British forces arrive in Greece.
March 11—President Roosevelt signs the Lend-Lease Act.
March 27—A coup in Yugoslavia overthrows the pro–Axis government.
April 3—Pro-Axis regime set up in Iraq.
April 6—Nazis invade Greece and Yugoslavia.
April 14—Rommel attacks Tobruk.
April 17—Yugoslavia surrenders to the Nazis.
April 27—Greece surrenders to the Nazis.
May 1—German attack on Tobruk is repulsed.
May 10—Deputy Führer Rudolph Hess flies to Scotland.
May 10/11—Heavy German bombing of London; British bomb Hamburg.
May 15—Operation Brevity begins (the British counter-attack in Egypt).
May 24—Sinking of the British ship *Hood* by the *Bismarck*.
May 27—Sinking of the *Bismarck* by the British Navy.
June—Nazi SS Einsatzgruppen begin mass murder.
June 4—Pro-Allied government installed in Iraq.
June 8—Allies invade Syria and Lebanon.
June 14—United States freezes German and Italian assets in America.
June 22—Germany attacks Soviet Union as Operation Barbarossa begins.
June 28—Germans capture Minsk.
July 3—Stalin calls for a scorched-earth policy.
July 10—Germans cross the River Dnieper in the Ukraine.
July 12—Mutual assistance agreement between British and Soviets.
July 14—British occupy Syria.
July 26—Roosevelt freezes Japanese assets in United States and suspends relations.
July 31—Göring instructs Heydrich to prepare for the "Final Solution."
Aug. 1—United States announces an oil embargo against aggressor states.
Aug. 14—Roosevelt and Churchill announce the Atlantic Charter.
Aug. 20—Nazi siege of Leningrad begins.
Sept. 1—Nazis order Jews to wear yellow stars.
Sept. 3—First experimental use of gas chambers at Auschwitz.
Sept. 19—Nazis take Kiev.
Sept. 29—Nazis murder 33,771 Jews at Kiev.
Oct. 2—Operation Typhoon begins (German advance on Moscow).
Oct. 16—Germans take Odessa.
Oct. 24—Germans take Kharkov.
Oct. 30—Germans reach Sevastopol.
Nov. 13—British aircraft carrier *Ark Royal* is sunk off Gibraltar by a U-boat.
Nov. 20—Germans take Rostov.
Nov. 27—Soviet troops retake Rostov.
Dec. 5—German attack on Moscow is abandoned.
Dec. 6—Soviet army launches a major counter-offensive around Moscow.
Dec. 7—Japanese bomb Pearl Harbor; Hitler issues the "Night and Fog" decree.
Dec. 8—United States and Britain declare war on Japan.
Dec. 11—Germany declares war on the United States.
Dec. 16—Rommel begins a retreat to El Agheila in North Africa.
Dec. 19—Hitler takes complete command of the German army.

1942

Jan. 1—Declaration of the United Nations signed by 26 Allied nations.

Appendix

Jan. 13—Germans begin a U-boat offensive along East Coast of the United States.
Jan. 20—SS leader Heydrich holds the Wannsee Conference to coordinate the "Final Solution of the Jewish Question."
Jan. 21—Rommel's counter-offensive from El Agheila begins.
Jan. 26—First American forces arrive in Great Britain.
April—Japanese-Americans sent to relocation centers.
April 23—German air raids begin against cathedral cities in Britain.
May 8—German summer offensive begins in the Crimea.
May 26—Rommel begins an offensive against the Gazala Line.
May 27—SS leader Heydrich attacked in Prague.
May 30—First thousand-bomber British air raid (against Cologne).
June—Mass murder of Jews by gassing begins at Auschwitz.
June 4—Heydrich dies of wounds.
June 5—Germans besiege Sevastopol.
June 10—Nazis liquidate Lidice in reprisal for Heydrich's assassination.
June 21—Rommel captures Tobruk.
June 25—Eisenhower arrives in London.
June 30—Rommel reaches El Alamein near Cairo, Egypt.
July 1–30—First Battle of El Alamein.
July 3—Germans take Sevastopol.
July 5—Soviet resistance in the Crimea ends.
July 9—Germans begin a drive toward Stalingrad in the USSR.
July 22—First deportations from the Warsaw Ghetto to concentration camps; Treblinka extermination camp opened.
Aug. 7—British general Bernard Montgomery takes command of Eighth Army in North Africa.
Aug. 12—Stalin and Churchill meet in Moscow.
Aug. 17—First all-American air attack in Europe.
Aug. 23—Massive German air raid on Stalingrad.
Sept. 2—Rommel driven back by Montgomery in the Battle of Alam Halfa.
Sept. 13—Battle of Stalingrad begins.
Oct. 5—A German eyewitness observes SS mass murder.
Oct. 18—Hitler orders the execution of all captured British commandos.
Nov. 1—Operation Supercharge (Allies break Axis lines at El Alamein).
Nov. 8—Operation Torch begins (U.S. invasion of North Africa).
Nov. 11—Germans and Italians invade unoccupied Vichy France.
Nov. 19—Soviet counter-offensive at Stalingrad begins.
Dec. 2—Professor Enrico Fermi sets up an atomic reactor in Chicago.
Dec. 13—Rommel withdraws from El Agheila.
Dec. 16—Soviets defeat Italian troops on the River Don in the USSR.
Dec. 17—British foreign secretary Eden tells the British House of Commons of mass executions of Jews by Nazis; U.S. declares those crimes will be avenged.
Dec. 31—Battle of the Barents Sea between German and British ships.

1943

Jan. 2/3—Germans begin a withdrawal from the Caucasus.
Jan. 10—Soviets begin an offensive against the Germans in Stalingrad.
Jan. 14–24—Casablanca conference between Churchill and Roosevelt. During the conference, Roosevelt announces the war can end only with an unconditional German surrender.
Jan. 23—Montgomery's 8th Army takes Tripoli.
Jan. 27—First bombing raid by Americans on Germany (at Wilhelmshaven).
Feb. 2—Germans surrender at Stalingrad in the first big defeat of Hitler's armies.
Feb. 8—Soviet troops take Kursk.
Feb. 14–25—Battle of Kasserine Pass between the U.S. 1st Armored Division and German Panzers in North Africa.
Feb. 16—Soviets retake Kharkov.
Feb. 18—Nazis arrest White Rose resistance leaders in Munich.
March 2—Germans begin a withdrawal from Tunisia, Africa.
March 15—Germans recapture Kharkov.
March 16–20—Battle of Atlantic climaxes with 27 merchant ships sunk by German U-boats.
March 20–28—Montgomery's 8th Army breaks through the Mareth Line in Tunisia.

April 6/7—Axis forces in Tunisia begin a withdrawal toward Enfidaville as American and British forces link.
April 19—Waffen SS attacks Jewish resistance in the Warsaw ghetto.
May 7—Allies take Tunisia.
May 13—German and Italian troops surrender in North Africa.
May 16—Jewish resistance in the Warsaw ghetto ends.
May 16/17—British air raid on the Ruhr.
May 22—Dönitz suspends U-boat operations in the North Atlantic.
June 10—"Pointblank" directive to improve Allied bombing strategy issued.
June 11—Himmler orders the liquidation of all Jewish ghettos in Poland.
July 5—Germans begin their last offensive against Kursk.
July 9/10—Allies land in Sicily.
July 19—Allies bomb Rome.
July 22—Americans capture Palermo, Sicily.
July 24—British bombing raid on Hamburg.
July 25/26—Mussolini arrested and the Italian Fascist government falls; Marshal Pietro Badoglio takes over and negotiates with Allies.
July 27/28—Allied air raid causes a firestorm in Hamburg.
Aug. 12–17—Germans evacuate Sicily.
Aug. 17—American daylight air raids on Regensburg and Schweinfurt in Germany; Allies reach Messina, Sicily.
Aug. 23—Soviet troops recapture Kharkov.
Sept. 8—Italian surrender is announced.
Sept. 9—Allied landings at Salerno and Taranto.
Sept. 11—Germans occupy Rome.
Sept. 12—Germans rescue Mussolini.
Sept. 23—Mussolini re-establishes a Fascist government.
Oct. 1—Allies enter Naples, Italy.
Oct. 4—SS Reichsführer Himmler gives speech at Posen.
Oct. 13—Italy declares war on Germany; second American air raid on Schweinfurt.
Nov. 6—Russians recapture Kiev in the Ukraine.
Nov. 18—Large British air raid on Berlin.
Nov. 28—Roosevelt, Churchill, Stalin meet at Teheran.
Dec. 24–26 1943—Soviets launch offensives on the Ukrainian front.

1944

Jan. 6—Soviet troops advance into Poland.
Jan. 17—First attack toward Cassino, Italy.
Jan. 22—Allies land at Anzio.
Jan. 27—Leningrad relieved after a 900-day siege.
Feb. 15–18—Allies bomb the monastery at Monte Cassino.
Feb. 16—Germans counter-attack against the Anzio beachhead.
March 4—Soviet troops begin an offensive on the Belorussian front; first major daylight bombing raid on Berlin by the Allies.
March 15—Second Allied attempt to capture Monte Cassino begins.
March 18—British drop 3,000 tons of bombs during an air raid on Hamburg, Germany.
April 8—Soviet troops begin an offensive to liberate Crimea.
May 9—Soviet troops recapture Sevastopol.
May 11—Allies attack the Gustav Line south of Rome.
May 12—Germans surrender in the Crimea.
May 15—Germans withdraw to the Adolf Hitler Line.
May 25—Germans retreat from Anzio.
June 5—Allies enter Rome.
June 6—D-Day landings.
June 9—Soviet offensive against the Finnish front begins.
June 10—Nazis liquidate the town of Oradour-sur-Glane in France.
June 13—First German V-1 rocket attack on Britain.
June 22—Operation Bagration begins (the Soviet summer offensive).
June 27—U.S. troops liberate Cherbourg.
July 3—"Battle of the Hedgerows" in Normandy; Soviets capture Minsk.
July 9—British and Canadian troops capture Caen.
July 18—U.S. troops reach St. Lô.
July 20—German assassination attempt on Hitler fails.
July 24—Soviet troops liberate first concentration camp at Majdanek.
July 25–30—Operation Cobra (U.S. troops break out west of St. Lô).
July 28—Soviet troops take Brest-Litovsk. U.S. troops take Coutances.
Aug. 1—Polish Home Army uprising against

Appendix

Nazis in Warsaw begins; U.S. troops reach Avranches.
Aug. 4—Anne Frank and family arrested by the Gestapo in Amsterdam, Holland.
Aug. 7—Germans begin a major counter-attack toward Avranches.
Aug. 15—Operation Dragoon begins (the Allied invasion of Southern France).
Aug. 19—Resistance uprising in Paris.
Aug. 19/20—Soviet offensive in the Balkans begins with an attack on Romania.
Aug. 20—Allies encircle Germans in the Falaise Pocket.
Aug. 25—Liberation of Paris.
Aug. 29—Slovak uprising begins.
Aug. 31—Soviet troops take Bucharest.
Sept. 1-4—Verdun, Dieppe, Artois, Rouen, Abbeville, Antwerp and Brussels liberated by Allies.
Sept. 4—Finland and the Soviet Union agree to a cease-fire.
Sept. 13—U.S. troops reach the Siegfried Line.
Sept. 17—Operation Market Garden begins (Allied airborne assault on Holland).
Sept. 26—Soviet troops occupy Estonia.
Oct. 2—Warsaw Uprising ends as the Polish Home Army surrenders to the Germans.
Oct. 10-29—Soviet troops capture Riga.
Oct. 14—Allies liberate Athens; Rommel commits suicide.
Oct. 21—Massive German surrender at Aachen.
Oct. 30—Last use of gas chambers at Auschwitz.
Nov. 20—French troops drive through the "Belfort Gap" to reach the Rhine.
Nov. 24—French capture Strasbourg.
Dec. 4—Civil war in Greece; Athens placed under martial law.
Dec. 16-27—Battle of the Bulge in the Ardennes.
Dec. 17—Waffen SS murder 81 U.S. POWs at Malmedy.
Dec. 26—Patton relieves Bastogne.
Dec. 27—Soviet troops besiege Budapest.

1945

Jan. 1-17—Germans withdraw from the Ardennes.
Jan. 16—U.S. 1st and 3rd Armies link up after a month-long separation during the Battle of the Bulge.
Jan. 17—Soviet troops capture Warsaw.
Jan. 26—Soviet troops liberate Auschwitz.
Feb. 4-11—Roosevelt, Churchill, Stalin meet at Yalta.
Feb. 13/14—Dresden is destroyed by a firestorm after Allied bombing raids.
March 6—Last German offensive of the war begins to defend oil fields in Hungary.
March 7—Allies take Cologne and establish a bridge across the Rhine at Remagen.
March 30—Soviet troops capture Danzig.
In April—Allies discover stolen Nazi art and wealth hidden in salt mines.
April 1—U.S. troops encircle Germans in the Ruhr; Allied offensive in North Italy.
April 12—Allies liberate Buchenwald and Belsen concentration camps; President Roosevelt dies. Truman becomes president.
April 16—Soviet troops begin their final attack on Berlin; Americans enter Nuremberg.
April 18—German forces in the Ruhr surrender.
April 21—Soviets reach Berlin.
April 28—Mussolini is captured and hanged by Italian partisans; Allies take Venice.
April 29—U.S. 7th Army liberates Dachau.
April 30—Adolf Hitler commits suicide.
May 2—German troops in Italy surrender.
May 7—Unconditional surrender of all German forces to Allies.
May 8—V-E (Victory in Europe) Day.
May 9—Hermann Göring is captured by members of the U.S. 7th Army.
May 23—SS Reichsführer Himmler commits suicide; German High Command and Provisional Government imprisoned.
June 5—Allies divide up Germany and Berlin and take over the government.
June 26—United Nations Charter is signed in San Francisco.
July 1—U.S., British, and French troops move into Berlin.
July 16—First U.S. atomic bomb test; Potsdam Conference begins.
July 26—Atlee succeeds Churchill as British prime minister.
Aug. 6—First atomic bomb dropped, on Hiroshima, Japan.
Aug. 8—Soviets declares war on Japan and invade Manchuria.
Aug. 9—Second atomic bomb dropped, on Nagasaki, Japan.
Aug. 14—Japanese agree to unconditional surrender.

Sept. 2—Japanese sign the surrender agreement; V-J (Victory Over Japan) Day.
Oct. 24—United Nations is officially born.
Nov. 20—Nuremberg war crimes trials begin.

1946

Oct. 16—Hermann Göring commits suicide two hours before his scheduled execution.

BIBLIOGRAPHY

Angolia, John R., and David Littlejohn. *Labor Organizations of the Third Reich.* San Jose, CA: R. James Bender, 1999.

———. *Uniforms, Organizations and History of the NSKK and NSFK.* San Jose, CA: R. James Bender, 1995.

Angolia, John R., and Adolf Schlicht. *Uniforms and Traditions of the German Army, 1933–1945.* Vol. 2. San Jose, CA: R. James Bender, 1986.

Ayçoberry, Pierre. *La Société allemande sous le IIIe Reich.* Paris: Editions du Seuil, 1998.

Benoist-Méchin, Jacques. *Histoire de l'armée allemande.* 2 vols. Paris: Editions Laffont, 1938.

Bessel, R. *Political Violence and the Rise of Nazism.* New Haven, CT: Yale University Press, 1984.

Broszat, Martin. *The Hitler State: The Foundation and Development of the Internal Structure of the Third Reich.* London: Longman, 1981.

Bullock, Alan. *Hitler: A Study in Tyranny.* New York: Penguin, 1952.

Carsten, F.L. *The Rise of Fascism.* London: Methuen, 1967.

Cartier, Raymond. *Hitler et ses généraux.* Paris: Librairie Arthème Fayard, 1962.

Cecil, Robert, ed. *Hitler's War Machine.* New York: Salamander, 1975.

Commager, Henry. *Pocket History of the Second World War.* New York: Pocket Books, 1945.

Cook, C., and Stevenson J. *Weapons of War.* London: Artus, 1980.

Cowdery, Raymond. *Nazi Para-Military Organizations and Their Badges.* Minneapolis: North Star Commemoratives, 1985.

David, Claude. *Hitler et le nazisme.* Paris: Presses Universitaires de France, 1979.

Davis, Brian. *German Army Uniforms and Insignia 1933–1945.* London: Brockhampton, 1971.

Dekker, Alex. *"Ook gij behoort bij ons!" Nederlanders bij het NSKK.* Alkmaar: Published by the author, 2007.

Droz, Jacques. *Histoire de l'Allemagne.* Paris: Presses Universitaires de France, 1945.

Dutch, Oswald. *Les 12 apôtres d'Hitler.* Trans. Gilles Baratier. Paris: Editions Corréa, 1940.

Ehrlich, C. *Uniformen und Soldaten—Ein Bildbericht vom Ehrenkleid unserer Wehrmacht.* Berlin: Verlag Erich Klinkhammer, 1942.

Ellis, Chris. *The German Army, 1933–1945.* Shepperton: Ian Allan, 1993.

Feder, Gottfried. *Das Programm der NSDAP und seine weltanschaulichen Grundgedanken.* Munich: Eherverlag, 1933.

Fitzgibbon, Constantine. *A Concise History of Germany.* New York: Viking, 1973.

Fleischer, W. *Feldbefestigungen des deutschen Heeres, 1939–1945.* Wölersheim-Berstadt: Podzun-Pallas Verlag, 1998.

Frischauer, W. *Rise and Fall of Hermann Göring.* New York: Ballantine, 1951.

Funcken, Liliane, and Fred Funcken. *L'Uniforme et les armes des soldats de la guerre, 1939–1945.* Vol. 1. Tournai: Editions Casterman, 1974.

Gallo, Max. *Night of the Long Knives: Hitler Liquidates the Brown Shirts, June 29–30, 1934.* New York and London: Harper and Row, 1972.

Gorlitz, Walter, and Herbert A. Quint. *Hitler: Eine Biographie.* Paris: Presses-Pocket, 1962.

Guichonnet, Paul. *Mussolini et le fascisme.* Paris: Presses Universitaires de France, 1966.

Halcomb, Jill, and Wilhelm P.B.R. Saris. *Headgear of Hitler's Germany.* Vol. 1: *Heer, Luftwaffe, Kriegsmarine.* San Jose, CA: R. James Bender, 1989.

Bibliography

Hart, S. *The German Soldier in World War II.* Osceola: MBI, 2000.

Heiden, Konrad. *Hitler.* Zurich: Europa-Verlag, 1936.

Hughes, Matthew. *Inside Hitler's Germany: Life Under the Third Reich.* Dulles: Brown Partworks, 2000.

Jones, Nigel. *The Birth of the Nazis.* London: Constable and Robinson, 2004.

Kammer, Hilde, and Elisabet Bartsch. *Jugendlexikon National-Sozialismus.* Hamburg: Rowohlt Taschenbuch Verlag GmbH, 1985.

Keegan, J. *Encyclopedia of WWII.* Feltham: Bison/Hamlyn, 1977.

Keizer, Jasper. *Dienen onder het hakenkruis.* Leeuwarden: Friese Pers, 2000.

Kissel, Hans. *Der Deutsche Volkssturm 1944/45: Eine Territoriale Miliz im Rahmen der Landesverteidigungs.* Frankfurt am Mein: Mittler and Sohn, 1962.

Landemer, Henri (Mabire, Jean). *Les Waffen SS.* Paris: Editions Balland, 1972.

Leach, Barry. *German General Staff.* New York: Ballantine, 1973.

Lepage, Jean-Denis G.G. *German Military Vehicles of World War II.* Jefferson, NC: McFarland, 2007.

Makowski, Josef. *Wehrmachtgefolge.* Warsaw: Czytelnik, 1962.

McInnes, C., and G.D. Sheffield. *Warfare in the 20th Century.* London: Unwin Hyman, 1988.

Mollo, A. *German Uniforms of World War II.* London: Macdonald and Jane's, 1976.

Montgomery, B.L. *A Concise History of Warfare.* Ware: Wordsworth, 2000.

Newton, John, series ed. *The Third Reich: Descent into Nightmare.* Alexandria, VA: Time-Life, 1992.

Peukert, D.J.K. *Inside Nazi Germany.* New Haven: Yale University Press, 1987.

Pia, Jack. *Nazi Regalia.* New York: Ballantine, 1971.

Reuss, Eberhart. *Hitler's Motor Racing Battles: The Silver Arrows Under the Swastika.* Yeovil: J.H. Haynes, 2008.

Schellens, J.J., and J. Mayer. *L'Histoire vécue de la seconde guerre mondiale.* Verviers: Editions Gérard (Marabout Université), 1962.

Schmitt, Carl. *Staat, Bewegung, Volk.* Hamburg: Hanseatische Verlagsanstalt, 1934.

Schönleben, Eduard. *Fritz Todt.* Oldenburg: Verlag Gerhard Stalling, 1943.

Smelser, R. *Robert Ley Hitler's Labor Front Leader.* Oxford: Berg, 1988.

Speer, Albert. *Inside the Third Reich.* New York: Avon, 1970.

Stern, J.P. *Hitler: The Führer and the People.* Glasgow: W. Collins Sons, 1975.

Stoffel, Grete. *La Dictature du fascisme allemand.* Paris: Editions Internationales, 1936.

Tagg, M. *De Wereld in Oorlog.* Harmelen: Ars Scribendi BV, 1993.

Thalmann, Rita. *La République de Weimar.* Paris: Presses Universitaires de France, 1986.

Thomas, Nigel. *Wehrmacht Auxiliary Forces.* Men-at-Arms No. 254. Oxford: Osprey, 1995.

Trevor-Roper, H.R., ed. *Hitler's Secret Conversations.* New York: Signet, 1953.

Wheal, Elisabeth, and Steven Pope. *Dictionary of the Second World War.* 2d ed. London: Macmillan, 1998.

Wheeler-Bennett, J.W. *The Nemesis of Power: The German Army in Politics, 1918–1945.* New York: Macmillan, 1967.

Whiting, Charles. *Siegfried: The Nazis' Last Stand.* New York: Stein and Day, 1982.

_____. *World War II: The Home Front: Germany.* Alexandria, VA: Time-Life, 1982.

Wilmot, Chester. *The Struggle for Europe.* London: Fontana, 1952.

Wistrich, Robert. *Who's Who in Nazi Germany.* New York: Bonanza, 1982.

Wykes, Alan. *Hitler.* New York: Ballantine, 1971.

Zeller, Thomas. *Driving Germany: The Landscape of the German Autobahn, 1930–1970.* New York: Berghahn, 2007.

Index

Adenauer, Konrad 6
Air raid shelter 33, 54, 55, 57, 58
Albania 23, 87
Alcoholism 61, 62
Allgemeine SS 142, 187
Alpine fortress 52
American Automobile Association 108
Anschluss 77, 194
Arbeit adelt 81, 101, 102
Arbeitsbuch 72, 73, 81
Armband 24, 27, 29, 31, 32, 37, 65–67, 73, 74, 80, 91–93, 101, 124, 129, 145–148, 160, 168, 181, 185, 187
Armored trains 181
Aryan 36, 60, 63, 76, 86, 89, 108, 117
Atlantic Wall 16, 20, 21, 23, 24, 26, 36, 38–41, 44, 58, 87
Attrappe 110, 112
Auschwitz 179, 195, 196, 198
Autarky 82
Autobahn *see* Motorways
Award 16, 26, 44, 68, 91, 101, 102, 105, 124–127, 173, 177

Balkans 26, 33, 92, 118, 122, 124, 166, 181, 198
Ballooning 170, 172–174
Battle of Britain 23, 115
Battle of the Atlantic 43, 48
Battle of the Bulge 138
Battle of the Nations 139
Bautruppen 85

Beauty of Work 68
Berger, Gottlob 142
Berghof 53
Bismarck (ship) 42, 195
Bismarck Youth 155
Blitzkrieg 112, 159
Blut und Boden 64
Blut und Ehre 168, 169
Bodyguard 6, 53, 90, 162
Bonaparte, Napoléon 139, 154
Bormann, Martin 15, 18, 24, 25, 62, 104, 121, 141, 142, 167
Brassard 124, 132; *see also* Armband
Brauchitsch, Manfred von 109
Braun, Eva 54
Braun, Werner von 49
Braunhemden see Storm Troops
Brest 23, 44
Britain 14, 15, 23, 39, 43, 51, 115, 122, 175, 191, 194, 195–197, 201, 202
Brüning, Heinrich 73

Camouflage 52, 53, 136, 165, 167
Canada 194
Caracciola, Rudolf 109–111
Carr, Michael 10
Casberg, Paul 181
Cathedral bunker 45, 46
Chancellor 6, 73, 105, 109, 155, 193
Christiansen, Friedrich 171, 177

Coffee bean cap 94
Cold War 190, 191
Concentration camp 1, 19, 26, 33, 36, 38, 53, 119, 143, 154, 163, 164, 179, 193, 196, 198
Corruption 58, 65
Crash helmet 106, 109, 130, 133, 134, 136
Croatia 23, 86, 166

D-Day (June 6, 1944) 40–42, 197
Dachau 38, 193, 198
Dagger 101–103, 114, 125, 159, 160, 171, 174, 181
Dalüge, Kurt 184
Darré, Walter 64
Dawes plan 73
Death's Head units 163
De Clerq, Gustave 86, 117
Degrelle, Léon 118
Dekker, Alex 105
Denazification 117, 189, 190
Deutsches Afrika Korps 132, 135
DFS gliders 175
Dopo Lavoro 68
Dorpmüller, Julius 16, 178
Dorsch, Xaver 16–21, 25, 26, 36
Dragon's teeth (*Höckerhindernis*) 9
Driver's award (*Kraftfahrbewahrungsabzeichen*) 124, 126

Eagle's Nest 53
Eastern Wall 43

Index

Egypt 54, 57, 114, 194, 196
Einheitsfeldmütze 33, 95, 136
Eperlecques 50, 51
Esser, Hermann 70

Fangrost 44, 45, 47
Fatigue suit 27, 29, 31, 92, 93, 129
Feder, Gottfried 5
Feldmütze 33, 95, 98, 136
Festungen 9, 44, 46, 52, 155
Final Solution of the Jewish Question 179, 195, 196
Fire brigade 183
Fire storm 57
FlaK 42, 44, 52, 55, 57, 67, 88, 93, 94, 98–100, 119, 177
Foreigners 18, 19, 23, 26, 31, 33–35, 58, 70, 86, 87, 117–120, 121, 123, 142, 154, 160, 162, 164, 167; German attitude toward foreign volunteers 119, 120
France 10, 15, 16, 21, 23, 24, 26, 33, 37, 39–45, 47, 50, 53, 86, 87, 96, 111, 113, 115, 117, 122, 138, 165, 190, 191, 194, 196–198, 201, 202
Freikorps 18, 74, 148, 154, 162, 163
Freikorps Sauerland 154
Freiwillige 120
Fritz Todt prize 14, 16
Fritz Todt ring 14, 16
Führer Chancellery bunker 19, 54

Gauleiter 16, 83, 144
Gendarmerie 96, 146, 148, 182, 183
Geneva Convention 2, 77, 115, 123
German Navy 1, 26, 39, 41, 42, 44, 46, 47, 49, 58, 67, 77, 114
German Red Cross 71, 189
Gestapo 72, 182, 193, 198
Gleichschaltung 59, 60, 105, 158, 160
Glider 173, 174, 175, 176, 178
Göbbels, Joseph 16, 52, 62, 83, 140, 141, 154, 155
Golden Age of Nazism 72

Gorget 96, 126, 131, 148
Göring, Hermann 13–15, 17, 18, 24, 25, 34, 49, 61, 72, 115, 163, 170, 171, 195, 198, 199, 201
Gothic line 23
Great Wall of China 43
Greatcoat 32, 93, 94, 99, 119, 127, 144, 145, 149, 174, 180, 182
Greece 8, 23, 87, 195, 198
Gruber, Kurt 169
Guderian, Heinz 105, 112
guerrilla 87, 156
Gypsies 36, 160

The Hague Convention 35, 146
Harris, Arthur 141
Hausser, Paul 164, 168
Headgear 33, 65, 94, 95, 97–100, 124, 127, 133, 144, 148, 163, 166, 173
Heer 1, 57, 77, 85, 118, 121, 134, 145, 164, 166, 167, 189, 201
Hellmuth, Otto 83
Hennes, Ernst 7, 110
Hess, Rudolf 15, 20, 82, 105, 117, 195
Heusinger, Adolf 140
Hierl, Konstantin 74, 75, 76, 81, 85, 88, 90, 94
Hilfsgemeinschaft auf Gegenseitigkeit der Angehörigen der ehemaligen Waffen-SS (HIAG) 168
Hilfswillinge 119, 121
Himmler, Heinrich 24, 25, 38, 49, 72, 84, 104, 111, 141, 142, 161–165, 182, 197, 198
Hitler, Adolf 1–20, 24–27, 34, 36, 39, 42, 43, 48, 50, 52–54, 58, 59, 61–63, 66, 68, 69, 71–73, 77, 79, 82–85, 91, 100–102, 105–114, 116, 118, 120, 138–143, 147, 155, 158–162, 164–170, 174, 176–179, 185, 186, 189–191, 193–198, 201, 202
Hitler salute 83
Hitler Youth 68, 78, 79, 105, 108, 109, 113, 143, 155,

168–170, 174, 177, 185, 186, 189
Hoheitszeichen 65, 124, 127
Holland 138, 165, 194, 198
Hühnlein, Adolf 104–106, 108–110, 113, 115, 116, 121, 129
Hungary 23, 33, 166, 195, 198

Icarus 172, 175
Identification disk 148
Italy 20, 23, 43, 52, 69, 96, 117, 121, 143, 194, 197, 198

Japan 49, 191, 194, 195, 196, 199
Jews 19, 25, 33, 34, 36, 37, 63, 70–73, 76, 84, 87, 89, 108, 142, 158, 160, 164, 165, 168, 179, 191, 193–197
Junkers Ju-160 plane 186

Kamikaze 49
Kammler, Hans 49
Kampfbinde 92; *see also* Armband
Kampfzeit 104
Kannenberg, Arthur 54
KdF *see* Kraft durch Freude
Keitel, Wilhelm 1
Keller, Alfred 171
Kennedy, Jimmy 10
Kennedy, John F. 51
Kennedy, Joseph 51
Klintzsch, Johann 168
Koch, Erich 140
Kraft durch Freude 7, 65, 68, 69, 71, 73, 87, 189
Kraus, Erwin 111, 116, 117, 121, 142
Kübelwagen 71, 110

Labor book 72, 73, 81
Lang, Hermann 110
Lanz, René 26
La Rochelle 23, 26, 45, 46, 47
Laval, Pierre 86
Lebensraum 43
Légion des Volontaires Français contre le Bolchévisme (LVF) 26
Lenk, Gustav 168

Index

Ley, Robert 16, 24, 59, 61, 62, 65, 67, 68, 69, 70, 71, 72, 76, 81, 84, 85, 202
Limesprogramm 12
Lokau, Werner 42
Lorient 23, 44, 45, 46
Lufthansa 170, 186
Luftwaffe (Air Force) 1, 8, 18, 23, 49, 56–58, 77, 85, 88, 93, 98, 99, 100, 115, 117, 119, 120, 121, 130, 132, 134, 145, 146, 170–176, 186, 189
Lutze, Viktor 68, 161

M 1935 helmet 30, 92, 97, 119, 131, 134, 148
Maginot Line 11, 13
Manziarly, Constance 54
Mauser rifle 30, 93, 150, 151
Medal 14, 26, 101, 112, 125, 126, 129, 159, 173
Mein Kampf 53, 193
Mercenaries 118, 120, 166, 168
Mimoyecques 50, 51
Mittelwerk 51
Mobilization 34, 84, 85, 87, 88
Morgenthau plan 140
Motor Schau 111, 112
Motorways 6–9, 13, 14, 52, 82, 106, 115, 178

Nacht und Nebel 1
Nagel, Wilhelm 116, 121
Nazi Party (National Socialist German Workers' Party (*Nationalsozialistische Deutsche Arbeiterpartei*, NSDAP) 5, 14, 16, 21, 25, 33, 34, 59, 61, 62, 65, 66, 69, 73–76, 78, 102–105, 112, 116, 117, 120, 129, 141, 142, 144, 145, 148, 154, 158, 159, 161, 162, 167–169, 171, 172, 178, 201
Nazi People Welfare Organization 71
Nazi racist system 35–38, 63, 70, 73, 76, 89, 108, 120, 165
Nazi regalia 102, 159
Nazi *Weltanschauung* 156
Nero decree 19, 156

Netherland 25, 46, 47, 86, 108, 113, 117–119, 122, 139, 171, 176, 194; *see also* Holland
Neubauer, Alfred 109
Night of Long Knives 75, 161, 193, 201
Nonprofessional militia 139
North Africa 41, 116, 126, 132, 153, 136, 137, 194–197
NSDAP *see* Nazi Party
Nuremberg Trials 19, 34, 62, 75, 136, 168
Nuvolari, Tazio 110

Obersalzberg 17, 52, 53
Ohnesorge, Wilhelm 16, 187
Ordensburgen 61, 84
Ostwall 84
Overall 129, 131, 174, 181
Overcoat (Mantel) 32, 37, 67, 93, 94, 99, 119, 123, 127, 144, 145, 149, 174, 180, 182
Overlord operation 41

Panzer uniform 132, 133, 135, 136
Panzerfaust 145, 146, 148, 150–154
Panzerschreck 151–153
Panzerwaffe 112
Panzerwurfmine L 153
Paratroopers 176, 177
Pas-de-Calais 38, 42, 43
Patrol service 30, 32, 96, 115, 143
Pétain, Marshal Philippe 86, 120, 127
Petersen, Wolfgang 46
Phoney War 10, 12, 13
Pimpf Deutsches Jungvolk (Junior Hitler Youth) 169
Pioneer of Labor Award (*Ehrenzeichen Pionier der Arbeit*) 68
Pioneerprogramm 11
Pith helmet 136
Poland 10, 20, 34, 35, 85, 86, 113, 194, 197, 200–202
Porsche, Ferdinand 71, 105, 106, 109, 110
Postschutz 187
Purge 33, 59, 63, 75, 161, 164, 184, 193

Racial extermination 36, 37, 38, 73, 179
Radar 42, 44, 55, 57
Ranks 22, 26, 27, 89, 90, 123, 124, 128, 149, 165, 166, 172, 180, 181, 184, 187, 190
Re-enactors 190
Regelbau 12, 39
Reichsluftfahrtministerium 171
Reichswehr 1, 74, 105, 161
Reichszeugmeisterei 102, 103
Retaliation weapons 48–50
Rex Party 118
Rifle association 143
Rivalry in Nazi leadership 23, 24, 66, 115, 141, 116
Robin Hood hat 95
Röhm, Ernst 64, 75, 105, 142, 159, 160, 161, 170
Röhm's second revolution 161
Romania 23, 33, 86, 122, 195, 198
Rommel, Erwin 40, 132, 137, 195, 196, 1980
Roosevelt, Franklin Delano 140, 193, 196, 198
Rosemeyer, Bernd 8, 110, 111

SA *see* Storm Troops
Saint-Nazaire 23, 39, 44
Sauckel, Fritz 34, 36, 62, 85, 88
Sauckel children 88
Schirach, Baldur von 68, 169
Schmelcher, Siegfried 52
Schmidt, Mathias 19
Schreck, Julius 6
Schrepmann, Wilhelm 142, 161
Schutz-Staffeln 6, 35, 36, 51, 53, 54, 72, 155, 160, 161, 162
Schutzpolizei 25
Scientists 159
Scorched-earth tactics 19, 156, 195
Sealion operation 39, 122, 194, 195
Seaman, Richard 110
Serbia 23, 86
Shako 182
Shaped charge 153

Index

Sicily 110, 197
Siegfried Line 10, 121, 198; see also West Wall
Slave labor 9, 19, 20, 25, 33–37, 49, 51, 58, 154
Slogan 60, 101, 125, 140, 141, 160
South Wall 42
Soviet Union 1, 23, 34, 87, 122, 139, 191, 194, 195, 198, 201, 202
Spain 69, 164, 175, 193
Speer, Albert 5, 12, 16–21, 24, 25, 34, 36, 54, 62, 68, 104, 116, 121, 156, 202
Speer miracle 19
Sport kit 94, 97, 169
SS see Schutz-Staffeln
SS-VT see Waffen SS
Stahlhelm 73
Stalingrad 1, 196
Storm Troops 26, 33, 59, 65–68, 75, 104–108, 142, 159, 160, 161, 168, 172
Stoßtrupp Adolf Hitler 162
Strasser, Gregor 64
Stuck, Hans 109, 111
Student, Kurt 176
Sturmgewehr rifle 151
Submarine 23, 26, 43–49, 87; see also U-Boat
Swallows' nests 80

Tallboy bomb 49, 51
Targa Florio 110
Tarnjacke 165, 167
TeNo (*Technische Nothilfe*) 184, 185
Tessenow, Heinrich 16
Thillo, René van 86
Todt, Fritz 6–9, 13, 15, 17, 21, 25, 82, 202
Totenkopf (Death's Head) 133, 163, 164, 166
Track suite 94, 97
Trade union 59, 61, 63, 64, 160
Traffic aid service 108
Tropical uniform 132, 135
Tuchmütze 94, 101
Type XXI submarine 48

U-Boat 2, 15, 43–48, 91, 122, 130, 194–196
Uhlenhaut, Rudolf 109
United States of America 15, 18, 43, 61, 190, 191, 193, 194–196, 200–202

V1 flying bomb 49
V2 missile 49, 139, 141
V3 gun 48, 50
V4, piloted V1 49
Valentin bunker 48, 49, 51
Van Doorne Company 113

Versailles treaty 1, 10, 106, 168, 170, 171, 191, 193
Veteran 73, 74, 150, 157, 161, 170, 171, 190
Vichy 86, 120, 127, 194, 196
Volksdeutsche 33, 165, 166, 119, 179
Volksgemeinschaft 60, 158
Volksjäger 52
Volkswagen 7, 70, 71, 84, 106

Waffen SS 26, 58, 86, 113, 118, 120, 123, 151, 158, 162, 165–168, 170, 184, 197
Wall Street Crash 73, 193
Wannsee conference 179, 196
War crimes 34, 123, 168, 199
Weber, Christian 104
Werlin, Viktor 112
West Wall 9–13, 20, 26, 38, 77, 84, 115
Winter suit 136 161
Wizernes 50, 51

Yugoslavia 33, 87, 110, 166, 195

www.ingramcontent.com/pod-product-compliance
Lightning Source LLC
Chambersburg PA
CBHW081556300426
44116CB00015B/2908